Networking Practitioner

The importance of teachers' learning about their practice has been increasingly recognised as central to the development of schools and classrooms in the last few years. *Networking Practitioner Research* is about the ways in which schools can improve through participating in research networks.

The book provides a strong theoretical framework for the field of research done within networks of schools. It includes a wide-ranging, critical review of school-based research to give readers a comprehensive knowledge of what is currently known about schools' attempts to learn from engagement in networks.

Chapters cover:

- The identification of questions that ought to be asked about research networks;
- An up-to-date analysis of current research, issues, conflicts and debates relating to school research networks;
- Teachers' collaborations in learning about and developing their practices;
- Extensive case studies of a number of international school networks, using examples from the UK, USA and Australia;
- The experiences and reflections of participants in these networks;
- The future and potential value of school research networks and the conditions and strategies that might lead them to be as fruitful as possible.

This book will be an invaluable resource to teachers, school leaders, academics and postgraduate students in education, facilitating informed decisions about the usefulness of research networks and ways of maximising their potential.

Colleen McLaughlin is Senior Lecturer at the Faculty of Education, University of Cambridge, UK. **Kristine Black-Hawkins** is Lecturer at the Faculty of Education, University of Cambridge, UK. **Donald McIntyre** is the Senior Researcher at the Faculty of Education, University of Cambridge, UK. **Andrew Townsend** is Associate Professor of Education at the University of Warwick, UK.

Networking Practitioner Research

Colleen McLaughlin,
Kristine Black-Hawkins
and Donald McIntyre
with
Andrew Townsend

Routledge
Taylor & Francis Group

LONDON AND NEW YORK

First published 2008
by Routledge
2 Park Square, Milton Park, Abingdon, Oxon OX14 4RN

Simultaneously published in the USA and Canada
by Routledge
270 Madison Ave, New York, NY 10016

Routledge is an imprint of the Taylor & Francis Group, an informa business

© 2008 Colleen McLaughlin, Kristine Black-Hawkins,
Donald McIntyre and Andrew Townsend

Typeset in Times New Roman and Gill Sans by
Florence Production. Ltd., Stoodleigh, Devon
Printed and bound in Great Britain by
Antony Rowe Ltd, Chippenham, Wilts

British Library Cataloguing in Publication Data
A catalogue record for this book is available
from the British Library

Library of Congress Cataloging in Publication Data
Networking practitioner research/Colleen McLaughlin . . . [et al.].
    p. cm.
    Includes bibliographical references and index.
  1. Education – Research – England.   2. School improvement
programs – England.   I. McLaughlin, Colleen.
LB1028.N356 2008
370.7'2 – dc22   2007021597

ISBN10: 0–415–38845–7 (hbk)
ISBN10: 0–415–38846–5 (pbk)
ISBN10: 0–203–08611–2 (ebk)

ISBN13: 978–0–415–38845–0 (hbk)
ISBN13: 978–0–415–38846–7 (pbk)
ISBN13: 978–0–203–08611–7 (ebk)

Contents

Acknowledgements

We would like to thank all those in the Networked Learning Communities' Programme who supported our research and, in particular, Jane McGregor, Mark Hadfield and Julie Temperley. We are very grateful to all members of the networks studied, including the staff and students in the schools and classrooms we visited. In particular we would like to thank those who co-ordinated our visits:

Sue Anstey
Caroline Eastes
Linda Curtis
Jean Hart
Stefani Shedden
Jacqui Smith
John Westwell

Finally, we would wish to thank Philip Mudd of Routledge and Lyndsay Upex for her patient and careful work on preparing the manuscript.

Illustrations

Figures

Tables

Box

Chapter 1

Introduction

Schools learning through networking and researching

Donald McIntyre

WHAT THIS BOOK IS ABOUT

This book is about ways in which schools can improve through enabling their managers and teachers to learn. The particular approaches to school improvement on which it is focused are research by schools and networking among schools, and especially the combination of these, research done by networks of schools and through school networking. This is not, however, an evangelical book, aimed at converting readers to a new truth that will save us all. It is instead a critical book, aimed at informing readers about what is known so far from research on schools' attempts to learn from engagement in research networks and at helping readers to form judgements about the usefulness of this approach and about the conditions necessary for it to be useful. It is written on the basis of our own direct experience of one such network (McLaughlin *et al.*, 2006), on our research into a number of such networks in England, and on our reading about similar networks in other countries.

KEEPING THINGS IN PERSPECTIVE

Schools are of course all about helping children and young people to learn. If their primary purpose were not the facilitation of their students' learning, schools would be very different from the easily recognisable institutions that they are. The world has become accustomed during the last two centuries to schools that consist largely of collections of classrooms, places where teachers teach and, it is hoped, students learn. Far from wanting to challenge this accepted reality, we want to re-assert it. However, it has been only gradually over these two centuries that we have come to realise that successful classroom teaching is a very demanding and complex task. Furthermore, the complexity of the task has increased greatly over these two hundred years as our aspirations for what we should achieve through schooling have steadily escalated. In the twenty-first century we still want everyone to become competent in the basic skills of 'the three Rs', but now it is not sufficient for only the self-selecting highly motivated few to pursue more ambitious educational goals. The task of classroom teaching now has to encompass such ambitious goals as enabling all students to develop their capacity for unlimited future learning (see Hart *et al.*, 2004). It is therefore a task that is dependent not just on high levels of expertise on the part of teachers, but also on their creativity and continuous new learning.

This need for teachers to be ongoing and intelligent learners has been increasingly recognised in the last few decades. It was in the 1960s in the UK that we began to engage in 'in-service education' for teachers. The idea quickly became quite normative. Hoyle (1974), for example, suggested a highly evaluative contrast between a 'restricted professional' conception of the teacher's role, involving a high level of competence in and commitment to classroom teaching, with an 'extended professional' conception, involving also a commitment to theorising and learning about practice and to taking a wider perspective on it. Recent surveys of English teachers' views of teacher professionalism (Maddock *et al.*, 2007) show that such a distinction, if viewed in less evaluative terms, remains useful. Although a very high level of consensus is apparent among teachers in their commitment to a core concept of professionalism focused on doing the complex job of classroom teaching well, teachers vary in their commitment to a view of professionalism that includes a strong emphasis on continuing professional development.

Teachers are right to show some scepticism about in-service education, especially where that scepticism is based on a view that the most important learning for practising teachers is learning from their own teaching experience. Several decades of experience of in-service courses suggest that, although teachers often find such courses interesting, they equally often have great difficulty in using such courses to improve their practice. If the courses are delivered without close reference to teachers' own teaching contexts, as has tended to be the case, and if there is nobody in the school contexts to give teachers informed support and encouragement in relating the course to their own practice, the task of using general innovative ideas in particular complex situations can easily be just too difficult. On the other hand, teachers do learn, deliberately or intuitively, from their own classroom experience; and much of that learning is certainly useful, making their teaching more fluent, more satisfying and more fruitful for their students. It would be immensely counter-productive, but also entirely unrealistic, to suggest that teachers should not learn from their own classroom experience. Nonetheless, learning from experience does have severe limitations: teachers are unlikely to learn from experience about the value of teaching approaches that they have never tried; and only unusually arrogant teachers would assume that nobody else had developed practical ideas from which his or her teaching could benefit. Furthermore, what individual teachers learn in isolation from their experience must inevitably vary in quite arbitrary ways.

The problems that detached in-service courses tend to have limited practical benefits, and that the learning from experience of isolated individual teachers also has severe limitations, both suggested a need for some kind of mediating framework, close to practice but broader in scope than the individual teacher's classroom experience. This apparent need, combined with the developing idea that schools themselves should accept responsibility for the quality and improvement of their own work, led to what in retrospect seems the quite obvious idea that school improvement might depend on schools themselves providing such mediating frameworks. As Fullan (1992) claimed, 'teacher development and school development must go hand in hand' (p. 114) and 'By and large, schools are now not places where teachers can learn to become more effective' (p. 116) School development necessarily depended on teacher development, but teacher development would in turn depend on schools providing frameworks to help teachers to learn both from reflecting on their own experience and from ideas from elsewhere (Bradley *et al.*, 1994; Hargreaves, 1994).

The question then becomes: how can schools best contribute to their own improvement through fostering the professional development of their teachers? There are a number of important ideas that can contribute to this, and we shall not be seeking in this book to deal with all of them. All such ideas, however, have one thing in common: they all involve schools, *because* they are all about helping children and young people to learn, in creating protected time and space for another purpose, that of helping teachers to learn. That is not something that just happens incidentally. Serious energy, resources and thought need to be committed to making it happen.

TWO IMPORTANT KINDS OF TEACHER ACTIVITY

Among the professional traditions readily available to schools for fostering teachers' learning, two are especially relevant to the theme of this book: the two traditions of collaboration among teachers and, linked to that, teachers as researchers.

It has always been the case that the most obvious source from which teachers could learn is other teachers. Teachers have been well aware of this, as is reflected in their professional associations, and especially in their subject teaching associations. Teachers of mathematics, science and English, for example, have recognised the value of sharing ideas about good practice and about the dilemmas they face, and have established mechanisms for doing this, such as regular conferences and professional journals. Within secondary schools, teachers have often identified most closely with their subject departments and have used their departments as frameworks for collaborative thinking about their teaching tasks.

At the same time, the history of classroom teaching has been one of teachers valuing the *privacy* of their classrooms, and of being reluctant to expose their teaching to the gaze of other adults (see Lortie, 1975). Classroom teaching, including the relationships that teachers form with their classes, has tended to be a very personal activity. The nature of the classroom teaching task means that doing it effectively depends not just on a technical expertise that can be replicated from one teacher to another, but also on an investment by teachers of their own selves and personalities into their teaching. Furthermore, the complexity of classroom teaching means that a great deal of teachers' expertise is necessarily intuitive and tacit: it is not only very personal but also, like personal behaviour in other contexts, not such that the individual teacher has a tidy and explicit awareness of it. Teachers are aware that their teaching is different from that of their colleagues, that to a considerable extent it embodies their own personalities, and also that colleagues are likely to judge it in terms of their own distinctive conceptions of good practice. For all these reasons, teachers can easily feel that to share their classroom lives with colleagues is to invite encroachment into their personal and private world, and to feel very vulnerable about doing so. And so there has been a tendency to maintain the privacy of classrooms as much as possible.

This historical tendency for teachers to treat classrooms as their private domains is therefore an inherent characteristic of the classroom teaching system, not a perverse weakness on the part of teachers. It has nonetheless been a counter-productive characteristic of the system, because it has reduced the amount of collaboration among teachers in their thinking about the most important part of their work, their classroom teaching. To counteract this tendency, there have been active movements in several countries (e.g. Biott and Nias, 1992; Little, 1982, 1990a; Smyth, 1991) to promote and to explore collaborative learning among teachers, within and across schools. The promotion and exploration of the value of collaboration among teachers have fed into debates and research about the closely associated ideas of collegiality and of communities of practice, and about the conceptual and strategic problems of clarifying what kinds of collaboration are valued and on what grounds, and of the conditions in which such valued collaboration might thrive (e.g. Fielding, 1999; Hargreaves, 1991, 1999; Little and McLaughlin, 1993; Little, 1999). Because the research and scholarship that have been conducted into collaboration among teachers provide such an important foundation for this book's theme of research networking among schools, Chapter 3 is devoted to reviewing this work.

Teachers as researchers is another international tradition that provides an equally important foundation for this book's theme. It is not an entirely disconnected idea, however, as collaboration among teachers has been a strong element of the teacher research tradition. Groundwater-Smith and Dadds (2004), for example, give 'towards responsible communities of practice' as the sub-title of their chapter on practitioner research in the *International Handbook on the Continuing Professional Development of Teachers* and explain that the chapter is arguing 'for the development and authentic improvement of schools to be based upon systematic practitioner inquiry undertaken as a collegial activity embedded within the culture of the school'. It is a movement with many roots, including the seminal thinking of key individuals such as Kurt Lewin, Stephen Corey and Lawrence Stenhouse. Elliott (1991), however, describes the origins of educational action research in England as including the collaborative efforts of innovative teachers in secondary modern schools in the 1960s who, through debate and investigation, were able to challenge and change their schools' curricula.

It was Stenhouse (1975) who articulated a key element of the rationale for teachers being researchers as the fact that in practice teachers are the most important decision-makers in education systems. As it is teachers who in practice determine the fate of proposed innovations, and whether or not they maintain the practices they have inherited, it is teachers who implicitly or explicitly evaluate the merits of different practices. Stenhouse argued that a critical element of 'extended professionalism' was that teachers should make such decisions consciously and deliberately. This does not mean that teachers need to be constantly questioning the merits of all aspects of their practice; but it does mean that they should identify critical elements of their practice for evaluation. Nor does it mean that teachers are under any obligation to engage in formal research investigations, nor that they should write and publish their findings; but it does mean that teachers should identify the kinds of evidence that are relevant to their evaluations and that they should collect evidence of these kinds. Others who have worked with teachers in this tradition, such as Elliott and Adelman (1974) and Carr and Kemmis (1986), have highlighted not only the practical value of having the help of others in collecting relevant evidence, such as one's colleagues or one's students, but also the critical importance of gaining access to the different perspectives that such others can provide.

Stenhouse's basic rationale for teachers being researchers still stands today, although others (e.g. Kemmis, 1995) have certainly developed and refined it. One problem is of course that it is very demanding and time-consuming for teachers to engage seriously in research, with the result that only energetic enthusiasts tend to do so. (In some eyes it is perhaps more realistic for teachers to aspire to the more recent, less demanding and vaguer ideal of being 'reflective practitioners'.) Elliott (1991) emphasised that a crucial facilitating condition for teachers engaging in research was having the right kind of school management, one 'which supported a "bottom-up" rather than a "top-down" change process', 'a collegial, rather than an individualistic or bureaucratic form of accountability' and which fostered 'a 'free, open and tolerant professional discourse' among all the school staff. His account of his experiences does not however suggest that he found such facilitation from senior management to be commonly self-generating. The evident dependence of teachers as researchers on a conscious commitment of senior management to support such activity is one evident element of the rationale for researching schools.

RESEARCHING SCHOOLS AND NETWORKING SCHOOLS

In this book, our task is to consider critically two ways in which schools can improve through facilitating learning by teachers, and especially the potential of combining these two ways of facilitating teachers' learning. Both these approaches are still in their infancy. We shall be describing these infants as they currently are and pointing out their achievements. They are of course just the achievements of infants, their first faltering steps and their first two-word or three-word sentences; and so, although we shall attempt to be critical, we shall also seek to be forbearing in our judgements and shall hope that our audience will be similarly forbearing. Our particular interest, however, is in the partnership of these two infants, and our primary focus will be on what happens when they work in partnership. The main challenge for us is not to evaluate what has been achieved but rather their potential as a partnership. Could they complement each other appropriately as partners? To what extent do they share the same philosophy? Do they have complementary strengths and limitations? By observing them playing alongside each other as infants, if not actually together, what can we learn about how they might work together in their maturity?

As we have noted, the idea of researching schools has to owe a lot to the much older idea of researching teachers. But we must not exaggerate the continuity between these two ideas. As we have noted, Stenhouse's (1975) idea of teachers as researchers was very much concerned with teachers focusing on their own individual classrooms, investigating and developing their own practice, albeit with some collaboration among individual teachers. Elliott's (1991) account of his extensive experience of teachers working as researchers is primarily about successive projects in which enthusiastic small groups or individual teachers have collaborated with university-based researchers. Other commentators, such as Carr and Kemmis (1986), have promoted a kind of teacher research aimed at offering a radical critique of established structures and assumptions in education. Unlike all of these versions of teacher research, researching schools are probably necessarily led by senior managers of schools, who aim to encourage and support teachers to engage in research that both the teachers and the managers believe will in some way lead to school improvement. This must leave open the question of how far researching schools can build on earlier experiences of teachers as researchers.

Historically, furthermore, the link is not easy to trace. Much the most outspoken and articulate prophet of researching schools in the UK has been David Hargreaves (1996; 1999). The primary focus of Hargreaves' 1996 lecture was the lack of practical usefulness of most research conducted by academic educational researchers, and how badly they compared with the much more productive record of medical researchers. A major part of his solution to this problem was for a large proportion of the resources available for educational research to be allocated to schools rather than to universities. In his 1999 paper, he followed this up with a much more detailed and closely argued account of how 'the knowledge creating school' would work and of the conditions necessary for the success of such an enterprise. The important point in this context is that in neither of these papers did Hargreaves mention a teacher research tradition on which his proposed developments could build. (When he delivered the latter paper at the British Educational Research Association 1998 conference, there were members of the audience who claimed that teacher researchers had been doing what he wanted for many years; but Hargreaves explicitly rejected these claims as invalid.)

However much or little continuity there may be, the concept of the researching school is both relatively new and not necessarily very clear. How far are such schools committed, as Hargreaves suggests they should be, to 'knowledge creation'? If they are, is such knowledge specifically for their own use, or is it for other schools too? Or are such schools primarily concerned with the process of teacher researching, with the teacher development that stems from the thinking and questioning involved being more important than any research findings? Nor is it clear how such schools can operate most effectively? How, for example, can the need for a senior management plan – or ideally a consensual school plan – for school improvement be compatible with the importance in research of individual imagination or with the unpredictability of where research will lead?

The idea of networking schools has become very fashionable in English education during the last few years, having been strongly promoted by official agencies, notably the National College for School Leadership (NCSL) through its Networked Learning Communities (NLC) initiative. As it seems quite a new idea in England, it may be surprising to find Lieberman and Grolnick (1996) suggesting that the most important study of educational networks was done by Allen Parker twenty years earlier. They quote Parker (1977) as concluding from his study of over sixty educational networks that five 'key ingredients' are needed in successful networks:

- a strong sense of commitment to the innovation
- a sense of shared purpose
- a mixture of information sharing and psychological support
- an effective facilitator
- voluntary participation and equal treatment.

These 'key ingredients' reflect some of the important ways in which the idea of 'networks' has come to be used in educational contexts. First, networks are first and foremost frameworks for collaboration, involving 'a mixture of information sharing and psychological support'. Just as it had become clear that teachers' learning was limited by working in the isolation of their classrooms, so it more slowly became apparent that schools' learning equally tended to be limited while they worked in isolation: networks are frameworks for collaboration among schools. Second, networks are not just groups of people who communicate regularly with each other: they are purposeful, and the purpose is to promote innovations. Lieberman and Grolnick (1996, p. 9) suggest that one of Parker's key insights was that members 'have a sense of being part of a special group or movement'. Third, the emphasis on 'voluntary participation' indicates that networks are to some extent 'outside the system': Lieberman and Grolnick note how, at an early stage in their own work, 'we recognized that these reform networks, unlike more permanent institutions, were intentionally constructed without rigid borders, buildings or permanent structures' (ibid). Fourth, the emphasis on 'equal treatment' indicates that there is no particular intended direction of influence, neither 'top-down' nor 'bottom-up'; the intention is instead one of 'working laterally' (Hargreaves, 2003a), with members of networks influencing each other through sharing their ideas and experiences.

These then are the two ideas for schools' and teachers' learning that we want to explore in this book: 'researching schools' and 'networking schools'. But why should these two ideas be brought together? One rationale for doing so is offered by Hargreaves (1999) who, having explained what a 'knowledge-creating school' might be like, went on to argue that:

> What the single school can achieve here is limited, but if a group of schools, either in a local or 'virtual' consortium, works on the same topic of professional knowledge creation and validation through a process of external networking, national progress in advancing the quality of teaching and learning could be rapid and cumulative. ICT provides opportunities for networking for professional knowledge creation, shared tinkering and concurrent dissemination on a scale and at a rate that has hitherto been unimaginable ... Networks are the key to this different model of dissemination in which *all* schools can now be linked through ICT and so *all* can take part in the activities of professional knowledge creation, application and dissemination.
>
> (Hargreaves, 1999, pp. 138–9)

We were less certain than Hargreaves that this was the way forward, but it certainly seemed a valuable enough idea for us to explore it through actively participating in one research network of schools and through studying several others. In doing so, we were again following Hargreaves' (1999) advice, when he suggested that one of the four ways in which university researchers could contribute to the development of school-based research was by 'making the study of the networked creation, validation and dissemination of professional knowledge a focus of university-led research' (p. 140).

THE STRUCTURE OF THIS BOOK

This book is in three sections. Part 1 is about identifying from the literature questions that ought to be asked about research networks of schools. In the next three chapters we shall review what the literature can tell us about the ideas, practices and problems associated with the different strands of thought that contribute to the idea of school research networks. First, in Chapter 2, we shall review critical issues that have been identified regarding researching schools, including questions of how they can build on the teacher researchers tradition. Chapter 3 will identify critical issues with regard to teachers' collaboration in learning about and developing their practice; and Chapter 4 will similarly examine what we can learn from the literature on networking schools. Then, on the basis of these three chapters, Chapter 5 will identify questions arising from the literature to be explored in the rest of the book.

In Part 2, we shall first in Chapter 6 review three school research networks in different countries, and shall then report both our own case studies of six English school research networks and a survey of the experience and reflections of participants in these networks. Chapter 14, at the end of Part 2, will identify further questions that have arisen from the study of these nine networks.

In Part 3, we shall aim to consider the questions arising from Parts 1 and 2, both about the potential value of school research networks and also about the conditions and strategies that might lead them to be as fruitful as possible.

Part I

The foundations of networking practitioner research

Researching schools, collaboration and networks

Chapter 2

Researching schools

Donald McIntyre

INTRODUCTION

In this chapter, we shall aim to outline what is known from previous research and theorising about researching schools, that is schools that have in some sense committed themselves to engaging as organisations in research or enquiry, or perhaps to facilitating research and enquiry by teachers. Doing this seems a necessary first step towards our consideration in this book of exploring the idea not just of researching schools, but of research networks. However, even the concept of the researching school is relatively new and not necessarily very clear. We need to consider, because it is far from obvious, what such schools aim to achieve, and why. And then we need to examine such evidence as there is about what enables or helps such schools to achieve their purposes effectively.

As we suggested in our introductory chapter, one significant issue concerns the extent to which the idea of researching schools incorporates and builds on the much more widely established idea of researching teachers. The likelihood that this must be so necessarily leads us to start by outlining key features of that stronger tradition. Given, however, that there are many excellent accounts of the literature on teachers as researchers readily available (e.g. Groundwater-Smith and Dadds, 2004; Zeichner and Noffke, 2001), we shall not attempt a comprehensive critical review of that literature. Our concern will rather be to consider the strengths of the teacher researcher tradition on which researching schools can build and the limitations of that tradition which it needs to overcome.

The greater part of the chapter will be concerned with reviewing evidence about what researching schools have aimed to do and about what has helped or hindered their efforts. Then a further section of the chapter will consider the rationale offered by Hargreaves (1999) for researching schools, a rationale focused on the ambitious ideal of 'the knowledge-creating school'. Finally, we shall begin to consider the implications of this chapter for the idea of researching networks.

TEACHERS AS RESEARCHERS

Dewey (1929) described teachers' contributions to educational research as an 'unworked mine'. This theme is echoed in the work of later writers, including in the UK Stenhouse (1975; 1981), Elliott (1991) and Hargreaves (1999), who have argued for teachers to be more than the subjects and consumers of educational research and for teacher research and enquiry to have a particular role in the generation of educational knowledge. However, there have been very different conceptions of the nature and purposes of teacher research and enquiry and much debate about its status and its quality.

Several different threads tend to get entangled in discussions of teacher research and enquiry. Somekh (1994), discussing action research as the type of research most characteristically undertaken by teachers, illustrates the intertwined nature of these different threads:

> If action research is not recognised as a research methodology, the knowledge generated from action research is neither taken seriously nor disseminated widely and effectively. The knowledge is seen merely as an outcome of a professional development process, devalued into something that concerns only the individual who carried out the action research – local, private and unimportant. In this way, the operation of power in the social system works to neutralize the voice and influence of practitioners and promote the hegemony of traditional academic researchers.
>
> (Somekh, 1994, p. 28)

As is clearly reflected in this quotation, one thread concerns contrasting purposes with which teachers can engage in research and enquiry. There is a long tradition of tension between two contrasting aspirations for practitioner research and enquiry. One is that teachers should investigate their own practice to improve it. The other is for teacher research to contribute to public knowledge about teaching and learning. The first of these aspirations is perhaps most closely identified with Stenhouse (1975) who argued for teachers espousing an 'extended professionalism' which involved three main elements:

- the commitment to systematic questioning of one's own teaching as a basis for development;
- the commitment and skills to study one's own teaching; and
- the concern to question and to test theory in practice.

(Stenhouse, 1975, p. 143)

Stenhouse (1975; 1981) thus saw teacher researchers as the main immediate beneficiaries of their own research and the appropriate wider audience for it, if any, as being 'the village' of the teacher's own colleagues, not the wider research community. However, other advocates of teacher research including Somekh (1994), as is clear from the above quotation, have seen the proper purpose of teacher research as being to contribute to public knowledge.

A second thread concerns the *methodological rigour* of action research and more generally of teacher research. As Zeichner and Noffke (2001) clearly demonstrate in their account of the history of teacher research in North America, it has been difficult for teacher research to establish itself as sufficiently rigorous to be 'taken seriously' and 'disseminated widely and effectively'. This has been partly because of the distinctive methodological problems that action research raises, although these problems have lessened as a multiplicity of research traditions have increasingly been accepted by academic researchers. Partly, however, the problem has been that teachers' normal working conditions make it practically difficult for them to spend sufficient time on their research to attain the standards of rigour expected by, for example, academic journals, and perhaps also culturally difficult for them to take these academic standards very seriously. Ruthven (2005), reviewing 'recent stock-taking of teacher research by some of its leading advocates' (Cochran-Smith and Lytle, 1999; Elliott and Sarland, 1995; Elliott *et al.*, 1996; 1997; Zeichner and Noffke, 2001) (p. 412), concludes that:

> practitioner research has been treated primarily as a form of professional development, in which respect it has been judged successful in contributing both to deepening insight and improving practice. However, teacher research has a much weaker record of contributing to the accumulation of trustworthy public knowledge ...
>
> (Ruthven, 2005, p. 417)

A third important thread in debates about teacher research is the suggestion that it is or should be of political significance. Two closely linked facets of this may be distinguished. One is the suggestion that teacher research and enquiry should be primarily directed towards goals of greater democracy and justice in education. Although there is general consensus that an immediate purpose of teacher research should be to improve educational practice, the debate here is about the need for critical perspectives on the ideologies and structures by which schools are controlled and for emancipatory action derived from these critical perspectives (see Carr and Kemmis, 1986; Freire, 1970). The other related facet, clearly evident in the above quotation from Somekh (1994), is the idea that teacher research should be seen as a way of giving teachers a more powerful voice in educational affairs. It is widely suggested that teacher research loses its political power when it is 'colonised', by national, district or school managers or by university departments (Elliott and Sarland, 1995; Elliott *et al.*, 1997) for school improvement or professional development purposes.

One fairly recent arguable example of such colonisation of teacher research in England is the Best Practice Research Scholarships (BPRS) scheme promoted and financed by the English Department for Education and Employment in 2000. Over several years, teachers received scholarships to support small specified research projects, which they generally conducted individually with some support from academic mentors. Presage *et al.* (2003) argue that the scheme was primarily aimed at raising pupil standards, as defined by DfEE, and that this was in tension with teacher development. However that may be, the scheme certainly did not support any critical or emancipatory aspirations that teachers might have had. Furthermore, the scale of the funding and of the mentoring somewhat predictably led to a situation in which the research reports produced by teachers were judged by academic evaluators to be generally methodologically weak (Furlong *et al.*, 2003), as had been the case with similar earlier schemes.

Although in practice much teacher research is conducted by isolated individuals, there is widespread agreement that it tends to be greatly facilitated and much more fruitful if it is conducted collaboratively. Whether in formulating the research questions to be explored, in gathering evidence, or in interpreting the evidence gathered, the help and the different perspectives of people other than the central teacher researcher can be crucially valuable. These other people may come from different positions, including very fruitfully the students in teachers' classes (e.g. the Ford Teaching Project, Elliott and Adelman, 1974). Teachers' colleagues tend however to be among the most helpful collaborators, as they are well placed to engage in critical questioning of a teacher's assumptions, in deliberation about both the design of the research and the meaning of evidence, and in data-gathering such as observation of each other's teaching. Working collaboratively can also be crucially valuable in providing teacher researchers with the emotional support that helps them to sustain the research when the work gets harder than anticipated, when its value seems questionable, or when the findings are disappointing.

As noted above, teacher research has not as yet made a very significant contribution to public knowledge about education. Its contribution to teachers' lives and professional development is not however disputed. In addition to its direct impact on teachers' classroom practice, engaging in research has been shown (e.g. by Dadds, 1995; Elliott, 1991) to make teachers' work more intellectually stimulating, to give them renewed feelings of professionalism, pride in being a teacher and excitement about teaching, to enable them to develop a broader sense of how their work matters and to 'reconnect' them to their colleagues.

It is not easy however for teachers to engage in research. In addition to the need to be highly motivated, teacher researchers need to have supportive conditions. Internally, the support of senior school managements is likely to be crucial, both in practically facilitating the research and also in recognising its potential usefulness and in being ready to consider changes in school practices in the light of research findings. External support, often from university colleagues, can be very important too, in providing research knowledge, training and guidance and also access to libraries and other information sources. And, as noted above, doing research as a member of a group that provides both support and critical debate generally makes the enterprise much more feasible and more rewarding.

Implications for researching schools

In the light of this brief outline of the teacher research tradition, we need to ask about strengths of this tradition on which researching schools (and networks) can build and also about limitations, which researching schools might be able to overcome.

One thing is immediately clear. Researching schools and networks are institutional arrangements that at the very least need the support of school managers and are generally likely to work most productively if they stem from considered school policies. This means that some of the more romantic elements in the teacher research tradition, involving individual teachers ploughing isolated, lonely research furrows, or emancipatory action research projects aimed at subverting established power structures, are unlikely to be elements that are incorporated into the work of researching schools. On the other hand, some of the major frustrations that individual teacher researchers have experienced should be reduced in the context of researching schools. The explicit support of school managers for research activity should mean that steps are taken both to facilitate the research, for example by treating the research as a recognised part of teachers' work, and to take advantage of its findings in consideration of schools' policies and practices. Similarly, the support of school managers should facilitate both collaborative research work within the school and the development of research partnerships with, for example, local universities.

It is not obvious, however, that the development of researching schools or networks is likely to differ from the teacher research tradition in bringing about a clear resolution of that most fundamental of debates, whether teacher research should be aimed primarily at the development of new validated public knowledge or simply at the professional development of the teachers involved. We can be confident that schools will be motivated to pursue the second of these agendas, with the further intention that teachers' professional development should contribute to whole school improvement. But it is difficult to predict whether schools are likely to aspire to the more ambitious goal of knowledge creation, or – if they do – whether they will see the knowledge created as distinctively local knowledge for use only within the school, or as knowledge to be made available, and likely to be useful, to a wider population. Associated with these questions is the further issue of whether schools will wish to invest sufficient resources into their research to make it possible for methodological rigour to be a reasonable aspiration, or indeed to develop school cultures in which methodological rigour is a matter of concern. These would seem to be questions that can only be resolved empirically.

SCHOOLS AS RESEARCH INSTITUTIONS

This section involves a significant shift of perspective from that of the previous section. Whereas the latter was concerned with the very robust and well established tradition of individual teachers engaging in research or enquiry on their own or in collaborating groups, here we have to concern ourselves with the idea of schools as institutions committing and organising themselves to conduct or support, and to use, educational research. This shift from personal projects to institutional projects has profound implications.

There is of course some considerable continuity in the ideas involved. Most fundamentally, there is continuity in that the primary purposes are to question current or proposed practices and so to improve the quality of educational practice. Just as the research of individual teachers has been most commonly aimed at their own professional development, and thus the improvement of both their educational understanding and their professional practice, so the dominant concern of schools as research institutions is with their institutional learning, and thus with the improvement of both their policies and their practice. And just as the aspirations of some individual teachers have been to go beyond development of their own thinking and practice, to challenge and enhance existing understandings, settlements, policies and practices more widely, so there has been some aspiration at the school level for schools not just to be concerned with their own improvement but also to become 'knowledge-creating' institutions.

It may even be argued that it is historically misleading to distinguish strongly between the tradition of individual teachers engaging in research on their practice and schools seeking to become research institutions. Elliott (1991), for example, in his account of the origins of educational action research in England, suggests that in the 1960s some secondary modern schools developed in which innovative teachers were able, through debate and enquiry, to challenge and change the schools' curricula. His account suggests that, although it was collaborating individual teachers who were the prime movers in such developments, one crucial facilitating condition was 'a management structure which supported a "bottom-up" rather than a "top-down" change process, and "a collegial, rather than an individualistic or bureaucratic form of accountability"' (p. 7). He emphasises too the importance of a 'free, open and tolerant professional discourse among all the school staff, fostered by frequent face-to-face interactions' (p. 6). As Elliott's account develops, however, the initiative continues over the subsequent decades to lie with individual teachers, usually collaborating with external academics such as himself. And although Elliott clearly recognises the importance of facilitation from people in senior management positions, this facilitation was not found to be self-generating or self-perpetuating: 'It was as if the internal facilitators required their strategies within schools to be validated by a strong external support team possessing influential sponsorship' (ibid., p. 41). More generally, the idea of schools developing themselves as research institutions has seemed to be much more complex than that of teacher-as-researcher, and one that has developed more slowly.

It is important to note here, however, a striking resemblance between the picture that Elliott paints of these innovative secondary modern schools of the 1960s and the characteristics of schools identified in the 1990s as those in which staff have operated as 'professional learning communities'. The use of this concept for thinking about schools was stimulated by the work of such organisation theorists as Senge (1990) and Sergiovanni (1994). Hord (1997), reviewing research findings on professional learning communities as the staff of 'change-ready schools (those that value change and seek change that will improve their schools)', emphasises inclusiveness: all teaching staff should understand the proposed mission for change and should be involved in deciding about change. School principals in such schools work supportively as peers and colleagues with teachers, engaging with them in professional development, being in the middle of things, easily accessible and making opportunities to stimulate conversation about teaching and learning. Active support is given by leaders to teachers seeking to develop their teaching strategies and skills. A culture of enquiry and questioning, searching for new ideas, critical thinking, dialogue, debate and collective problem-solving is deliberately fostered. This is done partly by creating conditions for teachers to work together, protected time and space being crucial resources, and partly through policies that prioritise effective communication, collaboration and an undeviating focus on meaningful student learning. Emphasis is placed too on fostering community solidarity within the staff and the development of trust and mutual respect among colleagues. Conflicts are not avoided but are actively addressed and resolved through discussion and debate. Fullan (1992, p. 353) is quoted approvingly as recommending 'a redesign of the workplace so that innovation and improvement are built into the daily activities of teachers'. These then are the suggested characteristics of schools in which staff are committed to learning and to changing their practices in the light of that learning. These might then be necessary but probably not sufficient conditions for schools to become research institutions.

It was primarily in the 1990s that the idea of schools as research institutions developed, apparently in close relationship to ideas about schools as self-improving institutions. Building on the already well established idea that teachers' professional growth can most fruitfully be based on their thoughtful research into their own practice, the idea was promoted that school improvement was closely tied to teachers' professional development (Bradley *et al.* 1994; Hargreaves, 1994) and so to teachers' research. The movement for schools improving themselves through becoming research institutions has however been internally quite diverse. At least five different and not closely related strands may be distinguished, and although it is the fourth of these that is most central and that will merit most attention, all five are potentially significant facets of such schools:

* schools using academic research
* schools making use of their 'data-rich environments'
* school self-evaluation
* corporate engagement of teachers as action researchers
* involving students and other members of schools as researchers.

But it would be wrong to suggest that the only important argument that has been advanced for schools becoming research institutions is that it is a way in which each school can improve itself. A quite different argument that has bubbled for decades is that the kinds of research done by university departments of education have not generally been helpful to schools and that, given the necessary resources, schools might themselves do more useful kinds of research. Here the focus shifts from schools engaging with research for their individual improvement to schools becoming generators of knowledge for much wider use. In recent years arguments for this kind of development have been advanced most strongly and coherently by Hargreaves (1996; 1999), and in the following section we shall seek to review these arguments.

THE CONTRIBUTION OF RESEARCH TO SCHOOL IMPROVEMENT

'During the last ten years a number of school improvement strategies have been developed in order to . . . provide the coherence and sense of strategic direction missing from previous efforts' (Gray *et al.*, 1999, p. 25). Deliberate engagement with research has been one important strand in some of these strategies for school improvement. But what 'engagement with research' means has, as noted above, not been uniform or straightforward.

Schools using academic research

If educational research is to contribute to school improvement, the most obvious way for that to happen is for schools to be able to take advantage of the large amounts of research that is done by academic researchers. There has been longstanding concern that this does not happen at all effectively, in England or elsewhere, but also uncertainty about the main sources of the problem and therefore about likely solutions to it. Criticism has been primarily directed at academic researchers, but the Hillage Report (1998), commissioned by the DfEE to make recommendations for 'the pursuit of excellence in research relating to schools' (ibid., p. ix), is not unusual in spreading the responsibility more widely:

> Practice among researchers on dissemination varies considerably, but the conclusions and implications of much research are not reaching their intended audience and those who could benefit from it. However, this is not just an issue for researchers. Practitioners and policy-makers (e.g. teachers and local and central government officials) need to be 'research aware', i.e. open to and interested in research, and have an understanding of what it can offer. They also need to have access to intermediary support to be able to interpret research and assimilate findings into their decision-making processes.
>
> (ibid., p. 52)

and later:

> whatever the relevance and the quality of the research and the user-friendliness of the output, its eventual impact will depend on the willingness and capacity of policy-makers and practitioners to take research into account in their decision-making and actions. This relies on a commitment to the principle, an understanding of what research can offer, and the practical capacity to interpret research . . .
>
> In our view, one of the biggest weaknesses of the current system is the absence of the interpretation of research findings to help inform decision-making and actions at all levels. It is not easy to articulate a solution to this issue succinctly, as effective mediation depends crucially on the context, the nature of the research and the knowledge of the practitioner or policy-maker, but it lies at the heart of a system that effectively integrates research, development, policy formation, implementation and reflective practice.
>
> (ibid., p. 53)

It may be suggested that the Hillage Report underestimates greatly the complexity and uncertainty of 'understanding what research can offer'. Baumfield and McGrane (2000) provide an interesting account of the slow process whereby teachers move, through engaging in research, from rather crude expectations that research should reveal 'what works' to necessary but more subtle concerns with 'why' and 'how' questions; and they conclude that, 'It does seem to be the case that the catalyst for productive engagement with research is engagement in research'. The Hillage Report is surely right, however, in its emphasis on the inadequacy of present provision for interpreting research findings to help inform decision-making and action. It is in university contexts, both in initial teacher education and in subsequent professional development programmes, that teachers most commonly are helped to learn about research and to reflect on its implications. But experience suggests that such decontextualised learning about research findings often does not help even individual teachers to develop their practice, far less help whole schools to do so. If schools are to use academic research to improve their practice, it is clear that becoming informed about relevant research and interpreting it in relation to a school's needs have to be integrated into the processes of generating and implementing the school's development plans. If McIntyre (2005) is right that the knowledge properly and characteristically generated by academic research and the knowledge necessarily used by teachers in their classroom teaching are of sharply contrasting kinds, and that a whole spectrum of intermediate kinds of knowledge is necessary in order to bridge the gap between them, this task of interpreting research and integrating it into school planning is far from straightforward.

Schools could in principle develop their own structures and personnel resources for doing this, but a more efficient way might be for continuing professional development (CPD) courses to be jointly planned by groups of schools with similar research-oriented agendas working with university faculties of education. One good example of this is the Masters course jointly planned by Hertfordshire Local Educational Authority (LEA) (as part of its own development plan), some of its schools and Cambridge University's Faculty of Education (Frost et al., 2003). Although the LEA involvement here does add a valuable extra dimension, any network of around ten schools, prepared to commit resources for (say) two teachers from each at any one time to be engaged on such a Masters course, could reasonably expect enthusiastic collaboration from a local faculty of education. Such a collaborative programme should of course be expected to go much further than selecting and interpreting academic research relevant to the schools' planning; it should also support schools in developing other facets of their own research agendas.

Using 'data-rich environments'

Changes in recent years, in England and elsewhere, have meant that schools have available to them very much more information (or 'data') about themselves than ever before. As many of those data come from official sources and are directly related to government agendas for what schools should view as most important (e.g. Standard Assessment Tasks (SATs) and GCSE results, OfSTED reports, Pupil Achievement Trackers (PATs) and Performance and Assessment Data (PANDAs)), an obvious starting point for becoming a researching school is to make active use of such already available data, using them to ask questions about the school's strengths and weaknesses and about how the school might set about improving (Ofsted, 2005). The 'data-rich environments' in which schools find themselves can thus perhaps offer both stimuli and tools for schools to become researching institutions.

Earl and Katz (2005) offer one thoughtful analysis of the possibilities that such data richness offers for school leaders. One important distinction that they make is between the 'extrinsic' and the 'intrinsic' motivation that can be aroused by data about schools. It is the extrinsic impact of externally provided data that is most likely to be apparent. For example, referring to the impact of national or state testing programmes, Earl and Katz report that 'certainly, there is considerable evidence that such assessments have been the impetus for awareness or conscious attention to educational issues that might not have been considered without them' (ibid., p. 5). They note that such awareness raising and the actions that follow from it can be desirable or undesirable, intended or unintended.

It is of course the less obvious 'intrinsic' motivation that data can arouse, where school staff are stimulated to ask and to investigate their own questions, that is most potentially valuable and most relevant to schools as researching institutions. It is in the context of thoughtful questioning of this kind, Earl and Katz suggest, that 'data provide tools for the investigation necessary to plan appropriate and focused improvement strategies' (ibid., p. 9). 'But', they go on to note, 'using data is not a mechanistic process. It is a skill and an art and a way of thinking'; and the greater part of their paper is devoted to elaborating the many conditions necessary for the use of data to be productive and helpful.

For example, Earl and Katz perceptively comment that 'data almost never provide answers. Instead, using data usually leads to more and more focused investigation and to better questions' (ibid., p. 13). Put another way, this means that careful and thoughtful use of the data available to schools almost always leads them to a realisation that such data are not good enough, and that quite new data will be needed to deepen understanding and to improve practice. There are two very good reasons for this. First, it is obvious that the data needed for answering any question have to be relevant to that question and data collected for another purpose are not likely to have that relevance: in particular, data from national agencies are unlikely to be relevant to school improvement strategies. Second, even where data collected for one purpose superficially seems relevant for another purpose, the quality of data will frequently be inadequate for that other purpose, so great caution is needed in using them.

If schools are stimulated by their data-rich environments to reflect thoughtfully on what they are doing, that may very well lead them to ask good questions about themselves and so to become researching schools. But among the basic characteristics of a researching school must surely be that it asks its own questions and that it evaluates critically the quality and the appropriateness of any available data for answering these questions.

School self-evaluation

The distinction between 'evaluation' and 'research' can be a fine one. It may involve nothing more than whether the main intention behind an investigation is research that is potentially generalisable to other contexts, or evaluation that is to help decision-making in one particular context. And in practice investigations often lead to ideas and insights that are less context-bound than was originally intended, or more so. So it must be expected that the practice of school self-evaluation, which has quite a long history, will have much to contribute to the development of schools as research institutions.

In the UK the idea of school self-evaluation appears to have developed in the first instance (e.g. ILEA, 1977) under the growing pressure in the 1970s for accountability. If schools had to be accountable for what they were doing, it was argued, then it was the schools themselves that should, at least in the first instance, assess their strengths and weaknesses. Although accountability to external audiences was the prime motivating force, there were those who from the beginning were arguing that self-evaluation did not make much sense unless it led to further research and development. For Elliott (1981), for example, this implied an action research framework for self-evaluation.

As it has developed over the last quarter-century, and as it can be seen in its fullest current manifestations (e.g. MacBeath, 1999), school self-evaluation has come to involve a number of key characteristics, all of which are highly relevant to schools as research institutions:

1. The primary premise for school self-evaluation, supported by extensive evidence, is that members of school communities know an enormous amount (and much more than non-members) both about their own good and bad school experiences and about what contributes to these experiences.

2. Whether or not external accountability is an important purpose of school self-evaluation, an important purpose should always be school self-improvement: school self-evaluation that does not lead to school improvement is demoralising; and valid school self-evaluation is a necessary condition for school improvement.

3. Schools are very complex organisations, so many different aspects of them need to be evaluated, many different criteria need to be used, and so many different sources and kinds of evidence are necessary.

4. Whether or not externally imposed or suggested criteria are used, valid school self-evaluation involves discovering and using the diverse criteria that are important for different groups in a school (different groups of students, of teachers and other staff, of parents, and also senior management and governors).

5. Considerable care and expertise are needed in order to develop and use valid procedures for gathering evidence for school self-evaluation, procedures that, for example, are comprehensible to the various groups of people involved, allow them to say what is important to them, and motivate them to express thoughtful and honest views. Comparable care and expertise are necessary for valid analysis and interpretation of the evidence gathered.

6. Self-evaluation procedures need not only to be valid but also to be credibly demonstrated to be valid. The usefulness of self-evaluation is likely to depend on such credible validation.

Taking all these considerations into account, it seems clear that valid self-evaluation can be of enormous value to schools, but is not a minor undertaking, depending as it does on quite considerable investment and planning. Furthermore, although as we have noted valid school self-evaluation does seem to be a necessary condition for school improvement, it is not a sufficient condition for school improvement. Although valid self-evaluation will certainly lead to better understanding of the school as it is, how to improve the school may remain far from clear. So something more is needed, and that something extra may well be the further move towards being a researching school.

MacBeath (1999) not only suggests that schools with whom he worked engaged in valid self-evaluation, but also offers a very clear (although quite demanding) framework to help other schools to do so. It does seem that we have reached a stage where both the value of becoming a self-evaluating school and also how to do so are relatively clear. So being validly self-evaluating could be a very useful platform from which a school might launch its efforts to become a researching school, something about which we do not know quite so much.

Corporate teacher engagement in action research

Enquiry for school improvement involves purposeful, focused and informed engagement with the context of the school as a means of learning about our practice and with a view to designing informed improvement interventions. It does not matter whether we start by finding out, or we start by deciding to act in a new or different way and then to study that action. The point is the purposeful engagement with the world of the school in a systematic, planned and collaborative way and to plan informed actions designed to improve practice, based upon what we are confident that we know.

(Jackson, 2002a)

At the core of the notion of the researching school is the idea of schools systematically encouraging and supporting teacher engagement in research. There is now a considerable literature giving accounts of such schools. Most, though not all, of these accounts explicitly suggest that the promotion of teacher research is directed towards school improvement.

On the other hand, it needs to be recognised that teacher research has not been a very widely used approach by schools seeking to improve themselves. And even where teacher research is viewed as important for school improvement, it tends to be adopted as one element integrated into a more overarching improvement strategy. It can be difficult, therefore, and perhaps misleading, to distinguish characteristics of the research element from other features of the overall improvement strategy. Often, furthermore, what might be seen as a research element is construed in broader and looser terms, with the word 'enquiry' frequently being preferred. Thus, although there is a frequent recognition that improvement is likely to be fostered by schools being 'learning organisations' or 'learning communities', there is often a vagueness as to the nature and extent of any research element implied by that. And while a general openness to learning is surely important in fostering improvement, there does not seem yet to be clear evidence about the specific importance of teacher research. Gray *et al.* (1999), for example, conducted twelve case studies of schools deliberately trying to improve and found strong correlations between 'improvements in effectiveness' and four 'change measures'. One of these four change measures was described as follows:

> the extent to which the school had begun to tackle the processes of teaching and learning at classroom level, including the use of classroom observation as part of the appraisal process, the fostering of collaborative work as a means of sharing good practice among teachers and the encouragement of discussion and an enquiry orientation towards teaching and learning.
>
> (Gray *et al.*, 1999, p. 130)

It is evident that such observation, collaboration and 'enquiry orientation' might or might not lead to something approaching research activity.

Most of the literature about schools fostering teacher research is in the form of accounts of particular school improvement schemes or of what has seemed important in particular schools or groups of schools. Most are insider accounts, offering rationales for what was done and/or insights about what facilitated or constrained success, and generally seeming both thoughtful and persuasive. Given both the specificity and the relative subjectivity of these accounts, but taking advantage of the common elements between them, we can infer some tentative hypotheses about what facilitates the corporate engagement of teachers in research in such a way as to be fruitful for school improvement.

Hypothesis I: The value for school improvement of teachers engaging in research depends on this being merely one element of an integrated strategy

A number of complementary policies for structural and cultural change or 'micropolitical strategies' (Johnson, 2003) are frequently mentioned in accounts of schools using teacher research as a strategy for school improvement (e.g. Baumfield and McGrane, 2000; Frost *et al.*, 2000; Johnson, 1998; Johnson, 2003). It is often not clear whether these strategies are seen primarily as instrumental to the development of researching schools or instead as complementary elements of overall strategies for school improvement. In practice, the distinction seems unimportant. Three such strategies may be highlighted. First is a strong emphasis on dialogue and collaboration, involving deep listening, sharing professional knowledge, sharing also the questioning of assumptions, openness about problems, and so ending the traditional privatised life of teachers. Second is an emphasis on multi-level or distributed leadership, where 'freedom to act, opportunity to experiment and authority to question historical assumptions' and 'emancipation through collaborative learning' are to be shared inclusively throughout the school. Third is establishing moral purpose (Johnson, 2003) whereby senior managers use moral arguments, including a discourse of hope and efficacy, about the need to do things differently in order better to foster students' well-being. This involves building a consensus around what members of the school community believe in, including asserting the nature of the problems to be confronted in terms that are calculated to overcome teacher weariness and cynicism and to establish a non-negotiable rationale for fundamental reform.

Hypothesis 2: The value for school improvement of teachers engaging in research depends on the overall commitment to this strategy of the senior management

One of the striking characteristics of schools that appear to make productive use of teacher research is the commitment to such research of senior management and usually the personal enthusiasm of the school principal. As a result, these schools seem to be pervaded by practices that are supportive to teacher research. For example, Ebbutt (2000) investigated staff perceptions of the conditions for research in six schools with which he was working as a research facilitator on behalf of Cambridge University. Also, knowing the schools well, he was able to rate the extent to which a research culture had developed in each. There was only one school that he judged to have an 'embedded research culture' and of it he reported that, 'What this school is seen by its staff to be providing is in part a swathe of conditions supportive to a culture of school-based research. But it is also the case that the school is seen by its staff to provide few disincentives or few conditions demotivating to research'.

It is not one or two particular things that help a school to take advantage of teacher research: it is the whole orientation of its senior management.

Hypothesis 3: The value for school improvement of teachers engaging in research depends on effective co-ordination of overall school development plans with research projects voluntarily undertaken by individuals or groups of teachers

Although there are some schools that recognise value in both whole-school research projects and small-group projects (e.g. Johnson, 1998), there seems to be a strong consensus about the merits of teacher research projects being initiated and conducted by small groups of teachers. The usefulness of such projects for school improvement depends of course on them relating to an agreed agenda for improvement, one that is supported and sustained by senior managers. Co-ordination is necessary between research activities and development agendas at any one time and also in a sequential way, with research findings being disseminated, used as a basis for reflection and planning, and also leading to further enquiry.

Such co-ordination can be problematic and there are conflicting views about how best it can be managed. For example, the Improving the Quality of Education for All (IQEA) approach (Hopkins *et al.*, 1994) was to create temporary new school structures, with a key School Improvement Group (SIG) involving teaching staff from all levels, with pairs or trios from the SIG each engaging in separate enquiries planned by themselves, but agreed, evaluated and critiqued by the whole SIG, and with changing SIG membership each year. But such complex temporary structures seem in some cases to have been difficult to manage and to be potentially divisive (Richards, 2003). A more radical solution has been to emphasise individual teacher leadership (Frost *et al.*, 2000, Frost and Durrant, 2003), placing on teachers the responsibility both to generate their own ideas for research and development and also to negotiate these ideas with senior staff so that their projects are integrated with school development plans. Either way, success seems to depend on senior management being prepared to take risks, committing themselves to the necessary support structures not only for the conduct of the research but also for the dissemination of the research findings within the school, and to their critical examination and possible use.

Hypothesis 4: The value for school improvement of teachers engaging in research depends on active, informed and sensitive support for their research activities from a university department of education

It is difficult to find examples of schools that have adopted this kind of approach to school improvement with apparent success but without having established a partnership with one or more university departments. Johnson (1998) for example notes not only the importance of such relationships with universities, but also some of the significant barriers that teachers have to be helped to overcome: fear of being judged by academic standards; fear of feeling inadequate in relation to academic discourse; a perception of academic knowledge as irrelevant to school realities. She discusses how dependent the success of her school's progress as a research institution was on academics who showed in practical ways that they valued the work and working context of the school, who became genuine respectful partners, and who shared with teachers both their knowledge and expertise and their enthusiasm for the joint research.

Hypothesis 5: An unresolved dilemma in relation to the value for school improvement of teachers engaging in research concerns the rigour and quality of the research that is necessary for school improvement purposes

> The word 'research' brings with it a number of associations related to rigour, reliability, validity, generalisability, ethics, scale, objectivity and so on. In reality, though, what we are talking about when engaging with school-based enquiry activities does not have to conform to the same exacting standards. There is a term known as 'good enough research' – which means generating research designs that are valid and reliable in relation to their purpose and their context, rather than to the purity of the knowledge or its generalisability. School-based enquiry is often 'good enough research'.
>
> (Jackson, 2002c, p. 5)

Jackson's comments capture very effectively three features of discussions in this field. First, they echo the views of many teachers that academic standards of rigour are quite inappropriate for their use of research for school improvement purposes. It is 'good enough' to think of what they wish to do as 'enquiry', without any aspirations to meeting academic research standards. Second, however, the questions of what kind of research or enquiry is 'good enough', and how one might decide this, are left unanswered. And third, there is equally little discussion of why, when research is seen to be valuable, normal research standards are seen to be unnecessary.

Teachers understandably experience diverse, conflicting feelings about this. On one hand, research is such a minor part of their work, and teaching is such a demanding and very different kind of discipline, that they are fully justified in feeling that it is unreasonable to ask them to meet professional research standards. On the other, suggestions that teachers cannot be expected to do research 'properly' can seem very insulting. Furthermore, teachers' views and feelings clearly change as they become more experienced in doing research and so in taking a research perspective. Johnson (1998), for example, documents the tensions that teachers felt as they were pressed into relying more on writing in their communications in order to take advantage of their research achievements. Baumfield and McGrane (2000), similarly, note how with experience in research teachers change their perspective, for example changing in their preferred research questions from 'What works?' to 'How?' and 'Why?'.

The solution to this dilemma will perhaps be found through working from the insights of Stenhouse (1975), who understood that the crucial research task that he was asking teachers to undertake in their classrooms was first and foremost an extension of their teaching work, not an imitation of academic research. The purpose of the classroom action research that he proposed for teachers was to examine critically the implications and merits of specific new or established elements of their practice, but to do so in context, without a need to make explicit the complex realities of their classroom situation and practice, which they knew intimately and necessarily took for granted in their daily work. This was research that was for their own professional purposes, not for wider public knowledge. (Teachers might of course wish to do research to add to public knowledge, but that would be a quite different matter.) Research for school improvement is of course different in that it is research addressed to members of the school community (or perhaps to a departmental community) not just for oneself. It may be, however, that it is possible to extrapolate, from Stenhouse's idea for individual teachers in their classrooms, the idea of doing research on certain highly selected themes within a community context where a great deal can be taken for granted. Working out what that would imply is likely to be a challenging task, but it may hold the key to what is 'good enough research' in the context of school improvement.

Hypothesis 6: The value for school improvement of teachers engaging in research depends on senior management's reliable provision of significant resources, especially resources of time, to facilitate both the research and its effective use

Every account of researching schools refers to the crucial importance of resourcing for research. Perhaps most fundamentally this includes the resourcing of support structures, including protected time for in-school groups to meet and also the expense of working in partnership with universities and possibly with other schools. Time is the most expensive commodity and therefore the most difficult to provide. Johnson (2003) for example emphasises the importance for senior management of protecting teachers' time from other school and external demands. Equally important, he suggests, is taking the lead in showing how the time and energies devoted to research fit within a coherent and realistic overall school plan for reform, and reframing talk about work intensification to emphasise teachers' capacity to make realistic changes in arrangements in the interests of students.

Among the environmental characteristics emphasised by Jackson as conducive to learning are, in addition to time, supportive social structures, information and knowledge sources, a caring management, inclusiveness, opportunities for teachers to observe each other's good practice, and fun and social cohesion support. The crucial importance of social and emotional supports is emphasised too by Johnson (2003), who quotes one of his informants: 'We spent a lot of time eating and drinking and socialising together but having professional discussions'.

Hypothesis 7: The value for school improvement of teachers engaging in research depends on a long-term commitment by the school, including its governors

Ebbutt (2000) judged that only two of the six School–University Partnership in Educational Research (SUPER) partnership schools that he studied had established research cultures (with one of the two having an embedded or taken for granted research culture). What was common to these two schools, in contrast to the other four, was that they had each been working at being research schools for some ten years. Fortunately we have detailed histories of these two schools as researching schools, from James and Worrall (2000) and from Richards (2003). Each of these histories gives us some understanding both of the distinctive individuality of each school's concerns, opportunities, aspirations and strategies and also of the complexities of the tasks involved for them in becoming research schools.

Two issues may be noted in addition to the considerable fruitfulness of the long-term efforts and commitment of the two schools. The first is that in both schools, despite all the encouragement and support given over ten years, there was still a substantial minority of teachers who wanted no part in the research culture and who were indeed opposed to such a culture. Johnson (2003) sensibly suggests that such dissent and resistance are to be expected and need to be consciously addressed using appropriate micropolitical strategies. Demonstration of respect for the resistant teachers and multiple opportunities for them to 'work things through' are of course the most constructive strategies but, as in the above two schools, that alone is unlikely to overcome all resistance. The deeper problem that this reflects is that teachers' working conditions are such that neither national government nor the governors of a specific school can reasonably demand of teachers that they should accept a researcher role as part of their basic contract. That would be taking a step too far. Before it would be possible to make such a demand of teachers it would be necessary to make other rather fundamental changes in teachers' conditions.

The second issue is no doubt related. In both schools, when the headteachers retired, there was a severe lack of continuity. Neither set of governors seemed, when appointing successors, to treat the researching nature of their schools as a matter of importance. In one school, the new head was initially quite hostile. He himself reported that:

> When I arrived I interviewed every head of department asking what the research that had been going on was all about and what results it had achieved. Several felt it was too low level and a waste of time. Only science remained enthusiastic, and they felt that their CASE work had been very successful and influential. I questioned the amount of time that had been devoted to research and decided that if research was to continue, it should be into what was valued in the school – cognitive acceleration . . .
>
> (Richards, 2003, p. 8)

In the other school, an even more serious crisis developed: after the appointment of a new head teacher the long-term hostility of the anti-research minority of the staff towards the deputy head teacher who had led the research for ten years was treated in such a way that she was left with little option but to take early retirement. Thus among governors too, even governors of schools that have made long-term commitments to research, the status of research as part of the work of schools can remain very fragile indeed.

Involving students and other members of schools as researchers

Teachers are of course not the only members of schools. Teachers are not only greatly outnumbered by their students but students are purportedly the people for whose benefit schools exist. In addition, increasing numbers of adults other than teachers are directly involved in the work of schools. And just as it has been argued that teacher research can contribute in important ways to school improvement, so it has increasingly been argued that members of these other groups could fruitfully be active as researchers. It is the case for students as researchers that has been pursued most vigorously, both in principle and in practice.

That schools can be greatly improved through much increased and improved consultation with, and listening to, their students has been very persuasively argued in recent years (e.g. Rudduck et al., 1996; Rudduck and Flutter, 2004); and there is now available a rich variety of tools for use in doing this (MacBeath et al., 2003). But the suggestion that students should themselves be researchers involves much more than seeking to give pupils an effective voice: it involves asking students to take on a new and demanding role, one which even the majority of teachers have not yet felt able to accept. Why should students be asked to undertake such a role?

Fielding (1998) argues that research by others about students, as about other less powerful members of a society, carries a number of endemic dangers. Information about students' ideas and practices can easily be accommodated so that it can be fitted comfortably into established ways of thinking about students. New information about students can be accumulated in ways that, far from empowering students, make it easier to monitor and regulate their lives. And through both these processes, researchers or users of the research can appropriate the research findings to validate their own views and to consolidate their own power. Fielding quotes Rudduck *et al.* (1996) to summarise these dangers: 'However much we convince ourselves that we are presenting their authentic voice, we are likely to be refracting their meanings through the lens of our own interests and concerns' (p. 177). He points out that these dangers are compounded if research about students is used as a basis for speaking for students, because among other things the research is necessarily conceived and conducted from the researcher's position, and because students have multiple identities, not just those of particular groups or categories that have been investigated.

On the other hand, Fielding points out, simply letting students speak for themselves may be no solution, because whether and how they are listened to will be shaped by the complex historical context in which they are speaking. He advocates in principle the idea of 'dialogic research' and in practice the involvement of students as co-researchers. Reviewing a number of initiatives involving students as co-researchers in North America, he notes that:

> All involve student volunteers who either have dedicated lesson time or institutionally supported external time to carry out their work. All started life and most continue as the brain child or particular enthusiasm of a person or persons external to the school. All have significant external expert help.
>
> (Fielding, 1998, p. 12)

Fielding and Bragg (2003) provide a wide range of examples of initiatives in which students have worked as co-researchers with individual teachers, with teams of teachers or departments and in whole schools. They explain that their own work with students as researchers is based on the following premises:

- Young people and adults often have quite different views of what is significant or important in their experience of or hopes for learning.
- Even when they identify similar issues as important, they can mean quite different things by them.
- These differences are potentially a source of creativity rather than unproductive conflict.
- If we start from students' questions and support their capacity to pursue their enquiries, we often find that new knowledge emerges

about learning, about teaching and about ourselves as teachers and
learners.
• For this process to be productive and engaging, we need to create
conditions of dialogue in which we listen to and learn from each
other in new ways for new purposes.

(Fielding and Bragg, 2003, p. 5)

'Students as researchers' is in practice a very important element of the
researching schools movement. It is quite difficult to find case studies of researching schools that do not assert the importance of students as researchers.
Yet there is a need for some caution. All the arguments advanced by Fielding
and others for students as researchers are powerful arguments for serious
consultation with students, but it is much less obvious why they should lead
to the conclusion that students should take on the role of researchers. The
most convincing arguments are those concerning the inherent limitations of
research about students by others, and those concerning the benefits for
students of the adoption of enquiry approaches in their school learning; but
neither of these are arguments for students being asked to act as educational
researchers. There is furthermore one additional problem: Rudduck *et al.*
(1996) and Fielding (1998) both rightly emphasise the crucial importance
of all students being consulted; yet in practice it always seems to be only a
minority who are involved in research. This is only one of a number of
dilemmas regarding students as researchers that remains unresolved and merits
further study.

KNOWLEDGE-CREATING SCHOOLS

In the previous section, the focus was on schools engaging with research
as a strategy for their own improvement. A quite different and much more
ambitious argument is that much of the research-based knowledge needed
for educational policy and practice might be better produced by schools than
it has been, or perhaps can be, by university departments of education. How
plausible is this argument and how far should schools' engagement with
research be influenced by it?

Hargreaves (1996) initiated recent debate on this theme by contrasting
sharply the close relationship between research and practice in medicine and
the severe lack of such a relationship in education. He related this difference
to the fact that much medical research, but very little educational research,
is done by practitioners. The solution, he suggested, would include much
more research being focused on generating evidence about effective practice,
and much of this research being done in schools by teacher researchers, with
the necessary finance being diverted from universities to schools in order to
make this possible. Three years later, Hargreaves (1999) pursued this theme

more analytically, and developed it in terms of schools as organisations, by exploring what a 'knowledge-creating school' might involve.

Hargreaves is well aware that this idea is a visionary one, with little basis in either current practice or current knowledge: 'the knowledge-creating process and its management can be analysed from two perspectives – the characteristics of knowledge-creating schools and the dynamics of knowledge-creating activities. As yet little is known about either' (Hargreaves, 1999, p. 125). Furthermore, when he speculatively but plausibly lists fifteen 'conditions and factors favouring knowledge creation in schools', he notes that:

> There is only a limited overlap between these features and what has now become the standard characterization of the effective school, from which many school improvement schemes derive. Not all schools that are effective by such conventional criteria will succeed in professional knowledge creation.
>
> (Hargreaves, 1999, p. 127)

In arguing for the idea of the knowledge-creating school, Hargreaves convincingly suggests that the practice of teaching is based largely on tacit and local contextual knowledge and that this practice can be influenced by new ideas only through processes of the 'externalisation' of tacit knowledge and its 'combination' with new ideas. He recognises too the great difficulty of doing useful high-quality research on teaching and in particular emphasises the great challenge for the knowledge-creating school of applying the necessary 'demanding forms of knowledge validation to supply evidence of the effectiveness of its new practices' (p. 129). And he agrees that, 'it is not merely that researchers and teachers are in different locations, making intensive interaction difficult to achieve, but each side starts from a very different knowledge-base' (p. 135), thus making it difficult for the parties to work together in the creation of usable knowledge. He recognises too that in their present working conditions it is difficult for teachers to do research of high quality.

In the light of such problems, Hargreaves concludes that radical change is needed: 'If the objective is the creation of high quality knowledge about effective teaching and learning that is applicable and actionable in classrooms, then practising teachers have to be at the heart of professional knowledge creation and researchers will have to get closer to them' and therefore 'both knowledge creation and its dissemination (need to be) reconceptualised' (Hargreaves, 1999, p. 136). The model that Hargreaves offers for this reconceptualisation is Mode Two knowledge production (Gibbons *et al.*, 1994), a new pattern of knowledge production that, it is claimed, has evolved in recent years in science and technology. Among the core characteristics of Mode Two knowledge production (as summarised by Gibbons *et al.*, 1994, pp. 3–8) are that:

- 'knowledge is produced in the context of its application': it is produced by people who need to solve a practical problem of their own;
- the knowledge is 'transdisciplinary', being produced within the distinctive evolving framework of the problem it is created to solve;
- it is undeniably a contribution to knowledge, with 'its own distinct theoretical structures, research methods and modes of practice', and its 'cumulative' development;
- 'the diffusion of the results is initially accomplished in the process of their production'. Subsequent diffusion occurs as the original practitioners move to new problem contexts;
- 'knowledge production is heterogeneous in terms of the skills and experience people bring to it . . .' In Mode Two, flexibility and response time are the crucial factors and because of this the types of organisation used to tackle these problems may vary greatly . . . people come together in temporary work teams and networks that dissolve when a problem is solved or redefined;
- 'Social accountability permeates the whole knowledge production process . . .': working in the context of application increases the sensitivity of scientists and technologists to the broader implications of what they are doing . . . because the issue on which research is based cannot be answered in scientific and technical terms alone;
- 'Criteria to assess the quality of the work and the teams that carry out research in Mode Two differ from those of more traditional, disciplinary science'.

In relation to this final issue of quality control, Gibbons and his colleagues are at pains to emphasise continuity with Mode One research and its rigorous standards, but also the importance of additional criteria such as efficiency and usefulness: 'This does not mean that 'anything goes' or that standards will be lowered. Rather traditional scientific criteria will have to be qualified by other criteria that can claim equal legitimacy.' (Gibbons *et al.*, 1994, p. 153).

There is too a strong focus in Mode Two knowledge production on specific problems in specific contexts: 'The dynamics of Mode Two knowledge production is . . . a matter of . . . an interest in concrete and particular processes and systems rather than in general unifying principles' (ibid., p. 43); '. . . a pluralism of approaches which combine data, methods and techniques to meet the requirements of specific contexts . . .' (ibid., p. 44).

The importance of Mode Two knowledge production for this book is enhanced by the centrality to it of concepts of webs and networks. Hargreaves quotes the following passage:

The . . . firm, then, takes on some of the characteristics of a spider's web. Each node is a problem-solving team possessing a unique combination of skills. It is linked to other bodies by a potentially large number of lines of communication. To survive, each firm must be permeable to new types of knowledge and the sector as a whole becomes increasingly interconnected.

(Gibbons *et al.*, 1994, p. 122)

and suggests that here we have 'an intimation of what might be more than the knowledge-creating school, but a knowledge-creating school system – a web of interlinked knowledge-creating schools' (Hargreaves, 1999, pp. 139–140).

For Hargreaves, the key characteristic of Mode Two knowledge is that it 'evolves within the context of its application', and he rightly suggests that it would be a radical step for serious educational research to be undertaken in these terms. However, some of the other characteristics of Mode Two knowledge production would not involve radical changes for educational research. Whereas one of Mode Two's most radically new features is said to be its transdisciplinary nature, educational research is already transdisciplinary. Indeed, the account by Gibbons *et al.* of how different teams of specialists come together in Mode Two, according to the specific nature of the problem to be tackled, is highly reminiscent of the way in which teams already come together in university faculties of education for specific research projects. Similarly, the broadening of quality control criteria in Mode Two beyond traditional scientific criteria would not be at all new for educational researchers. But does the parallel with Mode Two offer us a helpful way forward for thinking about researching schools?

Evaluating the proposal

One of the attractions of this way of thinking about the researching school is that it seems well conceived for bridging the gap between research-based knowledge and the knowledge used in practice by teachers (see McIntyre, 2005). On one hand, it takes its starting point as the practical classroom craft knowledge of teachers, and is concerned with articulating and problematising that knowledge. It goes substantially further than Stenhouse's conception of teachers investigating ideas for their individual use through classroom action research, as it is collaboratively planned research aimed at generating knowledge for much wider use. In relation to the research end of the continuum, on the other hand, this kind of research is both concerned with practical suggestions for teaching, taking account of all the wide range of criteria that this implies, and also research conceived and conducted in and for a specific context. So do this kind of research and the knowledge that it generates obviate the need for all the complex processes that are otherwise necessary for bridging the gap between research findings and the practices of teaching and learning that these findings are intended to inform?

Hargreaves (1999) rightly highlighted two problematic issues that he hoped could be solved through this reconceptualisation of research: these were the problems of validation and dissemination. Considering first the latter of these two issues, a clear convergence of insights is apparent between the idea of Mode Two knowledge production outlined by Gibbons *et al.* (1994) and recent educational research initiatives in England involving practitioners. From the former, we learn that, 'the diffusion of the results is initially accomplished in the process of their production. Subsequent diffusion occurs as the original practitioners move to new problem contexts' (Gibbons *et al.*, 1994, p. 5). In practice this has important implications: 'In Mode Two, knowledge production and knowledge appropriation converge. The outcomes are likely to be commensurate with the degree of involvement. Only those who take part in knowledge production are likely to share in its appropriation' (ibid., p. 165).

Sally Brown (2005) quotes several examples from the Teaching and Learning Research Programme suggesting that teachers' engagement with research findings tends to be dependent on them having been actively involved with the research, or at least having some special grounds for seeing the research as being linked to themselves. She notes too the importance not only of this sense of personal relevance, but also of 'the level of teachers' familiarity with the particular ideas that are the focus of the research evidence (and) how these ideas relate to the ways in which they already make sense of their own classroom work' (p. 395).

Simons *et al.* (2003), reflecting on their evaluation of the Teacher Training Agency's School-based Research Consortium Initiative, in which four consortia investigated pedagogical themes, conclude not only that, 'Many teachers did find that engaging *in* research themselves was a prerequisite for engaging in a meaningful way *with* research carried out by other people' (p. 353), but also that other teachers within the same schools and consortia were able to learn from the research only if quite demanding cognitive, affective and social conditions were met:

> Generalisation takes place ... but only if the relationship to the given situation is sufficiently retained for others to recognise and connect through common problems and issues. However, this seems a necessary but not a sufficient condition for generalisation. Our evidence also suggests that generalisation is made possible by relational and situational factors, such as the confidence and trust that sharing teachers have in each other ... The appeal to validity in this setting is not confined to methodological canon, still less to abstract notions of the weight of evidence. It is also grounded in professional agreement as to the usefulness or significance of particular insights, and in the trust and confidence that may be placed in the colleagues offering them. Evidence is still subjected to

testing, but testing within these confidence limits, and against criteria agreed among colleagues.

(Simons *et al.*, 2003, p. 359)

Simons *et al.* (2003) emphasise especially the importance of social influence in the context of such collaborative research initiatives:

> In the context of the consortia, a decision to adopt practices on the basis of evidence produced by teachers, and by teachers and researchers working together, was not simply individual. It was commonly a process of collective judgement and shared confidence in the findings that had already been demonstrated through the process of collectively researching and analysing the data.
>
> (ibid., pp. 360–1)

It seems clear then that those teachers who have been active in such research are likely to benefit from it, as too, given some very demanding conditions, may others within the same schools and even in wider networks; but there is certainly no expectation that institutions other than those actively involved in the research will benefit. There is then no magical solution here to the problem of 'dissemination'. In place of the complex processes currently necessary for effectively bridging the gap between research and practice, we have a vision of a new kind of research system from which the only schools likely to benefit will be knowledge-creating schools, with a new demanding kind of dissemination system within, and going no further than, networks of knowledge-creating schools. This is an attractive vision if and only if *all* schools can be enabled to become knowledge-creating schools.

There remains however the matter of the validation of knowledge claims based on the research done in knowledge-creating schools. Such claims will generally tend to be about teachers' practices, sometimes about the qualities of the practices or the conditions in which they are viable, but primarily about their effectiveness, and the conditions for their effectiveness, in facilitating useful learning or other benefits for pupils. Unless clear, and clearly valid, claims of these kinds can be made, the argument for knowledge-creating schools as a way of resolving the gap between research and practice becomes empty. And indeed, in a context where quality control is more broadly based, validation is likely to become a more complex concern, with practices having to be validated not only in terms of their effectiveness, but also in terms of their educational merits, cost-effectiveness, social acceptability and general practicality.

This task is further complicated by the priority that Hargreaves rightly gives to research strategies that take teachers' newly developing or established practices as their starting points. The great advantages of such strategies are that the practices with which they are concerned are already tuned to the complex realities of schools and classrooms in general and of the particular contexts in which the teachers are working, and that they are therefore likely to have high credibility to other teachers in these schools and networks. The problem of validating such practices, in a way that makes them useful to others, is that of abstracting their key effective generalisable features from the enormously complex real personal practices of the individual teachers. The problem is not that high-quality school-based research is any more complex than university-based research, but rather that it isn't any simpler. However, that is a matter of some controversy. As noted earlier, many proponents of researching schools take the view that traditional academic quality criteria and standards are unnecessary for their research. For the limited purpose of improvement of the individual school, this view might have some merit if it were clearer why normal research standards are seen to be unnecessary and also what other criteria would be appropriate. On the other hand, if the intention is that the research of a 'knowledge-creating school' should generate knowledge that has a wider validity, then there is no reason why the validity criteria for such research should be less stringent than those applied in academic research. Although both Gibbons *et al.* (1994) and Hargreaves (1999) seem to accept the need for such rigorous research designs, evidence and inferences, it is not at all clear that such acceptance is widespread among enthusiasts for school-based research.

Overall, then, Hargreaves' conception of the knowledge-creating school remains an exciting and attractive proposal but not yet one that has proved its worth. There is a great deal to be said for taking the practices that teachers have developed and about which they are enthusiastic as the starting points for research on teaching. But, although the traditional problem of effective dissemination of useful research findings is certainly transformed by this approach to research, it would seem to be solved only in so far as all schools can become knowledge-creating schools, and even then only partially. Meanwhile, the issue of quality criteria for school-based research remains unresolved and, indeed, not yet even adequately conceptualised.

CONCLUSIONS AND IMPLICATIONS

If schools are to improve, as they certainly must, then one of the best hopes for them doing so is through teachers' use of research based knowledge. And available evidence suggests that it is through their own serious engagement in research, in their own schools, and in collaboration with their own colleagues, that teachers are most likely to learn to use research based knowledge. But teachers can reasonably be asked to engage seriously in research only if their conditions of work change radically: their schools need to be firmly led and committed to being, in a serious sense, researching schools; teachers themselves can do serious research only if they are asked to do much less of other things, such as classroom teaching; they must be given time and other resources for research; they must be supported in learning to do research and in doing it; the social organisation of schools must facilitate collaborative research; and it must be rewarding for teachers to do research. At the same time, it must be recognised that there is still a great deal to be learned about what being a researching school means and implies, and about what such schools can reasonably be expected to deliver. One certainly should not be misled into thinking that Mode Two knowledge production would provide an easy option, either for school organisations or for teacher researchers.

Everything that we have learned about researching schools would seem also to be relevant to research networks of schools. On one hand, research networks might seem to offer exciting possible solutions to some of the problems faced by researching schools. For example, as Hargreaves (1999) clearly foresaw, the very interpersonal mode of dissemination of research findings that seems to be characteristic of school-based research might seem to imply that such research is not likely to offer proportionate benefits from the investment needed if it is to be well done; but if the research were to be network-based rather than merely school-based, that problem could possibly be overcome. On the other hand, some of the conditions that we hypothesised to be necessary for effective school-based research might be even more difficult for networks than for schools to meet. For example, how can the development plans of all the schools in a network and the research enthusiasms of teachers across the network be effectively co-ordinated? In some respects, it might seem that different conditions can best be met at different levels; for example, whereas long-term commitments to research and the development of research cultures might properly be the responsibilities of individual schools, it might be at the network level that flexibility would be important, with groups of teachers from across the schools forming for only two or three years to focus on particular research projects.

Chapter 3

Teachers learning through collaboration in schools

Colleen McLaughlin

INTRODUCTION

Collaboration between teachers is the keystone of much current educational architecture and policy-making. In many cases it is a taken-for-granted good. Those who advocate networks and new forms of educational reform, including knowledge creation, assume or advocate for a collaborative mode of working, as these quotations demonstrate:

> [Collaboration has become] an articulating and integrating principle of action, planning culture, development, organisation and research.
> (Hargreaves, A., 1994, p. 245)

> In short at the heart of educational transformation are networks of communities of teachers who are passionate about transferred innovation.
> (Hargreaves, D., 2003a, p. 18)

> Collaborative Enquiry as a 'way of being' in schools has the potential to transform the way practitioners think about and relate to the core business of teaching and learning, and in that sense is able to support the transformation of schools.
> (Street and Temperley, 2005, p. 9)

This chapter will examine the journey within education that has led to this thinking and will also explore the research that demonstrates the benefits, complexities and challenges that collaborative working in schools presents. This will be done by reviewing the major research and thinking on collaborative modes of working over the last thirty years.

WHY DO IT? THE VISIONS AND HOPES

The current emphasis on collaborative working between teachers has many roots. It is rooted in the work on the school as a workplace, the importance of collegial relations, as both a source of school satisfaction and motivation amongst teachers, and the significance that they have in school improvement (Liebermann and Miller, 1984; Little, 1990a; Nias *et al.*, 1989). The pervasiveness of teacher isolation and the perception of its potential to limit the development of teaching and learning for pupils and staff also drove this work (Lortie, 1975). More will be written about this later. Hargreaves and Dawe (1990) argued that 'the failure at classroom level of most efforts to secure curriculum implementation and planned educational change more generally' was intimately connected to the professional isolation of teachers (p. 227). Liebermann wrote in 1996 of the importance for schools and school systems of building a professional culture of teaching that was more responsive and receptive to change.

The work of the 1970s, 80s and early 90s began a detailed exploration of the role and form of teachers working together. In the 1990s and early twenty-first century the language changed and the emphasis shifted to learning communities (Street and Temperley, 2005) and communities of practice (Wenger, 1998), with practitioner knowledge generation and sharing as a key theme (Hargreaves, 1999, 2003a, 2003b). The vision and the hope were that the learning of pupils, and schools as organisations, would be changed by collaboration among teachers, and Fielding (1999) in particular argued that this should be inclusive of pupils, parents and communities. The worthy hope and vision are that teachers would work together and would share, examine and create new practice in their own schools and, in many cases, work across schools and in networks. Hargreaves (2003b) wrote about creating 'peer-to-peer epidemics' that would transform knowledge creation. Stenhouse (1975) and Elliott (1991) argued too that practitioner research was enhanced and strengthened by collaboration in schools. There have also been critical debates that have helped us to clarify the nature of teachers' working lives and the assumptions that may be naive or ill founded (Huberman, 1993). So what do we already know about collaboration between colleagues in schools? What can we learn from the fine-grained studies of collaboration in schools?

DEFINITIONS AND DISTINCTIONS

Already different words have been used to describe the activity of working together – collegiality, collaboration and joint working. There have been hot debates about the terms and their definitions (see Fielding, 1999; Hargreaves, 1999; Little, 1999). Many use these terms interchangeably. For the purposes of this chapter and at the risk of being simplistic, we will focus on the verb to collaborate. What happens when 'teachers work together' (Hargreaves, 1991) and particularly when they learn together with a specific focus on when they enquire into their practice? This necessarily connects to notions of teachers as colleagues and cultures of collaboration or non-collaboration

(Nias *et al.*, 1989). What is clear is that there is a range of practices that come under this heading, and some of the distinctions between them will be discussed later. There is also a range of possible collaborations: teachers collaborating with colleagues, teachers collaborating with people outside of the school and teachers collaborating with colleagues in networks. This chapter focuses primarily on the first of these, as the following chapter focuses on wider collaborations, but clearly many of the issues raised are common to all collaborations. Finer distinctions are made in the field and these will be alluded to in the following sections.

THE NATURE OF CLASSROOM TEACHING

In the last thirty years in particular there have been research studies that have focused on the characteristics of teaching and the working lives of teachers. The debates were on the isolation, loneliness and individualism of teaching (Hargreaves, 1993; Huberman, 1993; Liebermann and Miller, 1990; Lortie, 1975). Huberman (1993, p. 11), in challenging 'the vision of the schoolhouse as a bonded community of adults and children', raised some very important questions. Are the constraints to collaboration bound up with the social organisation of work in schools, the very nature of the profession and the nature of teaching? He proposed an artisan model of teaching that is 'a response to and determinant of the ecology of classroom teaching' (p. 13). He characterised teaching as a task of tinkering and likened it to being a bricoleur, 'a do it yourself craftsperson who can put to use a host of material lying around at various stages of a construction or repair job' (p. 14). Teaching is fast moving, requiring on-the-spot thinking and its general purpose is to inform rather than a pre-planned process that will flow easily. He warned against comparing teaching to other professions such as medicine. Teaching is necessarily pragmatic and individual – it has to be, given that we choose to organise schools in the way we do: individual teachers alone with 25 – 30 children in predetermined slots of time. He also argued for strong distinctions to be made between the culture and norms in relation to collaboration in primary or elementary schools and secondary schools. The classroom has an ecology that is complex, unpredictable, dynamic and difficult to manage – not linear (p. 20). Here Huberman (ibid.) argued teaching is similar to being in a jazz band, a 'succession of instructional acts [that are] dictated by the drift of events after the initial stimulus situation' (p. 21). It is what Yinger (1988) called 'a conversation of practice'. This means that teachers have difficulty in sharing a common knowledge or language to talk about their experiences, as their knowledge is shaped by experience, often tacit, and their concerns are highly pragmatic. Watkins (2005) makes the point that classrooms have not changed in shape for one thousand years. All of these factors have implications for teacher collaboration. 'Crudely put,

. . . teachers work alone, learn alone, and derive their most important professional satisfactions alone – or rather from interactions with pupils instead of with peers' (p. 23).

Andy Hargreaves (1993) took up this theme of individualism and isolation. He argued that individuality is often seen as heresy and as a barrier to professional development (p. 53). He saw this as ill-founded, and argued that individualism is part of the architecture of teaching in schools as constructed today. Hargreaves (1993) distinguished between constrained individualism, strategic individualism and elective individualism. Constrained individualism is when teachers are constrained by administrative and situational constraints; strategic individualism is 'the way in which teachers actively construct and create individualistic patterns of working as a response to the daily contingencies of their work environment' (p. 63); and elective individualism is the 'principled choice to work alone all or some of the time and sometimes when there are opportunities and encouragement to work collaboratively with colleagues' (p. 63). He concludes that it is foolish to presume 'that all teacher individualism is iniquitous' (p.74). The material reality of schools as presently constructed and school teaching as we organise it means that teachers necessarily work alone, isolated in their classrooms for the real work of teaching – human interaction with pupils. Their work is necessarily personalised.

Liebermann and Miller (1990) depicted this as 'social system understanding', i.e. the interplay between individual teacher experience and the social contexts of schools. The main features that they identified were the personalised style of teaching; the uncertainty of, and weak links between, teaching, learning and the knowledge base; that rewards are centred on students; the conflictual nature of goals; that control norms are necessary; that professional support is lacking and that teaching is an art.

Other work in the UK has emphasised similar aspects. Nias and Biott (1992) highlighted 'the occupational importance of control' in teachers' working lives:

> They [teachers] do not feel that they have attained a full professional identity until they are 'in control' and, customarily they believe that they are judged (by pupils, parents, superiors, peers) in terms of their ability to maintain discipline over children . . .
>
> (Nias and Biott, 1992, p. xvii)

Nias and Biott (ibid.) argued that this is particularly important when considering changes in working practice and in collaboration as it can lead to teachers being 'authority-dependent' and has its roots 'in the teacher's sense of moral responsibility for their students' and their learning (p. xvii). They also highlighted the characteristics of individualism and competition as key elements in the lives of teachers (Nias and Biott, 1992). This theme was echoed by Little (1990b) when reviewing studies of teachers as colleagues:

These studies draw our attention to the school as a whole, and to the ways in which teachers' involvement with one another as colleagues is fundamentally bound up – for good or ill – with their orientation toward their work as classroom teachers. In doing so, such inquiries also attend to the values that are expressed and the purposes that are pursued (or thwarted) through teachers' encounters with one another.

(Little, 1990b, p. 510)

These studies of the social reality of teaching draw attention to the possible tensions in terms of teachers' accountabilities, concerns and practices. The 'persistence of privacy' (Little, 1990a) can be seen as having some of its roots in the complexities and nature of the work. 'Research spanning more than two decades points consistently to the benefit of vigorous collegial communities', argued Little (2002b, p. 917) but she also warned that the persistence of privacy is not a thing of the past. Others have argued that 'individualism' is in retreat 'in a number of areas' (Hargreaves, 1991, p. 227). Certainly what is clear is that the idea of collaboration raises important issues about teachers' professional identity, including the social and emotional aspects of their work.

Some writers have argued that the emotional dimension of teachers' work has been underplayed in discussions about collaboration, change and practitioner enquiry. (Dadds, 1993; Hargreaves, 1998; McLaughlin, 2003). Studies that have focused on the affective aspects of teaching have reinforced and deepened our understanding of some of the themes previously discussed. Holly and McLaughlin (1989) worked with teachers through journal keeping and found the recurring theme of the feeling of isolation. Hargreaves (1998), in arguing strongly for greater attention to teachers' emotions, echoed the theme already discussed of the moral purposes of teaching, and his work exemplifies the connection between those purposes and teachers' emotions. Nias (1993) too documented the sense of grief and bereavement that teachers felt when the highly rationalised and imposed curriculum meant teachers experienced a sense of loss of values.

A second theme that emerges in these studies is the fear of exposure in teachers' work (Salzberger-Wittenberg et al., 1983). As teachers' daily experience is to spend most of their time alone and in the presence of children, the fear of public, adult exposure is understandable, but Salzberger-Wittenberg et al. (ibid.) also showed that the 'publicness' of classrooms is linked to the fear of judgement by teachers. It is interesting to note that they were writing at a time when the judgements about individual teachers were far less frequent or public than they are now. So here we can see some of the social and emotional landscape of teachers' work and the possible implications for collaboration.

These searching discussions about the nature of teaching are not necessarily arguments against collaboration but are good reasons to think carefully about the forms of collaboration and the necessary conditions and supports. Huberman (1993), for example, in arguing for the artisan model concluded that it was who collaborated with whom that was an important area for consideration. As classrooms are constructed as they are, it would benefit teachers who share similar conditions to collaborate e.g. in departments. He also argued that we should not elide the differences between types of school, such as primary or elementary and secondary. But before going on to consider these matters further, it is also important to recognise that there are benefits for teachers and students in collaboration.

THE POTENTIAL BENEFITS OF COLLABORATION

Johnson (2003, p. 332) details the following as the averred benefits of collaboration which feature in the literature:

- it provides moral support by strengthening resolve and providing support in difficult situations
- it increases efficiency by eliminating duplication and removing redundancy
- it improves effectiveness by improving the quality of teachers' teaching
- it reduces overload by allowing for teachers to share burdens and pressures
- it establishes boundaries by setting commonly agreed boundaries
- it promotes confidence
- it promotes teacher reflection through dialogue and action
- it promotes teachers' learning from each other
- it leads to continuous improvement.

Many of these are borne out by our own research as reported in Chapters 7–14, especially the reduction in isolation that many teachers experience.

Hargreaves (1998), Nias and Biott (1992) and Street and Temperley (2005) all documented the joys of teachers' work with students and colleagues. Teachers experience a renewed sense of purpose and professionalism, a reduced sense of isolation and a passion for the exploration of their teaching and learning. Richert's (1996) study of the effects on teachers of engaging collaboratively in research and enquiry in the Bay Region IV Professional Development Consortium mirrors the findings of many others (Dadds, 1995; Elliott, 1991; McLaughlin and Black-Hawkins, 2004; TTA, 1998a; Zeichner, 2003). The effects were:

- it resulted in a renewed feeling of pride and excitement about teaching and in a revitalised sense of oneself as a teacher
- the research experience reminded teachers of their intellectual capability and the importance of that capability to their professional lives

- the research experience allowed teachers to see that the work that they do in school matters
- the research experience reconnected many of the teachers to their colleagues and to their initial commitments to teach
- the research experience encouraged teachers to develop an expanded sense of what teachers can and ought to do
- the research experience restored in teachers a sense of professionalism and power in the sense of having a voice.

However, these are neither inevitable nor unconditional. Johnson's own research (2003) showed that this was the case for the majority of teachers in the Australian study, however it was not inevitably the case for all the teachers. Hargreaves (1994) cautioned against uncritical acceptance of 'the collaborative solution'. Many (Achinstein, 2002; Blasé and Blasé, 1999) have argued that there are dangers at a micropolitical level and that the rhetoric of collaboration can mask other, less democratic processes. Anderson (1998; 1999) and Hargreaves (1991) have 'contrastingly pointed to the contrived and manipulative use of collaboration as a managerealist tool of control' (Johnson 2003, p.339). These debates show the need to interrogate and clarify what we mean by collaboration and to delineate carefully what research has shown us about the uses and benefits of collaboration, as well as the complexities of supporting such work. Despite the fact that researchers in the field emphasise the fragility and lack of spread of collaboration in schools (Achinstein, 2002; Hargreaves, 1991; Little, 1990b) they have also emphasised the potential power of it and, as was mentioned earlier, this has also been picked up by policy makers. The benefits are for both students and teachers.

BENEFITS FOR STUDENTS

The teacher–student relationship is the central obligation and reward of teaching, and Little (1990a) argued it must be the increased quality and productivity of the relationship with students that must be used as the measure of teacher collaboration. This is a consistent theme in the research and writing over the last thirty years (Street and Temperley, 2005). Some studies show that teachers' working together enhances life and learning for students considerably (Little, 1990b; McLaughlin and Talbert, 2001). The benefits include improvements in behaviour, achievement and the attitude of students. Our own research reported later in this book also shows that for teachers, despite the difficulties, when collaborative learning works well it outweighs the benefits of working alone for both students and teachers. However, Achinstein's (2002) study also shows that it can be at the cost of students, and her caution against unguarded optimism or promotion of collaborative research is one worth heeding. Little (1990a) warns of the difficulties and demands of early attempts at collaboration and that it can sometimes feel that being collaborative is like swimming upstream in the face of the 'immediacy' of the classroom. There is a need to accept that learning is involved in collaboration, it is difficult and it takes time.

THE CONDITIONS FOR FRUITFUL COLLABORATIVE WORK

What are the implications and consequences for collaboration between colleagues of the contexts in which they work? As the focus on the importance of professional community has progressed, so have the understanding of, and research into, the complexity of the collaborative endeavour in schools. Little (1982) argued that there were critical variables in the 'norms of collegiality and experimentation'. 'Particularly at issue here are the nature of role definition, the shape of role relationships and the degree to which existing role expectations permit or encourage teachers' professional development' (Little, 1982, p. 326). Her research documented the range of interactions that teachers engage in: from lending materials, through analysing practice and its effects to giving advice, asked or unasked. 'Each of these situated interactions places more or less extensive demand on teachers' time, knowledge experience and good will' (Little, 1982, p. 329). The work practices were characterised by their range, location, frequency, focus and concreteness, relevance, reciprocity and inclusivity.

Little (1982) concluded that:

> Continuous professional development appears to be most surely and thoroughly achieved when: Teachers engage in frequent, continuous, and increasingly concrete and precise talk about teaching practice (as distinct from the teacher characteristics and failings, the social lives of teachers, the foibles and failure of students and their families, and the unfortunate demands of society on the school). . . . Other things being equal the utility of collegial work and the rigor of experimentation with teaching is a direct function of the concreteness, precision and coherence of the shared language.
>
> (Little, 1982, p. 331)

Successful schools were distinguished as supporting 'critical practices of adaptability . . . discussion of classroom practice, mutual observation and critique, shared efforts to design and prepare curriculum and shared participation in the business of instructional improvement' (Little, 1982, p. 332). The degree to which the school permitted and encouraged this was important, as was the frequency of such interaction. The building of a shared technical culture or a shared language was important, demanding and potentially threatening. 'As demands escalate, so do teachers' requirements for "support" in the form of clear, public and visible sanctions for participation' (Little, 1982, p. 334). In 'successful schools', continuous professional development was seen as relevant and integral to teaching and interaction was characterised by reciprocity – a manner of acting and speaking with deference, respect and humility. Reciprocity also included equality of effort. Teachers who had this characteristic were able to appreciate how close discussion of practice was to discussion of competence and distinguish between them, thus being aware of and sensitive to the risks. Finally, teachers were able in their collaboration to appreciate the consequences for, and impact on, other colleagues. They had an inclusive mindset. Little (ibid.) concludes that the school as a workplace is 'extraordinarily powerful' and that there is a necessity for there to be a 'prevailing norm of collegiality' if teachers are to learn from each other.

How teachers resolve and engage with the social and emotional dimensions of their work varies considerably and is also dependent on the conditions and leadership they have. Little (1990b) warned that:

> Closely bound groups are instruments both for promoting change and for conserving the present. Changes, indeed, may prove substantial or trivial. Finally, collaborations may arise naturally out of the problems and circumstance that teachers experience in common, but often they appear contrived, inauthentic, grafted on, perched precariously (and often temporarily) on the margins of real work.
>
> (Little, 1990b, pp. 509–10)

Hargreaves and Dawe (1990) distinguished between voluntary and imposed collaborations or what they labelled 'collaborative cultures' and 'contrived collegiality'. They focused on the dimension of prescribed collaboration, which ran alongside the more centralised control and direction or 'managerialism' in education. They pointed out the 'peculiar paradox' that teachers are apparently being urged to collaborate more when there is less for them to collaborate about' (p. 228).

In 1973, Granovetter showed the importance of weak ties in networks. Little (2002b) developed this work and showed its importance in discussing the work of teachers. The professional literature has subsumed a wide array of teacher-to-teacher exchange under the broad heading of collaboration or collegiality and Little (1990b) highlighted four key activities: storytelling and scanning, sharing, [seeking] aid and assistance, and joint work:

> They are phenomenologically discrete forms that vary from one another in the degree to which they induce mutual obligation, expose the work of the each person to the scrutiny of others, and call for, tolerate, or reward initiative in matters of curriculum and instruction. . . . The move

from conditions of complete independence to thoroughgoing interdependence entails changes in the frequency and intensity of teachers' interactions, the prospects for conflict, and probability of mutual influence.
(Little, 1990b, pp. 511–12)

Nias and Biott (1992) and Nias *et al.* (1989) highlighted the importance of mutually supportive relationships, engaging constructively with the sense of powerlessness and loss of control, the willingness to ask for and take help, and most importantly '. . . the value of: support and reinforcement; enquiry and cognitive challenge; creating a common language for discussion; modelling alternative forms of behaviour' (p. xvii). The factors here are a mixture of the personal and interpersonal but they also highlight the social conditions of the workplace. The social conditions of collaboration in schools have been another area of productive and illuminating research. Nias *et al.* (1989) suggested the main components of a 'culture of collaboration' were 'beliefs and values, understandings, attitudes, meanings and norms (arrived at by interaction); symbols, rituals and ceremonies' (p. 18). Their detailed ethnographies of schools are helpful in showing us how to develop and nurture collaboration. As the research has developed, and as collaboration has become a focus of renewed interest and policy-making (e.g. McLaughlin and Talbert, 2001; Sergiovanni, 1994; Street and Temperley, 2005), so recent research has made even more fine-grained distinctions.

When engaged in collaborative learning through research and enquiry, which often focuses unflinchingly on teachers' classroom practice and necessarily involves critical debate and reflection, the emotional and social dimensions are to the fore. McLaughlin (2003) and Dadds (1993) have focused particularly on this. Dadds (ibid.) argued that 'passionate and committed teacher research is driven by affective as well as cognitive epistemologies' (p. 122). Abercrombie (1989) showed clearly the crucial and complex relations between the inner and outer worlds and, in particular, the link between the state of the perceiver and the judgements made. McLaughlin (2003) has argued that this has implications for collaborative work and for the support provided, i.e. it necessitates providing personal, learning and contextual support. So the nature of teaching itself and the emotional consequences have emerged as important factors in engaging in collaborative work. This work highlights the importance of trust and negotiation of risk as well as the centrality of group and individual support.

What is clear is that considerable risk is involved in sharing together and working together, as the discussion of the social and emotional dimensions of work has shown. The conditions in which teachers work will enable risk to be borne or not and in the face of this teachers will adopt different stances and will engage in different collaborative activities to different degrees.

Little (2002a) suggests that the research studies show that there is a developmental trajectory in groups, 'specially with regard to their capacity and disposition to dig deeply into matters of practice' (p. 918) – something that fits with more general group theory (Johnson and Johnson, 2006).

CONFLICT AND CHALLENGE

Stephen Ball has concentrated on other characteristics of schools that are relevant here:

> I take schools, in common with virtually all other social organisations, to be *arenas of struggle:* to be riven with actual or potential conflict between members: to be poorly coordinated; to be ideologically diverse. I take it as essential that if we are to understand the nature of schools as organisations, we must achieve some understanding of these conflicts.
> (Ball, 1987, p. 19)

Achinstein (2002), drawing on this central idea of Ball's, engaged in a close study of two teacher professional communities. She warned against ignoring the nuances of collaborative reform efforts, of pathologising conflict in teacher communities engaged in collaboration and of the need to understand 'how such communities form, cope and are sustained over time' (p. 422). She argued that 'the complexities of difference amid community' are very important in this debate. Her study illustrates the dangers of polarising conflict and consensus: 'Collaboration and consensus – critical elements that build community – actually generated conflict. Not only did the teacher professional communities experience multiple conflicts, but also the core norms and practices of collaboration that define teacher communities paradoxically raised the conflicts' (p. 440).

Collaboration makes public differences and difficulties that previously could remain hidden or non-public because of the tradition of individualism and privacy. Therefore she argued that conflict is an inevitable part of collaboration and 'an essential part of community', but one with which many teachers do not know how to engage constructively. Her case studies portrayed teacher learning and enquiry sometimes hampered by the desire not to engage in conflict. If the general culture in the school is that conflict is never made public then this will be the way collaboration is also engaged with. Thus when matters of principle and difference are met, the teachers will work to protect their social and professional relationships. She also reinforced and provided a vivid example of how teachers can maintain their own community's stability and cohesion by focusing on the failings of the pupils or other communities rather than engaging with the responsibility to examine and debate the differences in their own community. The emphasis in her research was on how varied are the ways that groups of colleagues negotiate difference and conflict. She provided a useful continuum of the different stances taken (see Table 3.1). She argued against viewing the negotiation of conflict in a

Table 3.1 Collaborative teacher learning in schools

Conflict	Avoidant	Embracing
Stances	exclude, rapidly absorb or transfer conflicts; seek harmony and unanimity; low levels of dissent; limited repertoire of mechanisms for public debate while active informal mechanisms privatise conflict *An approach has been implanted so we don't see the conflict. The principal uses the term consensus.* (Washington teacher)	acknowledge, solicit and own conflict by critically reflecting upon differences of belief and practice; active dissent and opportunities for alternative views; broad repertoire of mechanisms for public debate *'When conflict is brought to the surface ... that's when it becomes real. It will go somewhere.'* (Chavez teacher)
Border	*Unified/exclusive*	*Diverse/inclusive*
Politics	highly bonded social ties; homogeneity within community; rigid or impermeable borders that form barriers to outsiders *'We took those who disagreed and shot them.'* *'You send them out because you can't deal with them and they're infecting everybody else.'* (Washington teachers)	individual and sub-group identities upheld; heterogeneity of beliefs and participants fostered; fluid social arrangements; open boundaries that form bridges; sometimes fragmentation *'There's plenty of space for dissent here.'* *'We are not meeting the needs of our African American youth.'* (Chavez teachers)
Ideology	*Mainstream/congruent*	*Critical/counter*
	mainstream ideology about the purposes of schooling – to socialise students into current society; teacher's role is socialisation; inside school ideology congruent with dominant messages from the environment *'It's not about changing society. It's about bringing the students' scores up.'* (Washington teacher)	Critical ideology about the purposes of schooling – to build critical thinkers and actors to transform, rather than reproduce, current society; teachers as change agents; inside school ideology in conflict with dominant messages from the environment *'What education should be is liberatory. It's to challenge the existing social systems; to change it.'* (Chavez teacher)
Organisational change and learning	*Stability/static*	*Change/learning*
	solutions result in maintenance of existing social relations and norms *'Aren't we going to support our own?'* *(explanation for strengthening the existing discipline policy)* (Washington teacher)	conflicts result in questioning core norms; organisational change; potential for organisational learning *'Let's try it [IRISE] ... What's been going on certainly isn't working.'* (Chavez teacher)

singular fashion or as static. She used the three concepts of conflict, border politics and ideology, reinforcing, as did Nias and Biott (1992) and Little (2002b), the importance of the latter.

In her case study schools conflict and the negotiation of difference had a price to pay and were not easy. The challenge was to maintain the ties and connectedness while sustaining the constructive controversy and she recommended Gardner's (1991) notion of 'wholeness incorporating diversity'. This all matters because the potential for a community or organisation to learn is linked to the negotiation of difference and conflict. In making a plea for greater research and understanding on the phenomena inherent in teacher collaboration she said:

> Policy makers should reconsider naïve initiatives that put teachers in groups and expect them to learn and grow, disregarding the complexity of the collaborative process and the time needed to navigate differences. Practitioners who understand the micropolitics of collaboration also may be less alarmed when conflicts do arise . . .
>
> (Achinstein, 2002, p. 45)

This focus on difference and complexity is very pertinent to collaborative learning in schools that focuses on research and enquiry, for critical reflection and dialogue are central to the quality and rigour of the work. The sorts of issue raised in Achinstein's and others' work (Lima, 2001) are a necessary part of the landscape of collaborative enquiry in schools. For many years there has been a focus on criticality. Stenhouse argued that it was not necessary for teachers' research to be published, as 'what seems to me most important is that research becomes part of a community of critical discourse' (Stenhouse, 1981, p. 109). His view was based on Gramsci's (1971) concept of a deliberative college, i.e. that it should be face-to-face; local; collegiate; directed towards mutual learning; engaged in a rigorous struggle to avoid habits of dilettantism, improvisation, oratorical and declamatory solutions; and include writing notes and noting criticisms. We see from later research that these are complex and sophisticated processes that require skilled facilitating and fostering.

CRITICAL FACTORS

We can conclude that:

> Research spanning more than two decades points consistently to the potential educational benefit of vigorous collegial communities. Researchers posit that conditions for improving teaching and learning are strengthened when teachers collectively question ineffective teaching routines, examine new conceptions of teaching and learning, find

generative means to acknowledge and respond to difference and conflict and engage actively in supporting professional growth.

(Little, 2002a, p. 917)

This research on collaboration in schools suggests that there are three important levels of work which affect how well or vigorously those in schools engage in collaborative work. These are the individual level, the professional community level and the organisational level, in particular how well the organisation can support teachers and improvement in practice. At the individual level there are the tradition of privacy and autonomy; the power of values and their link to professional identity; the emotions involved in risk and how these are engaged with: a helpful or unhelpful set of attitudes and practices in relating to colleagues; and the professional ability to engage with difference.

At the level of professional community, critical factors are the ability to develop a shared language; to share purposes; to engage in a range of collaborative practices, accepting that this is a developmental task, especially in relation to 'the capacity and disposition to dig deeply into matters of practice' (Little, 2002b, p. 918); to understand and work with the risk; to work towards improvement in students' learning rather than improvements in collegial cohesion; to engage constructively in conflict and the discussion of difference; and to interact with a focus on practice, including distinguishing between focusing on practice and evaluating performance, and to interact frequently. These are highly sophisticated tasks. The discussion of practice and the development of a shared language in themselves are challenges requiring subject and pedagogical knowledge and containing many assumptions. Little (2002a), Fielding *et al.* (2005) and Wenger (1998) have also cautioned that the notion of transferring practice is neither fully understood nor simple. The research also suggests that there are differences between primary and secondary school settings and draws attention to the final critical factor – the institutional capacity to support teachers and improvements in practice.

Key features that emerge from the research (Little, 1990a; McLaughlin and Talbert, 2001) on organisations that enhance collaboration or the development of professional community are:

- most fundamentally, institutional policies committed to supporting teacher collaboration and collegiality, as reflected for example in symbolic endorsements and institutional policy statements that give rewards and importance to collaborative work
- school-level organisation of staff work and leadership: Little (1990a) reminds us that often this is to do with school structures. The facility and opportunity to meet vary considerably between types of school, as does the degree of autonomy given to teachers in their work. It is a mixture of opportunity and felt obligation. Distributed leadership and the extent of it are important in this domain. A UK study (McLaughlin

et al., 2006) found that the degree of alignment between policy and structure was key

- the degree of influence on important matters of curriculum and teaching and learning: this is particularly pertinent today in a climate of dictat and prescription. Clearly teachers' ability to influence is limited; however there is still considerable room for manoeuvre
- time and the timetable: the importance of these two items is clear and very important to teachers, although often underplayed by managers and administrators. It allows for meetings to occur and has great influence over the sustainability and scale of collaboration
- training and assistance: as has already been underlined in this chapter, the tradition of teaching is to work alone and be highly autonomous in the classroom. Assumptions are often made that teachers know how to work together in groups and have the skills and knowledge to do this. There is much research to show that training and assistance to support tasks, processes of working together and leading a group can be extremely beneficial (Johnson and Johnson, 2006; Little, 1990b; McLaughlin, 2003). Given the research finding that collaboration has a developmental trajectory, this is very important indeed. It relates also to the use made of external partners. Cordingley *et al.*'s (2003) study was one of many that have reinforced the value of using external partners to help with this development.
- resourcing and material support: this too is a matter of alignment between the policy and resourcing of the collaborative working. It refers to the availability of resources and space to undertake the work.

Two recent studies of teachers' learning through continuing professional development have reinforced these points (Bolam and Weindling, 2006; Wellcome Trust, 2006).

From this review we can see that the power of teacher collaboration is evident, as is the complexity and necessity of organisational support. Indeed the importance of changes in teachers' working contexts to allow for collaboration emerges as a key feature. What is also evident is the need for further study and engagement with innovations that are built on the bedrock of teacher collaboration. Little (2002a) argues very clearly for further work on teacher learning and innovations in practice. She echoes Wenger's (1998) caution against romanticising communities of practice and concludes:

> The urgency associated with contemporary reform movements, especially those targeted at persistent achievement disparities, has intensified the pressure on teachers and fueled policy interest in the collective capacity of schools for improvement. This is a timely moment to unpack the meaning and consequences of professional community at the level of practice.

(Little, 2002a, p. 937)

Chapter 4

Networking schools

Kristine Black-Hawkins

> Networking between schools is increasingly recognised as a key driver
> of school improvement in so far as it encourages professional collaboration,
> innovation, the spread of good practice, and the strengthening of mutual
> accountability and transparency across groups of schools and 'communities'
> of practitioners.
>
> (McCarthy *et al.*, 2004, p. 61)

In the previous chapter we reviewed the literature regarding ways in which
individual teachers develop their professional learning when working
collaboratively with colleagues. In this chapter we consider what the literature tells us about how learning takes place between schools when teachers
work collaboratively within networking schools. As McCarthy *et al.* note
above, there has been an increased interest in, and commitment to, schools
and teachers coming together in this way, in the UK and elsewhere. Examples
include the Teacher Training Agency (TTA) Research Consortia in England
(Cordingley and Bell, 2002); the Coalition of Knowledge Building Schools
in Australia (Groundwater-Smith and Mockler, 2002); and the Bay Area
School Reform Collaboration, in the US (BASRC, 2004). All of these are
considered in more detail in Chapter 6.

More generally, in England, the vast majority of schools already have some
kind of working relationship with other schools, albeit in a range of ways
and for many reasons. Some of these connections are small-scale, informal
and led by teachers, others are more widespread, formal and bureaucratic.
Recently, various government schemes have supported and formalised such
developments as part of their overall education reform agenda: for example,
Excellence in Cities (DfES, 1999), Specialist Schools (DfES, 2004a) and the
Leading Edge Partnership Programme (DfES, 2002a). In 2002, the first cohort
of Networked Learning Communities was funded by the Department for
Education and Skills (DfES), under the auspices of the National College
for School Leadership (NCSL, 2002a). By 2003 there was a total of 135
networks, comprising over 1,500 schools and forming, according to Hannon

(2005), the then largest educational networking programme in the world. We examine the experiences of six of these networks in Chapters 7–13. More recently the Primary Strategy Learning Networks (DfES, 2004b) have been introduced, setting out to involve some 9,000 primary schools in 1,500 networks. However, as Hannon argues, these and other programmes are part of 'a networking landscape which is at best confusing' (p. 7). She also notes that, although they 'belong to a broad family of collaboration . . . there are significant differences between them' which can not be overlooked (p. 8). Furthermore, such collaborations do not always co-exist easily alongside the prevailing 'standards agenda' in England which encourages competition between schools (Fielding *et al.*, 2005; Rudduck *et al.*, 2000).

Similar confusions and complexities emerge throughout much of the literature relating to school networks. In particular, there is a recurring concern about the difficulty of finding accurate ways of defining, portraying and evaluating the vast array of arrangements that are called 'networks' as well as the wide variety of actions that are identified as 'networking'. This is partly to do with the metaphorical nature of these rather nebulous terms. It is also partly to do with how networks function in practice. Their inherent plasticity allows them to develop and adapt to changing circumstances, which then makes them difficult to describe with any precision. Certainly, the literature presents us with a rich and diverse range of networks involving a wide variety of networking processes, activities and intentions.

Thus the following questions arise:

- Are there certain qualities that are fundamental to all school networks? And, if so, what are they?
- What does belonging to a networking school really mean?
- What are the advantages for such schools and what are the costs?
- In what ways does a school network support teachers' and students' learning?
- Why are some school networks more successful than others?

To address these questions, we begin by presenting two rather different, but complementary, views of educational networks so as to introduce the idea of common features across networks, as well as to note possible variations between them. In the next section, we focus on the concept of network itself, drawing on literature not only from education but also from other disciplines. In particular, we consider writings that explore and extend the network metaphor: for example, by developing ideas around 'knots', 'threads' and 'nodes'. We also reflect on the idea of social capital as a central notion in understanding the nature of relationships in networks. We then go on to consider an underlying assumption, within much of the literature, regarding educational networks as almost always worthwhile endeavours, capable of providing important opportunities to learn for teachers and students and also their schools. Subsequent sections of the chapter are structured around the 'who', 'why' and 'how' of networks. These are: teachers and schools (who); coming together for a purpose (why); so as to engage in activities (how). It is axiomatic to argue that no network could exist unless all three aspects were broadly present in some form. However, beyond this commonplace, understanding what is actually meant by 'who', 'why' and 'how' in particular networks, and the nature of the relationship between them, remains problematic. Where appropriate we draw on examples of networks which involve some form of practitioner research and enquiry, as an introduction to our discussion in Chapter 5. We end this chapter by considering network conditions that are likely to support learning between members of different schools, as well as tensions and problems that can inhibit such learning.

As noted earlier, the notion of school networks has become very popular in education and this has contributed to an even more recent proliferation of writing on the topic. However, in this chapter we primarily draw on literature available up until 2004. That is, we consider the ideas, arguments and concerns that informed the research we undertook at that time and as it is presented in Chapters 7–13.

BEGINNING WITH SOME COMMON FEATURES OF NETWORKING SCHOOLS

> Networks are purposeful social entities characterised by a commitment to quality, rigour and a focus on outcomes. They are also an effective means of supporting innovation in times of change. In education, networks promote the dissemination of good practice, enhance the professional development of teachers, support capacity building in schools, mediate between centralised and decentralised structures, and assist in the process of re-structuring and re-culturing educational organisations and systems.
>
> (Hopkins, 2000, p. 1)

> The kind of sharing that goes on in educational networks often has the effect of dignifying and giving shape to the process and content of educators' experiences, the daily-ness of their work, which is often invisible to outsiders yet binds insiders together . . . They encourage and seem to support many of the key ideas that . . . are needed to produce change and improvement in schools, teaching and learning.
>
> (Lieberman, 1999)

The first of these descriptions was constructed by the attendees at an OECD/CERI seminar, the purpose of which was to examine how networking amongst European schools has led (could lead) to innovative educational policies and practices. In contrast, the second provides what appears to be a more modest justification for educators working collaboratively in this way. Where Hopkins writes of large-scale, possibly international, 're-structuring of educational organisations and systems', Lieberman describes 'dignifying the daily-ness of teachers' work'. Despite their differences in scope, these two extracts highlight key elements of school networks which are reflected in much of the associated literature. That is, networks would ideally seem to involve people working together ('social'/'sharing'), have a clear focus ('purposeful'/'give shape'), and be primarily concerned with what actually takes place in classrooms and schools ('good practice'/'educators' experiences'). Finally, there should be a consensus that the overall purpose of any school network is to bring about improvement with a focus on outcomes, whether across a number of classrooms, a group of schools or entire educational systems.

EXAMINING THE CONCEPT OF NETWORKS AND NETWORKING

The recent expansion of the network phenomenon

Networks, educational or otherwise, are clearly not a new phenomenon. They have always existed in various forms and for a variety of reasons, as a way of supporting the human connections we have as individuals and as members of groups. Neither, of course, is the activity of 'networking' new. As Nardi et al. (2000) argue: 'The term networking, as in cultivating useful others, has been in use since at least 1940 . . . What is new, we will argue, is the intensity and absolute necessity of networking for practically everyone' (p. 3). The concept of networks, however, has become more recently an area for intense study in an attempt to make sense of recent global changes, and particularly in response to the extraordinarily rapid expansion in information technologies, communication systems, travel and trade, that has taken place in the last few decades. The work of Castells (2000) has been central to these concerns. He argues that understanding networks and networking is key to understanding ourselves and our relationships with others: professionally, politically, socially and culturally as well as locally, nationally and globally. 'Networks constitute the new social morphology of our societies, and the diffusion of networking logic substantially modifies the operation and outcomes in processes of production, experience, power and culture' (p. 500). His analysis clearly demonstrates not only the sheer momentum of what he has coined as the 'rise of the network society' but also the constantly shifting nature of its exchanges, which are both exciting and disturbing.

The growth of school networks can be seen as a part (albeit a minor one) of this larger phenomenon. Various examples of this expansion have been highlighted in the opening section of this chapter. In particular, it is claimed by some, networks that support teachers' professional development have become increasingly significant in recent years. Lieberman and Wood (2001) argue that 'the history of professional development for teachers is a landscape littered with failed approaches', in which teachers were 'passive consumers of prepackaged knowledge, or at best compliant participants' expected to absorb 'expert' knowledge (p. 174). In contrast, educational networks have grown in numbers because they create 'discourse communities' that encourage 'exchange among the members', thus allowing teachers 'flexibility' and 'self-determination' in their learning (Lieberman and McLaughlin, 1992, p. 676).

Kaplan and Usdan (1992) discuss the 'profusion' of 'education policy networks' in the US. They reflect wryly on the extent of the changes that have taken place: 'Back in the 1950s, the word network was still as noun, and educators would probably have considered it both socially and grammatically "unseemly" "to network"' (p. 665). However, they argue that this understanding of education is no longer viable:

> To function largely in isolation . . . is to volunteer for obscurity – even extinction. Finding and making common cause with people and groups of similar purpose and vision and so rising above professional roles and government jurisdictions is a necessity. Networks are in; anachronistic and mindless sovereignty is out.
>
> (Kaplan and Usdar, 1992, p. 672).

Network as metaphor

One of the difficulties that arises throughout the literature is that of clarifying what is understood by the term 'network' and then applying it to the practices of schools and teachers. This is also a common feature of other forms of network outside education. In their evaluation of international development networks, Church et al. (2002) describe their 'struggle for definition': 'We have consistently come up against the question "What, or who, is the network?"' (p. 14). This nebulous notion becomes even more inexact over time as networks shift and change. We have seen this in our own efforts to provide a narrative of SUPER (Schools–University Partnership for Educational Research): a network of which we have all been members and with which we have worked closely for a number of years (see McLaughlin et al. 2006).

In the paper referred to above, Church and her colleagues do, however, begin to untangle the concept of the network. They extend the metaphor to incorporate 'threads, knots and nets' (relationships, activities and structures) so as to develop a network typology that also seems helpful when considering networks of schools. They explain them as follows:

- 'The threads give the network its life. The threads link the participants through communication, friendship, shared ideas, relational processes, conflict, information.'
- 'The knots are where the threads the participants spin meet and join together. They are the joint activities aimed at realising the common purpose.'
- 'The net is the structure constructed through the relationships and the joint activities, a structure which allows for autonomy in community, a structure which participants create, contribute to and benefit from.'

(Church *et al.*, 2002, p. 16)

To return to educational networks, McCormick and Fox (2006) asked teachers and local authority (LA) co-ordinators to visualise and then construct a 'map' of the networks in which their school or the LA were involved (see also Carmichael *et al.*, 2006). Each map identified 'nodes', defined as 'actors (such as people, roles, organisations, groups and communities), places and events'; 'links between nodes'; plus, the 'structure of the overall map' (p. 6). In applying the metaphor of a map to that of the network, it became clear that understanding the relationship between schools and their networks depended on not only *when* a map was constructed but also *by whom.* 'When two respondents from the same school represented their school's networks these did not coincide (even though there were common elements) because they experience different network links or because they perceive them differently' (Carmichael *et al.,* 2006, p. 220). The writers refer to this as the 'ego-centred perspectives' of the individual map-makers and argue that, 'There is no assumption that individuals have oversight of *the* entire network, or even that *an* entire network exists' (ibid.).

Thus, another important aspect of network emerges, concerning the distinction between whole networks that can be comprehended as complete entities with clear boundaries, and others which are diffuse and open, interacting and overlapping with other networks. In terms of education, there are many example of both. The distinction between them also helps to untangle some of the differences between a *school network* and a *networking school.* The NLC scheme in England helps to illustrate some of this complexity: each individual NLC might be considered as a 'whole' or 'bounded' network, as indeed might the overarching national scheme (a school is either in an NLC or it is not). However, the vast majority of the individual schools also have allegiances to, and relationships with, other schools, institutions and organisations beyond their particular NLC structure. These additional elements – 'threads and knots' or 'nodes and links' – can be seen as enriching the work of teachers in the schools, although they also complicate our under-standing of any specific network. Granovetter's (1973) analysis of social networks also seems useful here. He discusses the value of a continuum of 'weak' and 'strong' ties across different groups, providing members with access to a wide range of different opportunities as well as associated levels of commitment.

This takes us back to Castells' work (2000) and the notion of the 'morphology of the network'. He argues that it is 'well adapted to increasing complexity of interaction and to unpredictable patterns of development arising from the creative power of such interactions' (p. 70). Indeed, Castells draws on the work of Kelly who provides yet another metaphor:

> The Atom is past. The symbol of science for the next century is the dynamical Net ... Whereas the Atom represents clean simplicity, the Net channels the messy power of complexity. .. The network is the least structured organisation that can be said to have any structure at all.
> (Kelly, 1995, pp. 25–7, cited in Castells, 2000, p. 70)

Social capital and the importance of trust in school networks

Networks are fundamentally about human contact in its myriad forms; about the ways in which people connect, relate and are tied to some rather than others. Social capital is an idea frequently used to explore the theory behind how and why networks function as they do. Sampson (2004, p. 18) suggests that, '[it] is typically conceptualised as being embodied in the social ties among persons'. Gilchrist (2004, p. 147) adds to this by stressing 'the collective value' of 'personal relationships and organisational connections' within networks. She goes on to argue that 'robust and diverse social networks enhance the health and happiness of individuals, and contribute to the well-being of society as a whole'. This sense of 'well-being' is paralleled in much of the literature focusing on educational networks. For example, it links to the discussion in Chapter 1, regarding Parker's (1977) insight into the value teachers place on belonging to 'a special group or movement' (cited in Lieberman and Grolnick, 1996, p. 6), or what Jackson (2004, p. 25) refers to as a sense of 'shared destinies'.

In his critique of the National Writing Project (NWP), Hargreaves (2004) suggests that the success of this US national network is based predominantly on the high levels of social capital it has generated. He argues that networks have two sides. The first is 'structural', or what he calls the 'the nature of the links between the nodes' (p. 84). The other is 'cultural ... which is usually encapsulated in the term *trust*', arguing that 'without trust, networks rarely prosper'. He explains that in the NWP, 'high levels of social capital were built up among the participants and crucial to the project's success was this generation of high levels of trust between teachers, rather than on the actual activities and structures in place' (ibid.). Thus, the focus and context of particular practices are less important than how far they 'may be successful in generating the high social capital that allows teachers to learn with and from their colleagues in a way that benefits their classroom practices' (p. 85). Thus networks that are characterised by high social capital may develop and be sustained spontaneously (continuing to generate social capital); networks that are deliberately constructed may, or may not, have these necessary characteristics.

Whereas Hargreaves (2004) argues that 'without trust, networks rarely prosper' (p. 84), Sampson (2004), in his work on inner city crime, offers a warning that, 'writing on social capital tends to gloss over its potential downside – namely that [it] can be drawn upon for negative as well as positive goals' (p. 161). He notes that, 'networks connect do-gooders just as they connect drug dealers. . . . It is important to ask *what* is being connected – networks are not inherently egalitarian or prosocial in nature' (p. 159). Although it seems highly likely that school networks will comprise teachers whose intentions are to 'do good' (although not in the negative sense of 'do-gooders') not all relationships formed will necessarily and unambiguously support such aims. Gilchrist warns that networks can 'reinforce a sense of belonging, of mutuality, based on somewhat transient notions of "us" and "them"' (p. 149), thus creating networks in which social capital strengthens relationships that are exclusive, insular and conservative. Lieberman and McLaughlin (1992) highlight this concern specifically with regard to educational networks. They argue the need to find a balance between 'overextension', on the one hand, which may lead to 'a kind of intellectual bankruptcy', and 'limiting membership', on the other, which may risk 'creating or aggravating a "them/us" divisiveness among teachers' (p. 676).

CONSIDERING THE 'TAKEN-FOR-GRANTED' GOOD OF SCHOOL NETWORKS

As noted earlier, however school networks are understood in theory and conducted in practice, they are almost unfailingly presented as worthwhile undertakings, of clear benefit to their members and also often to a wider community. For example, the Bay Area School Reform Collaborative (known as Springboard Schools, from 2005), based in San Francisco, has the following 'mission and vision . . . to transform schools across the Bay Area into vital places to learn and teach' (BASRC, 2004). These intentions are, of course, unquestionably right and proper and, as such, they resonate with the general intentions of many other networks. Underpinning the NLC initiative in England is the stated 'aspiration of generating morally purposeful partnerships between teachers and schools' (Jackson, 2002b, p. 3). As with BASRC, this aim cannot be disputed. However, it is through such statements, based on ethical stances, that networks *per se* may be given an uncontested legitimacy. This is generally expressed not only in terms of democratic values that encourage the contribution of a range of participants, but also through the commonality of their aims based on improving the educational experiences of students in schools.

Thus although some of the literature explores potential tensions and dilemmas in the processes of networking (for example, see Lieberman and McLaughlin, 1992), there is, it seems, little reporting of 'bad' or 'weak' school networks, or evidence regarding whether networking is necessarily the 'best' means by which to accomplish a particular set of ends. This sometimes unquestioning belief in the intrinsic rightness of school networks may detract from a more useful and rigorous critique of what does and does not work well, and why. To return to the extracts from Hopkins (2000) and from Lieberman (1999): they describe very clearly the potential strengths of schools working together in these ways, but it may be that in reality these opportunities are not always realised by all schools that set out to belong to networks.

There seem to be clear parallels here between schools working together in collaborative ways and individual teachers doing so. As noted in Chapter 3, the latter is also often seen as 'a taken-for-granted good'. However, as Hargreaves argues in his critique of the 'heresy of individualism' (1993, p. 53), there are, at times, certain benefits to be gained by some teachers when they choose to work independently of colleagues. In the same way, it may be that supporting collaborative working practices among colleagues *within* a school is, sometimes, more beneficial than collaborating or networking with colleagues in *other* schools. McLaughlin and Talbert (2001) have considered a range of organisational contexts of potential 'professional communities' to support teachers working in high schools in the US. These include the level of curriculum department, school, district and state. They argue that all have their strengths. They also observe that 'the level of community that is closest to the classroom is the most salient for teachers, and thus most able to influence their practice and career experiences' (p. 94). Thus for some teachers, membership of a small-scale and easily accessible department may, at times, provide a more worthwhile professional community than that of a more geographically wide-spread and disparate network, although there is no reason, of course, why teachers might not work closely with departmental colleagues and also within a broader network of other schools.

It is interesting to note that assumptions about the beneficial nature of school networks are not necessarily shared by those who analyse other forms of network. For example, McCarthy et al. (2004) emphasise the increasingly influential nature of national and global networks. However, they do so by presenting a number of powerful examples that span a continuum from the useful to the clearly harmful and unethical:

> Think about Al-Qaeda. The internet, eBay, Kazaa. The mobile phone, SMS. Think about iron triangles and old school ties . . . . Think VISA

and Amex, the teetering electricity grid, the creaking rail network. LHR to LAX. Think about six degrees of separation. Think small worlds, word of mouth.

(McCarthy *et al.*, 2004, p. 11)

They go on to argue:

[Networks] are all around us. We rely on them. We are threatened by them. We are part of them. Networks shape our world, but they can be confusing: no obvious leader or centre, no familiar structure and no easy diagram to describe them. Networks self-organise, morphing and changing as they react to interference or breakdown.

(ibid.)

They suggest that, while networks cannot be ignored or avoided, they are also too complex to be understood as morally neutral. Nevertheless, in discussions regarding school networks the notion of morality is rarely raised. There is, quite properly, an assumption that if schools come together to work collaboratively, whatever the specific focus of any ensuing network, their overarching aim will be to improve the experiences of their students. And this assumption is based, again quite properly, on the understanding that teachers as professionals are committed to improving the experiences of those they teach. Nevertheless, real networks function in the messy real world and, in practice, some might not be particularly effective or might be less effective than they once were. As Lieberman and Wood (2004) note, 'A crucial question left hanging, however, is whether or not network learning ever actually finds its way into classroom teaching and student accomplishment' (p. 66). The literature does, however, provide examples of the possible difficulties that a school network might face. For example, Lieberman and McLaughlin (1992) identify a number of potential 'nagging problems' (p. 675), and Lieberman (1999) describes networks as having 'to negotiate a set of tensions' (cited in Lieberman, 2005, p. 2). When Earl and Katz (2005) evaluated the NLC programme in England, the title of the report included 'inevitable tensions'. In all of these there is a clear implication that some networks may not be as successful as others, and also that any network may become less successful over time. However, none of them suggests that networks *per se* are not a force for good in education or that alternative approaches might be preferable. We consider the nature of these identified tensions and problems later in the chapter.

EXPLORING THE WHO, WHY AND HOW OF SCHOOL NETWORKS

School networks comprise three necessary elements that are closely related to each other. These are: people (*who*), with a shared purpose (*why*), organised so as to engage in activities (*how*). Such interconnections are clearly found in all networks, including those that involve school-based practitioner research and enquiry. *Who* participates in the research (in terms of the researchers and the researched as well as the users of research), *why* research is undertaken and *how* it is conducted and subsequently made use of, will shape and be shaped by the nature of each particular network. For example, the Educating Professionals for Informal Classrooms (EPIC) network in Ohio is part of the larger US Professional Development Schools networking project (see Darling-Hammond, 1994). It comprises teachers from four elementary schools, plus academic staff from Ohio University. The primary purpose of the network has been to improve teachers' day-to-day classroom practices through engaging in practitioner enquiry, supported by university staff. As one of the teachers explains:

> By becoming a PDS, we hoped to increase our capacity to engage in systematic inquiry into our practice by bringing together teachers' practical experience and knowledge with university faculty's theoretical and research expertise in joint inquiries into ways to meet the needs of all children.
>
> (Kirschner *et al.*, 1996, p. 206)

The relationship between the three elements of *who, why* and *how* can also be noted in the overall scope and scale of school networks. Consequently, larger networks, with more powerful membership, may well have more ambitious intentions and also more means by which to achieve them. Hopkins (2000, p. 11) offers a helpful typology of networks, organised into five levels. The first he describes as, 'Basic . . . simply groups of teachers joining together for a common curriculum purpose and for the sharing of good practice'. By the fifth level, however, networking is depicted as an activity involving a range of different interest groups, possibly with political influence, with the purpose of bringing about major changes through national and even international legislation. Hopkins describes this final level as, 'Groups of networks . . . act[ing] explicitly as an agency for system renewal and transformation'.

School networks, of course, necessarily involve real people engaged in real activities and therefore are unlikely to remain static in their composition, intentions or actions, (*who, why* and *how*). Such evolutions can be traced through the literature. For example, the description of the SUPER network as it was first formed in 1999 is both similar to and different from its incarnation some four years later (see Ebbutt, 2002; Black-Hawkins, 2003). Some schools have left, others have joined; key participants have been replaced in schools and the university; purposes have been developed; new structures have been introduced; changes have been made in funding arrangements. Yet even this does not tell a complete story. How the schools and the Faculty of Education first came together has its own history that continues to shape this network's current activities and its future possibilities (see, for example, James and Worrall, 2000, and McLaughlin et al., 2006).

Finally, however explicitly stated the aims of a network might be, members may interpret them, and how they might be fulfilled, in a variety of ways. Richmond (1996, p. 215), a lecturer at the University of Michigan, notes 'the particular challenges' posed by such tensions between herself and the science teachers with whom she sets out to collaborate. Somekh (1994) not only experiences similar concerns *between* university and school staff, but also comments on the potential for similar pressures *within* individual schools as well as *within* the university research team. And, in her persuasive defence of school-based collaborative enquiry, Groundwater-Smith (2004, p. 1) nevertheless reminds her readers not to overlook how 'schools are made up of individual practitioners with varying careers and social histories'.

Who are the members of a school network?

The literature provides many examples of groups of people who have come together to describe themselves as networks. Some are 'internal networks' (Hargreaves, 1999, p. 125) consisting of members from a single school or even an individual department within a school; for example, see Little (2002b) and also the work of the Southwest Educational Development Laboratory (SEDL) (Hord, 1997). Others involve members from a number of different schools. These may be locally based, such as the EPIC network noted above, or have a national base, like the NLC initiative referred to earlier. Some networks include participants from a range of organisations other than schools. In particular, networks of schools that set out to engage in practitioner research very often include members of universities. For example, the Coalition of Knowledge Building Schools not only comprises participants from several schools but also from the University of Sydney (Groundwater-Smith and Mockler, 2002). This model of schools and universities working together is similar to that of the four research consortia supported by the Teacher Training Agency (TTA) (see Cordingley *et al.*, 2002; Cordingley and Bell, 2002). However, in addition, each consortium included members of LAs. Furthermore, networking also took place not only within each consortium but across the group of four.

An additional consideration when examining the membership of a network is the numbers of people involved from its composite organisations. At one end of this continuum are those networks that comprise a small number of *individuals* from each school and other institutions. For example, the Pupil Autonomy in Learning with Micro-computers (PALM) network set out to research how the use of computers in the classroom might promote autonomy in student learning. This involved about one hundred teachers from across twenty-four schools (that is, maybe four or five teachers from each) plus members of the Centre for Action Research in Education (CARE) based at the University of East Anglia (Somekh, 1994). Some teachers participate enthusiastically in such networks because they cannot find the supportive, collaborative relationships they want within their own schools. 'When the climate of a school is difficult, [networks] provide teachers with knowledge, support and identity with a broader community that enable them to persevere' (Lieberman, 1996, p. 200). However, as Little and McLaughlin (1993) argue, this can bring conflict and a tension in loyalties: 'Such energetic participation earns teachers "good colleague" status in the network but sometimes brings disapproval in their schools or departments' (p. 4).

At the other extreme are networks that involve entire *institutions*, although this too requires further clarification. Describing a school as a member of a network does not necessarily mean that everyone working there has an involvement in, a commitment to, or even any knowledge of, the network and its purposes and activities. Indeed, this may not be necessary for its success. Participation may entail teachers only, or teachers plus students, or teachers, students and others, such as parents, governors, local community groups and so forth. Defining institutional membership for a school may therefore depend on a notion of critical mass and/or critical levels of active commitment from headteachers and other members of senior management teams. Even then, within a single network, there may be differences in terms of the level of institutional support. For example, in the SUPER network (McLaughlin and Black-Hawkins, 2004) there is an element of student involvement in network activities in each of its eight schools. However, the extent of that engagement and the numbers of students concerned varies greatly between the schools.

The difference between *individual* and *institutional* networks can partly be understood in terms of *teacher* networks and *school* networks. That is, they both provide frameworks for professional collaboration, but the former primarily offers opportunities for individual teachers to learn from other individual teachers across a number of schools and with no assumption that such learning will necessarily be shared with other teachers from those composite schools, whereas the aim of the latter is for schools to learn from each other and for that learning to have some form of institutional effect. In practice such distinctions are unlikely to be clear cut. For example, while the NWP focuses on the professional development of individual teachers it also provides a wide range of on-going support structures to encourage individual teachers to use their learning with colleagues in their schools. Furthermore, these arrangements and activities are made available at local and national levels, so that the membership of this network is fluid and can be interpreted in a variety of ways (see Lieberman and Wood, 2004). The notion of complete or open networks (as well as school *networks* or *networking* schools), as discussed earlier, is also helpful here.

Why be in a school network?

Lieberman and Grolnick (1996) suggest that, 'Networks must somehow demonstrate a compelling reason to convince people to participate in what is, after all, still another activity . . . [that] working together [will] be of mutual importance' (pp. 10–1). As already noted, the overriding intention of any school network is to improve, in some way, the experiences of students and staff. Within this overall framework, there are two related reasons why members of schools choose to get together in this way. First, they share a set of purposes regarding the educational improvement they want to bring about and, second, they believe that these purposes will be most effectively addressed by working collaboratively as a network rather than as separate institutions. Beyond these general considerations there exist amongst networks a vast range of objectives and intentions. This is clearly illustrated by Lieberman and Grolnick's (ibid., pp. 14–5) analysis of sixteen US school networks. In this they provide a summary of the purposes of each. These vary from the highly focused to the somewhat more open-ended. For example, the specific aim of the Foxfire Teacher Outreach Network is to support teachers of English in secondary schools who use the Foxfire scheme to teach writing to students, whereas the more loosely defined aim of the Network of Progressive Educators is to 'provide a professional network for people who share the same values and beliefs about progressive education'.

Whatever their particular intentions, schools and other institutions form networks because their members believe that in doing so their aims will be more effectively accomplished. 'What is achieved in the collaboration must be greater than what any of the members . . . could have achieved individually' (Richmond, 1996, p. 217). The importance of harnessing the inherent power of the group is reiterated throughout the literature on school networks. Jackson (2002b, p. 4), in describing the theoretical framework of the NLC programme, notes that 'a key mantra for the initiative [. . . is] working smarter together, rather than harder alone'. He argues that, in doing so, networks are able to 'provide a supportive context for risk-taking and creativity'. Similar advantages are noted by others. Hopkins (2000, p. 5) writes of opportunities for 'collaborative professional development'; 'the breaking down of isolation'; 'joint solutions to shared problems'; 'the exchange of practice and expertise'; 'the facilitation of knowledge sharing and school improvement'; and 'opportunities to incorporate external facilitation'. Fielding *et al.* (2005) suggest that these processes of sharing and exchange, within networks, might be better understood in terms of 'a "development" model rather than a "transfer" model'. That is, one that provides a 'strong commitment to reciprocity, both of respect and learning' (p. 90).

> Whilst the original practice remains central it does not remain static . . .
> the point is not just to transfer good working practices, but also to make

them better through mutual learning. The roles of originating and receiving institution thus become blurred or interchangeable.'

(Fielding *et al.*, 2005, pp. 90–1)

Hargreaves (2003a, 2003b) goes far beyond the local and specific in his advocacy of schools networks. Such organisational structures, he suggests, offer highly effective large scale opportunities for engaging both with and in school-based research, or, to use Hargreaves' terms, *'knowledge sharing'* and *'knowledge creation'* (see also Hargreaves, 1999). He argues that their purpose is not only to support the work of individual teachers, schools or even networks, but equally importantly to provide a critical means by which radical innovation can take place in schools, thereby bringing about a systemic transformation of UK education. Knowledge sharing through networking ensures that, 'The best professional practices . . . are not locked within the minds of a few outstanding teachers and restricted to the privacy of their classrooms, but are common property of all who might profit from them' (p. 25).

Hargreaves maintains that networking allows *knowledge creation* to take place in a more efficient and robust manner because groups of teachers, by 'working laterally', can draw on the combined intellectual, social and organisational capital of many schools. He criticises the more customary school-based practitioner research and enquiry conducted by individual teachers within their individual schools.

[A network] is so much larger than an individual school, it can prioritise a shared topic for knowledge creation and have a much more sophisticated design, both for sharing the innovative workload, so that each school undertakes a limited and variable amount of activity, and for testing it more rigorously than is ever possible in a single . . . school or department . . . generat[ing] a far more robust evidence base . . . in a far shorter time.

(Hargreaves, 2003a, p. 40).

In a later paper, he emphasises the importance of the social and collaborative characteristics of networks, not only in terms of knowledge transfer but also knowledge creation, or what he calls here 'innovation':

What we have traditionally called professional learning is very often a form of knowledge creation and knowledge transfer, alternatively conceived as innovation and the dissemination of such innovation. We now understand better than ever that innovation is very often a social, interactive process rather than one of individual creativity, and that networks play a vital role in the creation and the transfer of new knowledge and innovation.

(Hargreaves, 2004, pp. 84–5)

72 Networking practitioner research

How do school networks work?

How school networks structure, organise and conduct themselves, including the types of activity in which they engage, is clearly related to who constitutes their membership as well as the reasons underpinning why a group of institutions have elected to work together. Lieberman and Wood (2003) argue that 'networks flourish [when] they attract participants around compelling ideas'. Judgements about how are also shaped by pragmatic as well as ethical considerations: what is possible and reasonable, together with what is fair and proper. Both these concerns are certainly pertinent to networks that undertake school-based practitioner research.

There is also an inherent tension in the how of networks: they need to be both strong (to support the needs of members) and flexible (to respond to changes and new ideas). Hargreaves provides us with another network metaphor when he contrasts the construction of a 'cathedral' with that of a 'bazaar' (2003, p. 56). Once the former is built, he argues, it cannot be changed and thereby it is in danger of becoming outmoded. The latter, he maintains, is preferable because it is able to respond spontaneously to its users' ever-changing needs and creative developments. (Although it is, of course, possible to argue that a bazaar may lack the necessary stability and political authority to sustain embedded changes.) Hargreaves (2004) also argues that structures and practices *per se* are far less important than the 'culture' of a network and the levels of trust between its members; a successful network generates 'high social capital that allows teachers to learn with and from their colleagues in a way that benefits their classroom practices' (p. 85). Similarly, Darling-Hammond and McLaughlin (1996) emphasise the importance of flexibility as well as the nature of the relationship. They argue that networks are 'powerful learning tools' because:

> They engage people in collective work on authentic problems that emerge in their own efforts, allowing them to get beyond the dynamics of their own schools and classrooms to encounter other possibilities as well as people experiencing and solving similar problems.
>
> (Darling-Hammond and McLaughlin, 1996, p. 207)

It is possible to identify within the literature a number of features, conditions, structures, processes and activities that are considered likely to support collaborative working and learning by teachers in networks. Although there are variations in the texts and different degrees of emphasis (in particular between networks of *teachers* and networks of *schools*), certain elements recur sufficiently frequently to allow a composite list to be produced. In doing so, however, there is a danger that these elements are reduced to simplistic generalisations or even platitudes. Nevertheless, the following provides a synthesis of key points established by drawing on texts already referred to in this chapter (see Cordingley *et al.*, 2002; Earl and Katz, 2005; Hopkins, 2000; Jackson, 2002b and 2004; Lieberman, 1999; Lieberman and Grolnick, 1996; Lieberman and McLaughlin, 1992; McLaughlin and Black-Hawkins, 2007):

1   *developing and sustaining supportive and invigorating relationships:* providing both information sharing and psychological support; building social capital through openness and mutual trust; encouraging respect for the diversity of contributions made by different members by drawing on teachers' existing knowledge and valuing their experiences
2   *determining clear purposes and a strong commitment to the work:* developing a strong sense of identity through common core values and beliefs, particularly with regard to the purposes and usefulness of the network, including its direct relevance and application to classroom teaching and learning; establishing shared understandings of ownership of and accountability for the network
3   *ensuring voluntary participation:* ensuring that a variety of activities and structures are available to allow members to work flexibly and in a range of ways, with different levels of commitment, which suit their current needs, both professionally and personally
4   *engaging and maintaining the commitment of school leaders:* ensuring that leaders are fully committed to the network's purposes, will act as advocates for its work to support school improvement and encourage collaborative working practices; also leaders who will provide a range of leadership opportunities across the network, so that those who participate in the work are able to share new ideas and practices more broadly
5   *building effective and flexible communication strategies across the network*: setting up systems that support interactions between members and that recognise the importance of discussing practices and other shared issues rather than focussing on the 'business' elements of meetings; providing means of disseminating the work in ways which are useful to members from a range of different contexts
6   *learning from alternative perspectives within and beyond schools:* drawing on the knowledge and experiences of a range of members, including the views of students in schools; involving other institutions, such as universities, to provide training on research methods, where appropriate; developing longer-term critical friendships to encourage and challenge the network's development
7   *maintaining resources in terms of time, money and energy:* ensuring sufficient resources to get a network started and also to sustain it; recognising that teachers need extended time to build relationships, take risks and find creative solutions to shared problems.

IDENTIFYING TENSIONS AND PROBLEMS IN SCHOOL NETWORKS

There is far less emphasis in the literature on potential difficulties faced by members of networks, compared with the reporting of and advice on how to create and sustain successful ones. It would, of course, be possible to rephrase the seven elements in the previous section to provide some form of list of 'difficulties'; for example, replacing 'developing and sustaining supportive and invigorating relationships' with *not* developing such relationships or possibly 'developing and sustaining obstructive and debilitating relationships'. However, a more useful approach is offered by Lieberman and McLaughlin (1992) and also Earl and Katz (2005).

Lieberman and McLaughlin identify the following 'problems' (pp. 675–7), all of which they suggest need to be addressed if successful networks are to be sustained. We have summarised their main concerns in the form of questions:

- 'Quality': How can the quality of the work be assured, especially if developing trust among members may lead to the avoidance of challenging assumptions?
- 'Application': How far, and in what ways, can learning that takes place within networking activities be transferred into schools and classrooms?
- 'Stability': How can sufficient resources be sustained to ensure time for learning to take place?
- 'Overextension': How can popular networks avoid becoming too large and dissipating their resources, in terms of time, money and energy?
- 'Ownership': How can networks, and the teachers within them, maintain flexibility over networking decisions when other partners have more money and/or status?
- 'Expanding objectives': How can networks support teachers and other members to take on roles that will bring about systemic change in education, moving beyond their immediate classrooms and schools?
- 'Leadership': How can networks be led so as to ensure that they are well managed without becoming bureaucratic and inflexible?
- 'Evaluation': How can networks be made accountable in ways that reflect the nature of their work (such as changes in adult behaviour) and not simply in terms of measurable student outcomes?
- 'Goals': How can networks maintain the integrity of their goals against the demands of outsiders, including funding bodies?

Earl and Katz (2005, pp. 8–9) present their analysis of network problems in the form of a series of opposing tensions. A number of these resonate strongly with the concerns articulated by Lieberman and McLaughlin (1992), in particular those relating to the 'quality' of the work undertaken in networks.

The following three 'tensions' are especially pertinent in terms of ensuring that worthwhile learning takes place between teachers and across schools in networks. These are summarised below:

- 'ensuring quality control': providing opportunities to share knowledge and practice *and* ensuring that what is shared is of high quality
- 'focusing on compelling ideas with high leverage': being focused *and* ensuring that the focus is worthwhile and will make a difference to students and their schools
- 'using evidence in an era of rapid reform': encouraging teachers to use data and evidence to support their decision making *and* giving teachers the time and the skills to use that evidence well in routinely changing circumstances.

Of course, as already suggested, none of these problems and tensions exists separately from the others. For example, if the focus is worthwhile, then sharing knowledge and practice that are of high quality and based on sound evidence will be more likely. Furthermore, transferability, or 'application' will also probably be more straightforward, and all of these will benefit from supportive leadership, sufficient funding and appropriate forms of accountability. However, addressing these difficulties so as to develop and sustain any school network (*how*), which is then able to support the diverse and changing requirements of its members (*who*), in ways that allow its aims to be successfully addressed (*why*), is clearly far from straightforward. Endeavouring to do so continues to challenge and invigorate those of us who are involved in the messy and complex practice of networking schools.

Chapter 5

Key questions emerging from the literature on networking practitioner research

Colleen McLaughlin

Our concern in this book is how schools can facilitate teachers' ongoing learning about how to teach in ways that facilitate students' learning. More specifically, our concern is with the usefulness for that purpose not only of the two ideas of *researching schools* and *networking schools* but more especially with the usefulness of combining these two ideas. Is it sensible and useful to promote *networks of researching schools*? Do the two ideas share the same assumptions and values sufficiently for them to be easily compatible? And are they likely to be mutually helpful through having complementary strengths, so that each might contribute to overcoming the problems encountered in the development of the other? At this stage, having reviewed some of the literature about each, we should be well placed to know some of the key questions that should be asked about combining the two ideas. It is the task of this chapter to articulate such questions.

The previous three chapters should however make us quite cautious in undertaking this task. It is clear that neither the idea of researching schools nor that of networking schools is sufficiently developed in practice for any sure lessons to have confidently been learned about them. The amount of research into the practical use of these ideas has been very small indeed, in the UK and also internationally. We are not yet able to build on firm foundations of knowledge about the implications or problems of these two ideas, although we certainly do know more about the more fundamental ideas of *teachers as researchers* and *collaboration among teachers*.

KEY QUESTIONS FROM THE RESEARCHING SCHOOLS LITERATURE

We may start by considering what has helped or hindered the efforts of researching schools. To what extent could networks of researching schools build on the successes such schools have already achieved or overcome the frustrations they have experienced?

We found from the literature that the primary concern of most researching schools was with their own improvement and we formulated some hypotheses about factors that might contribute to their success in pursuing this purpose. So a simple extrapolation from these hypotheses would lead us to ask whether these same factors would be likely to be equally influential and whether or not they would be more evident in networks of researching schools than in individual schools. In pursuing this line of thought, it may in the first instance be helpful to focus on two obvious features that distinguish networks from individual schools. On one hand, networks of schools are generally larger in scale – in terms of the total number of teachers and pupils they include – than individual schools. On the other hand, individual schools are generally likely to have achieved much clearer identities and stronger internal coherence than networks of schools. What kinds of question or hypothesis follow from these simple considerations?

Issues of scale do seem to be relevant to some of our hypotheses about what would help schools to use research for their own improvement. There is, for example, the hypothesis that researching schools are more likely to flourish if they have the support of university departments of education; and it certainly seems likely that university departments will be more ready to establish frameworks for giving such support if there are a number of schools seeking it together. More tentatively, the hypothesis that the allocation of significant resources to research is an important condition for its fruitfulness may also indicate the value of the greater scale of networks: modest contributions from each of several schools may generate a sufficient budget for useful research; and the commitment of a number of schools to a joint research undertaking may also be helpful in attracting support from external sponsors.

However, our hypotheses about conditions for the effective use of research for school improvement also suggest some ways in which research networks might encounter greater problems than those faced by individual schools. Most basically, the hypothesised needs for strong and evident commitment of senior management to the research enterprise, and for this enterprise to be conceived as part of a coherent overall school philosophy might seem to be much more difficult to achieve in a voluntary network of several schools than in a single school with a single central management. Equally, it seems doubtful whether the hypothesised need for long-term commitment is compatible with the voluntary and flexible nature of networks. And it seems likely that the delicate task of effectively co-ordinating the voluntary engagement of teachers in research with whole school development plans would be greatly complicated by the need for plans to be made at the network level as well as at the school level. Therefore, what we learned from the literature about what helps schools to use research for their own improvement does suggest some questions about how working in research networks might be helpful and also some questions about how such networks might further complicate a task that schools find difficult even when working on their own. These then are questions about the value of research networks for the purpose of school improvement. But perhaps the major value of research networks is for the even more demanding purpose of knowledge creation. Hargreaves (1999; 2003) has argued strongly that, whereas the limited resources and limited horizons of individual schools may constrain their ability to work effectively on their own to engage in knowledge creation, networks of researching schools are well placed for the Mode Two kind of knowledge creation that he believes to be appropriate. That in itself is an important hypothesis. What other questions does it raise?

As we have argued in Chapter 2, the limited available literature on research conducted by networks of schools (Simons *et al.*, 2003) does suggest that knowledge generated by such research tends to be disseminated through interpersonal processes involving the people who have done the research in the context of their own work, just as the Mode Two model would suggest. It also suggests, however, that such dissemination depends on quite substantial cognitive and affective resonances among teachers and therefore on quite close social relationships. One set of questions that needs to be asked therefore is whether, how, and in what circumstances, research networks of schools manage to enable teachers both to engage in high quality research and also to establish and maintain the necessary empathetic social relationships with colleagues, not only in their own schools but throughout the networks.

This leads on to another question: what, in the context of such networks, motivates schools and teachers to invest the necessary time and energy in the rigorous research and cumulative development of knowledge necessary for such exercises to be useful? As Chapter 2 made clear, neither the well established 'teachers as researchers' tradition nor the more recent 'researching schools' tradition has been characterised by such concerns. What then might lead networks of researching schools to make such investments?

KEY QUESTIONS FROM THE TEACHER COLLABORATION LITERATURE

Chapter 3 showed clearly that many aspects of classroom teaching discouraged collaboration among teachers: 'The material reality of schools as presently constructed and school-teaching as we organise it mean that teachers necessarily work alone, isolated in their classrooms for the real work of teaching – human interaction with pupils' (p. 45).

But it also demonstrated the benefits to teachers that can come from collaborating. The benefits for teachers personally were seen to be in large measure emotional, reducing their sense of loneliness, strengthening their resolve and increasing their confidence. Collaboration, it was seen, could enhance teachers' sense of professional identity, giving them a new pride and sense of purpose, and an expanded conception of their role; and it seemed that teachers' collaborative research was one kind of activity that especially engendered both such renewed enthusiasm and such broader kinds of thinking about their role. At a very practical level, collaboration could reduce duplication of effort, thus increasing efficiency and possibly reducing overload. And, perhaps most significantly, collaboration could lead to the improvement of teaching, through teachers' learning from one another, through their learning together and through the reflection stimulated by dialogue among them. Collaborative engagement in research is recognised as one particular way in which collaboration can promote learning and improvement.

It was also clear, however, not only that collaboration in schools is not easily promoted and achieved but also that collaboration does not necessarily lead to such benefits. Much depends, it would seem, on the precise nature of the collaboration and on what motivates the collaboration. Considerable risks are involved, so clear thinking, caution and negotiation are needed; and, crucially, trust must be developed. Furthermore, the benefits of collaboration appear to be dependent on a recognition of the inevitability and potential fruitfulness of conflict, and on the development of constructive ways of responding to conflict. Even within schools, then, collaboration is neither simply achieved nor automatically beneficial.

The fundamental problem with collaboration in schools is that it seems to be going against the grain of the way teaching in schools is organised; so the potential benefits of collaboration, although substantial, are hard won. Is the same true of collaboration among schools? It can be argued that the potential benefits of collaboration among teachers across networking schools are similar to, but even greater than, the benefits of within-school collaboration. But is it also going against the grain to seek collaboration among schools? Schools are generally well established coherent entities, with considerable emphasis put upon their individual identities and on obligations of loyalty to them, whereas networks have only voluntary, fleeting and flexible identities. And especially in systems where a great deal of decision-making, of finance, and of accountability, rewards and punishments are devolved to individual schools, it might well seem that the benefits of collaboration across schools will be even more hard won than they are within schools. And it might be especially difficult to gain such benefits when they depend on doing something so complex and so little established in schools as research.

So key questions arising from Chapter 3 include: Are the benefits of research collaboration across schools similar to those of collaboration, and especially of research collaboration, within schools? If so, are the benefits enhanced or diminished by the cross-school nature of the collaboration? And what distinctive kinds of benefit, if any, are there from cross-school research collaboration?

Are the risks, costs and problems of research collaboration across schools also similar to those within schools? What distinctive kinds of risk are there, if any? What conditions and strategies are necessary to ensure that the benefits of research collaboration across schools outweigh the costs? Are networks able to cope better or worse than individual schools with the problems and conflicts that collaboration entails?

KEY QUESTIONS FROM THE NETWORKING SCHOOLS LITERATURE

As Chapter 4 demonstrated, 'networking between schools is increasingly recognised as a key driver of school improvement' (McCarthy *et al.*, 2004). It became clear that one of the main attractions and strengths of networks is the fact that they are not pre-existing organisations with their own prior purposes and so can be structured flexibly for their own specific temporary purposes. Kelly (1995) was quoted as saying that 'The network is the least structured organisation that can be said to have any structure at all' and Hargreaves (2004, p. 84) has suggested that successful networks depend primarily on the high levels of trust between members 'rather than the actual activities and structures in place'.

One question that arises for research networks of schools is therefore whether networks are the right kinds of organisation for learning through the necessarily highly disciplined procedures and critical questioning of research. Might networks, with their emphasis on flexibility and on trust, not be better fitted to other less disciplined and critical kinds of learning, as perhaps implied in the Chapter 4 quotation from Darling-Hammond and McLaughlin (1996), suggesting that networks are 'powerful learning tools' because 'they engage people in collective work on authentic problems that emerge in their own efforts, allowing them to get beyond the dynamics of their own schools and classrooms to encounter other possibilities as well as people experiencing and solving similar problems' (p. 207)?

Chapter 4 quoted Hargreaves, however, as arguing on the contrary that networks are necessary for ensuring that 'the best professional practices . . . are not locked within the minds of a few outstanding teachers and restricted to the privacy of their classrooms, but are common property of all who might profit from them' (Hargreaves, 2003b, p. 25) and as claiming that networks of researching schools are indeed well fitted for such disciplined work: '[A network] is so much larger than an individual school, it can prioritise a shared topic for knowledge creation and have a much more sophisticated design, both for sharing the innovative workload, so that each school undertakes a limited and variable amount of activity, and for testing it more rigorously than is ever possible in a single . . . school or department . . . generating a far more robust evidence base . . . in a far shorter time' (p. 40). We need to treat these claims as hypotheses that require critical testing.

A contrary hypothesis would be that individual schools are better placed than networks to develop research plans that are consistent with the many other demands on teachers' time and attention. McLaughlin and Talbert's (2001) claim that 'the level of community that is closest to the classroom is the most salient for teachers and thus most able to influence their practice and career experiences' (p. 94) might suggest that research planned at the school level would not only be more manageable but also more influential for teachers.

Several authors, including Lieberman and Grolnick (1996) and Richmond (1996), are quoted in Chapter 4 as emphasising the need for networks to have compelling attractions and ongoing benefits for schools and for teachers, because they require what is unambiguously extra work. There is no doubt that networking has many attractions for teachers, but whether or not, and in what circumstances, engaging in jointly planned research is one of these attractions remains an open question.

Finally, Chapter 4 synthesised from the literature a number of elements that are repeatedly suggested to be characteristic of successful networks:

- developing and sustaining supportive and invigorating relationships
- determining clear purposes and a strong commitment to the work
- ensuring voluntary participation
- engaging and maintaining the commitment of school leaders
- building effective and flexible communication strategies
- learning from alternative perspectives within and beyond schools
- maintaining resources in terms of time, money and energy.

We may tentatively hypothesise that these elements are characteristic of the particular kind of network with which we are concerned, networks of researching schools.

CONCLUSION

As yet, we know very little indeed about the potential benefits or the potential problems of networks of researching schools, nor of the conditions and strategies that are likely to enable them to succeed. In this brief chapter, we have sought to extrapolate from the preceding chapters' discussion of the literature on researching schools, on collaboration among teachers, and on school networks so as to identify some of the questions that should be asked about the ambitious idea of networks of researching schools. But of course, it is only through the efforts of those who try to develop such networks that we can really learn about them. In the next section, therefore, we shall first review the limited previous literature on networks of researching schools and shall then go on to describe each of six research networks that were supported by the Networked Learning Communities Project. On that basis, we shall hope in our final section both to begin to answer some of the questions that we have formulated here and also to consider some of the further questions that will arise from these case studies.

Part 2

Studies of researching networks

Chapter 6

A review of previous studies of researching networks

Kristine Black-Hawkins

The second part of this book considers the research that we undertook into six networks of researching schools. The purpose of this chapter is to provide some background to our work. To do so we consider studies of three previous networks, to reflect on what might be learnt from other teachers and schools working in similar ways but in different sets of circumstances. At the end of the chapter we introduce our own study. We describe the Networked Learning Communities initiative in England, which provided the national context for each of the six networks (NCSL, 2002a). We also discuss the research questions that shaped our work and the methodological approach we took.

DESCRIPTIONS OF RESEARCHING SCHOOL NETWORKS

This chapter offers descriptions of the following three researching school networks:

- the Bay Area School Reform Collaborative (BASRC) in the US
- the Coalition of Knowledge Building Schools in Australia
- the School-Based Research Consortia in England.

Our reasons for selecting these networks are threefold. First, they are all portrayed in the literature as ones in which practitioner research and enquiry are of primary importance. As discussed in Chapter 4, although there are many forms of school network, there are far fewer that are particularly intent on engaging teachers in research. Second, membership of, and research activities in, each of these three networks specifically aimed to go beyond individual or groups of teachers so as to bring about changes to schools at an institutional level. Third, and notwithstanding these shared characteristics, together they provide a wide range of examples of network and research practices.

We have structured each of the descriptions around the three elements of *who, why and how* of networking schools, as discussed in the second half of Chapter 4. Our intention is to illustrate the relationship between these elements as they are enacted within the context of 'real' schools and 'real' networks. Together they reveal that, although there are undoubtedly variations between these three networks, they also share certain concerns and characteristics. Decisions about where to place information did, at times, seem rather arbitrary. For example, unlike the other two networks, the early work of BASRC was supported with a substantial grant, donated through foundation and corporate sponsorship. This has relevance not only to *who* (the key involvement of charitable and business organisations), as well as *why* (such funding encourages schools to join a network), but also *how* (the effects of considerable resources on the conditions, structures, processes and activities of a researching network). Indeed, these interconnections need to be taken into account throughout all three descriptions. Differences and similarities are explored particularly with regard to the kinds of research knowledge and skill that are considered useful by practitioners and that can be exchanged between networking schools as well as the conditions and processes that might support or impede such activities.

Finally, the resulting portrayals are necessarily incomplete and unlikely to capture fully the complex and shifting nature of the networks or the range of perceptions held within them. For example, some details have been omitted so as to provide succinct summaries and information; other information that might have been useful was not always available in the texts; finally, each description can only offer a snapshot, fixed in time, and is unlikely to reflect accurately current circumstances of the networks or the schools within them. Furthermore, it is, perhaps, inevitable that much of the literature focuses on the positive experiences of those members who were engaged in research and network activities rather than on the views and understandings of those who were more passive or antagonistic (or even oblivious) to the accomplishments of the network of which they were ostensibly a part.

THE BAY AREA SCHOOL REFORM COLLABORATIVE

We have chosen to describe the work of BASRC partly because, in contrast to our case studies, it provides an illustration of a network from outside England and partly because it is distinctive in terms of its scale, in particular, the large number of schools involved and its extensive levels of funding. Another characteristic of BASRC is the clarity and range of materials provided by its website (see http://www.basrc.org), which has helped to inform much of this section. BASRC no longer exists as a network: in 2005 it became Springboard Schools and expanded its programme to cover the whole of the

State of California. (For information about these more recent developments see http://www.springboardschools.org.)

Who are the members of BASRC?

Since its inception in 1995, the school membership of BASRC grew steadily so that by 2004 it involved 120 schools (elementary, middle and high) from twenty-eight districts, based in and around the Bay Area of San Francisco, California. Different types of school membership, such as 'leadership' or 'membership', were available and these reflected the levels of funding received by individual schools as well as expectations about the roles and responsibilities they would undertake within the network. From 2001, BASRC also encouraged groups of schools within a single district to apply for joint membership and funding so as to work together as 'local collaboratives'. Within these broader structures a series of smaller networks was also established. Each of these focused on learning and enquiry and was intended to support the work of specific groups of individuals within BASRC (see BASRC, 2004). They included:

- 'Local collaborative coaches': These networks provided support for the 'field-based coaches' who worked with teachers in local schools, with the aim of raising students' academic performance. They comprised 'teacher leaders' and 'reform co-ordinators', as well as classroom teachers. Indeed, the role of 'coach' was fundamental to the overall school improvement and research aims of BASRC. Three main types of coaching were provided:
  i   intervention in identified low-performing schools
  ii district coaching and
  iii school coaching.
- Principals: The purpose of these networks was to support those with responsibility for leading systemic improvement in the teaching and learning taking place in schools. They included principals, assistant principals and other school leaders.
- District leaders: These networks were intended to support leaders with responsibility for directing district-level reform. They comprised superintendents, assistant superintendents, school board members and other district staff.

A range of other organisations also had links with BASRC (see BASRC, 2004), such as:

- A number of school–university partnerships: The most notable of these was with the Center for Research on the Context of Teaching at Stanford University, members of which undertook research in collaboration with BASRC.

- 'Just for the Kids-California': This state-wide organisation provided schools with access to data analysis tools and research-based best practices.
- The 'Consortium of Reading Excellence' (CORE): This organisation set out to help teachers to improve the way they taught reading, through the implementation of researched-based reading and literacy programmes.
- Members of private sector corporations and foundations: 'Corporate partnership programs' were established, in particular to encourage financial support, which was considered crucial in terms of sustaining the work of BASRC.

Why be in BASRC?

BASRC was initiated in 1995 by a small group of people, based in the Bay Area, and drawn from education, business and the community. Their overall intention was to bring about whole school change. To support this, the 'BASRC rubric', based around five key aspirations, was developed. These were: best practices of teaching and learning; high standards for students and teachers; systems to manage the change process; partnerships with stakeholders; and a professional learning community. Any school intending to join the network first had to provide evidence that it agreed with these aims and then show how it would work to fulfil them. The network also had the following overall 'mission statement':

> BASRC seeks to transform schools across the Bay Area into vital places to learn and to teach. We work with education leaders in both schools and districts to develop, assess and use the knowledge needed for schools to engage in a systematic and sustainable improvement process. BASRC aims to help create a future in which all students learn to high levels and where race, class, language, gender, and culture are no longer good predictors of educational outcomes.
>
> (BASRC, 2004)

This highlighted three interrelated principal purposes:

i   to advance social justice and equity ... 'all students ... race, class, language, gender, and culture'
ii to bring about whole school improvement ... 'systematic and sustainable improvement process' and
iii to engage in and with school-based research ... 'develop, assess and use ... knowledge'.

Thus in BASRC, research activity (purpose iii) was a means, albeit a crucial one, of bringing about school improvement (purpose ii), which in turn would contribute to the primary aim of increasing social justice (purpose i). Furthermore, this focus on research was expected to be undertaken at various levels within BASRC, including:

- Schools: 'Good schools practise shared inquiry to improve the learning of all students, and have a focused strategy for improving instruction'.
- Districts: '. . . regularly collect, reflect on, and share data about the effectiveness of their school-support strategies'.
- Networks (for coaches, principals and district leaders): '. . . are professional learning communities whose focus is engaging in collaborative inquiry with the goal of improving our professional practice and creating a more equitable system of schools' (BASRC, 2004).

How does BASRC work?

The conditions, structures, processes and activities that supported the work of BASRC evolved and developed over time, although its key purposes generally remained unchanged. BASRC noted these changes but described itself as being committed to providing, 'flexible support that helps the education system respond to changing policy mandates, funding levels, demographics, and local needs and priorities' (BASRC, 2004). It was also a large association, spread over a wide geographical area. It was therefore inevitable that individuals and institutions within it worked more closely with some rather than others and that these alliances developed working practices to suit their own particular needs. Nevertheless, there were certain characteristics that ran throughout the organisation and conduct of BASRC; for example, a central 'research service' was established to provide research support materials and 'tools'. For the purposes of this description the following five conditions, structures, processes and activities have been highlighted as having particular relevance to research and networking practices: These are:

1 foundation and corporate funding
2 notions of high performance and best practice
3 the 'Cycle of Inquiry'
4 the role of the networks within the network and
5 the dissemination of findings.

Foundation and corporate funding

The monies available to BASRC were considerable and therefore cannot be overlooked, especially when comparing the two networks described later in this chapter as well as the six networks that are described in Chapters 7–12. In 1995 fifty million dollars were donated as part of a 'matched funding programme'; by 1999 that requirement had been fulfilled bringing the total budget to one hundred million dollars. The BASRC (2004) website notes that; 'It is critical to engage the private sector in our efforts to mobilize the resources needed to transform teaching and learning for the children who need it most'. This strategy was not perceived as merely complementing adequate public funding, but rather as a necessary means of averting financial hardship in schools as well as more generally supporting economic growth in the Bay Area: 'Our response to the crisis in California's public schools today will directly affect the long-term economic viability and overall quality of life of the Bay Area for years to come'. Schools had to apply formally to BASRC to become members before any funding would be allocated. In the first round of grants, schools were asked to submit portfolios based on the BASRC rubric (outlined above). From this, eighty-seven 'leadership' schools were established, each receiving funding for three to five years of one hundred and fifty dollars per student, to pay for support service, school-based research, teacher professional development and so forth. Funding was also allocated to other institutions and organisations; for example, to support school–university partnerships and the series of networks operating within BASRC.

Notions of 'high performance' and 'best practice'

These related concepts were central to BASRC's research, informing and directing the school-based research that took place. There was a clear expectation that such work would focus on those students, classrooms, schools and districts with high performance test scores because they were considered to provide opportunities to investigate models of best practice. Findings from these studies were then introduced into other BASRC classrooms, schools and districts by BASRC 'coaches'. The assumptions underlying this approach were that what worked well in one school context could, to some extent, be transferred to another, and that findings on what worked 'best' would provide particularly useful research evidence to support more systemic changes. An example of this was the Best Practice Study, established in 2004, which set out 'to identify effective strategies . . . in high performing, high improving and gap closing schools and districts' (BASRC, 2004). Linked to this research project, a number of Best Practice Institutions were identified, which allowed researchers and other educators to explore 'how high performers get results [. . . thereby] improving student achievement . . . closing the achievement gap [and . . .] learning how high-performers address obstacles to success' (ibid.). In addition, schools and districts could make use of the Needs Assessment Tool Kit (provided by BASRC's research services). This provided, 'Diagnostic tools to compare current practices to the practices of sustained high performers, plus diagnostic tools to prepare another school system to conduct 'best' implementation of the other site's best practices' (ibid.)

The 'Cycle of Inquiry'

This was the key research strategy for BASRC, and was used at classroom, whole school and district level. Indeed, Copland (2002, p. 5) described it as 'The engine of BASRC's theory of school change'. As its name suggests it was conceived as a cyclical process, as is similar to other action research models. It comprised six steps:

1   identify problems (based on data)
2   refine the focused effort
3   identify measurable goals (school, grade, and/or departmental level)
4   build concrete action plan
5   take action
6   analyse results from the data

After completing the last of these, the cycle would begin again, by identifying new or adjusted problems, which were largely determined by the analysis of previous results. Thus the purpose of the cycle was to provide the information needed to bring about school change, through evidence based decision-making.

> Simply put, BASRC's Cycle of Inquiry aims to inform schools about the degree to which they are actually accomplishing what they think they should be accomplishing in terms of a focused reform effort and the consequences for students. Importantly, in defining and revisiting a focused effort, members of the school community are not just recipients of someone else's vision of what needs to be done.
>
> (Copland, 2002, p. 5)

Central to this process was that it would draw on the knowledge and experiences of a wide range of a school's community (teachers, but also parents, students and administrators). In this way collective decisions were made about which problems to address and what kinds of solutions should be developed. In addition, schools received practical support from the BASRC 'coaches' and could draw on the research services for associated materials, including videos and on-line training.

The role of the networks within the network

As already noted, BASRC set up a series of networks as part of its overall framework. They were conceived of as professional learning communities, focusing on collaborative research and enquiry. According to the BASRC (2004) website they fulfilled a number of purposes. That is, they provided different groups of 'reform leaders' with time and opportunities to meet, so that they could 'learn, collaborate and solve problems with their peers [. . . doing] similar work and confronting similar challenges'. In this way they would become increasingly effective in their roles and, in particular, learn how 'to best support inquiry-based reform in schools'.

Dissemination of findings

A challenge for many networks of researching schools is how to ensure the effective dissemination of their work both within and beyond the network itself. This is a concern that BASRC recognised and set out to address. In the guidelines produced by its research services it argues for the 'aggressive dissemination of findings to inform BASRC stakeholders, support practitioners and policy analysts and to build the field of education research' (BASRC, 2004). To this end, BASRC produced a wide range of its own publications, available to members through its website, which took into account the needs of differing audiences. Examples of these include: 'BASRC Works', produced five times a year to highlight ongoing work, including research taking place in schools and districts; 'In Depth', an issue-themed publication focused on school-based enquiry; Annual Reports, which summarised the overall progress of the collaborative; 'Policy Update', a monthly email newsletter, which summarised news about BASRC and broader state educational concerns; research reports, commissioned by, or undertaken in close collaboration with, BASRC (for example, by Copland (2002), Leadership of Inquiry and, by Symonds (2003), After the Test: How Schools are Using Data to Close the Achievement Gap).

Reflecting on BASRC as a network of researching schools

As with many other networks, it is not easy to assess precisely how far and in what ways the research work undertaken within BASRC contributed to the learning of teachers and students as individuals, or of their schools as institutions. To help us to do so in this section, we draw on two evaluations. The first of these, by McLaughlin and Zarrow (2001), focused on the process of the 'cycle of inquiry' as a way of supporting schools to move towards what they describe as a 'culture of inquiry' (p. 86). They suggest that, 'In many schools, we see the results of their inquiry process have led to new understandings about practice in their school and classroom' (p. 87), and in a smaller number of schools it 'has begun to mature into an accepted, iterative process of data collection, analysis, reflection, and change' (p. 89). They describe such schools as 'learning communities' (ibid.). They argue that in these schools, 'Patterns of knowledge use and learning define and are defined by the culture of the school's community of practice and [that] BASRC's strategies [have] shaped this culture' (p. 91). From their study, they identify five interrelated elements of a school's community that influenced how teachers participated in and benefited from research activities (pp. 91–6). These are:

- developing 'clear and shared goals' that are focused on students and their performance, at both the classroom and school levels
- teachers who adopt an 'inquiry stance' (see Cochran-Smith and Lytle, 2001) towards their own practice as well as towards the school more broadly
- teachers from across the whole school who have developed the 'learning skills' needed for research, as well as a growing body of knowledge about practice
- teachers who act as 'boundary spanners' by being active in a range of contexts outside the school and so are able to bring in new ideas to refresh and challenge members of the community
- involving other members of the school in the research processes, such as parents and students, and thus having 'broadened community boundaries'

The Center for Research on the Context of Teaching (2002) provides an evaluation of BASRC, focusing on the years from 1996 to 2001. The aim of this report is 'to address the question of whether BASRC mattered for students in the funded Leadership Schools' (p. 8). As with the study by McLaughlin and Zarrow (both of whom were contributors to this later evaluation), the report emphasises the role of the 'cycle of inquiry', but with a particular interest in how far, and in what ways, it had contributed to raising students' measurable achievements. To address this the researchers set out, 'To compare SAT-9 standardized test trends for BASRC schools with trends for a control group . . . . We also compare trends . . . on closing within-school gaps in student achievement [. . . and] on test scores of racial/ethnic and socioeconomic groups within schools' (pp. 8–9). The key findings of the report suggest that:

> Most BASRC Leadership Schools made progress on inquiry-based reform, and those most advanced in using evidence about student outcomes to evaluate and change their practice showed the greatest SAT-9 gains. Overall, [the schools] made significantly greater improvements in their students' performance on SAT-9 basic skills tests than did schools in the evaluation's control group.
>
> (Center for Research on the Context of Teaching, 2002, p. 11)

However, the report noted that the schools did not make particularly significant gains when compared with other schools in the Bay Area more generally. Furthermore, they did not do as well 'in closing within school achievement gaps' (p. 12). Finally, although BASRC's activities 'generally were rated favourably' by the member schools, the report argued that, 'Not all schools had the capacity to take advantage of, or profit equally from, the Collaborative – most particularly, those high poverty schools pressed on multiple fronts' (ibid.). These points seem particularly important as they relate closely to the key aim underpinning the whole BASRC initiative: that is, its commitment to notions of social justice and equity in terms of supporting the learning of all students, regardless of race, class, language, gender, and culture. What is difficult to assess is whether these desired systemic changes will take place eventually, but that a longer period of time is required before they can be more fully achieved; or, that the work of BASRC may need to be modified for the aims to be fulfilled; or, indeed, that other more radical and broader socio-economic and cultural developments are needed to support the efforts taking place in schools.

The report is, however, more positive about the role of research (and especially the 'cycle of inquiry') as a means of changing the culture of the network schools. Over a period of three years (1999–2001) schools were expected to 'document activities, accomplishments, and goals' relating to research. From this evidence, schools were rated as either 'beginning', 'emerging', 'systematic' or 'sustainable' with regards to their enquiry practice (p. 16). The report argued that 'steady progress' had taken place:

> More than half of all schools advanced from one stage to another over two years or maintained a *systematic* rating . . . . Among those schools for which 2001 ratings are available, the number rated as *systematic* jumped from 10 per cent in 1999 to 53 per cent in 2001
>
> (ibid., p. 17)

> As inquiry practices became more deeply engrained in school culture, teacher communities generated new, more probing, questions and deeper analysis of student outcomes and teaching practices. And in schools advanced in inquiry, this analysis took place at multiple levels – classroom, grade, department and school. Such interconnected inquiry cycles were essential to engaging instructional issues for the whole school. Without these interconnections, inquiry occurred in pockets and did not engage questions of school level practices or instructional decisions.
>
> (ibid., p. 18)

Thus, in agreement with McLaughlin and Zarrow (2001) as discussed earlier, the authors argue that if the 'inquiry practices' of individual and groups of teachers are to be effective they must take place within a school that is a researching institution. What remains problematic is how such work, in such places, is usefully connected with, draws on, and contributes to, the 'inquiry practices' of other teachers in other schools, to establish what then might be described as a network of researching schools.

THE COALITION OF KNOWLEDGE BUILDING SCHOOLS

In this section we describe the Coalition of Knowledge Building Schools, partly because it provides a second illustration of a network of researching schools from outside England and partly because, in contrast to BASRC, it is relatively small scale. The Coalition involves far fewer schools and does not formally receive any funding. Furthermore, it was established by members from the schools who, because of their shared interests, values and beliefs, chose to come together to work in collaborative ways; it was not, therefore, part of an external initiative or programme, which schools could then opt to join. This has allowed the Coalition greater independence and flexibility than either BASRC, or the School-Based Research Consortia discussed later in this chapter. Throughout this section we draw on the work of Professor Susan Groundwater-Smith who, as co-director of the Centre of Practitioner Research, based at the University of Sydney, Australia, has worked closely with the Coalition schools. She describes the Coalition as being, 'modest in size but committed to complexity and excellence' (Groundwater-Smith, 2006, p. 4).

Who are the members of the Coalition?

The membership of the Coalition comprises schools in and around Sydney, New South Wales. Over time, the number of schools that have elected to join the Coalition has grown and their geographical spread has widened. Its composition therefore seems more fluid than networks of schools that are structured by the demands of external schemes. The origins of the Coalition go back at least until 1998, when three independent girls' schools were each involved in an action research project. Teachers from these schools met together, through the initiative of the Centre for Practitioner Research, based at the University of Sydney, to discuss the methodologies and outcomes of their projects (Groundwater-Smith, 2006). In 2001, the Coalition was established more formally with six schools: three from the independent sector and three from the government sector (Groundwater-Smith, 2002). By 2004, the numbers had grown to nine, including three more government schools (Groundwater-Smith, 2004). By 2006, it had extended to thirteen schools, and in doing so, had spread its geographical area a little more widely to include some regional schools and one remote school. The other key institutional member of the Coalition is the Centre for Practitioner Research, referred to above. Its role has been described as 'critical' in terms of 'supporting the Coalition and providing it with some sort of institutional base' (Groundwater-Smith and Mockler, 2002, p. 6).

Why be in the Coalition?

Groundwater-Smith and Mockler (2002, p. 5) argue that from its very beginning the overall aim of the Coalition has been, 'The on-going improvement of the work of [the] schools through the systematic and public collection and discussion of evidence regarding teaching and learning within the lived life of the school'.

The focus of the Coalition therefore has been on 'building knowledge' in and across the schools through the careful gathering of evidence, while also appreciating and having due regard for the individual context of each school. Within this general framework the following purposes of the Coalition have been established by its members:

- to develop and enhance the notion of evidence based practice
- to develop an interactive community of practice using appropriate technologies
- to make a contribution to a broader professional knowledge base with respect to educational practice
- to build research capability within their own and each other's schools by engaging both teachers and students in the research process and
- to share methodologies that are appropriate to practitioner enquiry as a means of transforming teacher professional learning (Groundwater-Smith and Mockler, 2003, p. 1).

Underlying these purposes, and the work of the Coalition more generally, are a set of values and beliefs about the purposes of practitioner research in terms of its 'emancipatory and democratic possibilities' (Mockler, 2002, p. 2), and its contribution to the development of teachers, schools and broader educational systems. Groundwater-Smith (2002) argues that the foundation for these was in place early on in the life of the Coalition:

> The embryo coalition believed that by embedding enquiry practices into the daily work of the schools it would be possible to evolve an authentic workplace learning culture. They recognised that professional learning is not an exclusively individualistic enterprise but that learning and growth can take place at the organisational, or corporate level.
>
> (Groundwater-Smith, 2002, p. 5)

These values and beliefs are 'deeply rooted in principles of equity and social justice' and inform members' understanding of the identity of teachers as 'activist professionals'; that is, all teachers are concerned with the education of all learners in all schools (Groundwater-Smith and Sachs, 2002, p. 352).

How does the Coalition work?

In the Coalition, decisions about the conditions, structures, processes and activities that form its work are clearly shaped by the strongly held values and beliefs of its members, as outlined above. Indeed, Groundwater-Smith

(2002) argues that, because membership of the network is voluntary and it is independent of external demands and supports, these 'agreed principles' are necessary in terms of maintaining the network and its development:

> The strength of the Coalition is that it is just that, a loose coalition governed by agreed principles rather than regulation and fiat. The great challenge facing the Coalition will be not only the establishment of trust but its maintenance.
>
> (Groundwater-Smith, 2002, p. 13)

Shared principles help to strengthen 'trust' among schools, which is considered to be essential to ensure the quality of their collaborative work. 'Trust has gradually been built up between member schools to the point where in recent times we have begun to move beyond the celebratory to address some of the more difficult issues present in our work' (Groundwater-Smith and Mockler, 2002, p. 11).

Principles and the notions of 'knowledge-building' and 'evidence'

In the following quotation, a teacher in one of the schools defines the notion of 'knowledge-building':

> Our understanding of what it means to be a "knowledge-building school" relates primarily to the valuing of ideas and knowledge, whether those ideas are generated by "academics" or "practitioners", and regardless of whether those ideas are foremostly reflective of theory or practice. . . . At their best "knowledge-building activities" are generative for the teachers involved and for the school as a whole . . ., foster collaborative collegial relationships between teachers involved . . . and facilitate partnerships between school and university-based educators . . . to the benefit of both.
>
> (Mockler, 2002, p. 2)

This description helps to illustrate the relationship between the principles of the Coalition and the research activities and processes undertaken by the schools, which contribute to their building of knowledge. In particular, a clear theme runs through much of the writing on the Coalition to do with the nature of research evidence and, specifically, the notion of 'evidence based practice' (see Groundwater-Smith and Dadds, 2004). The Coalition does not look for 'that elusive, indeed we would argue impossible, goal "best practice"' (Groundwater-Smith and Mockler, 2002, p. 2), arguing that doing so contradicts their conceptualisation of evidence as needing to be understood in the 'lived life of the school' (ibid., p. 5). That is, what works well for one teacher, in one classroom and school, is not necessarily 'best' for other teachers in other classrooms and schools. Rather they have:

> A view that evidence was best considered in the forensic rather than adversarial environment; that is to say that it should be constructed and examined in ways which illuminate understanding rather than as a means of proving a particular case.
>
> (Groundwater-Smith, 2002, pp. 4–5)

Key processes to support the research work

Members of the Coalition have identified a number of key processes to support their endeavours, intended to encourage practitioners to undertake research that is collaborative in nature and that conceptualises evidence as being problematic. These are:

- developing new practitioner research methods;
- sharing methodologies which are appropriate to practitioner enquiry;
- engaging in cross-researching in member schools;
- considering forms of documentation;
- reporting and critiquing research;
- engaging in collaborative writing and reflection;
- planning professional development to support practitioner research; and
- considering ethics in practitioner research.

(Groundwater-Smith, 2002, p. 5)

The Coalition also offers explicit guidance about how research might be conducted in the schools. For example, it is suggested that evidence gathered by teachers should take into account the following three tests (Groundwater-Smith and Mockler, 2002, p. 4): First, 'Is it ethical?' (causing no harm and ensuring participants' protection). Second, 'Has it been triangulated?' (exploring several data sources). Third, 'Has it been intersubjectively verified?' (interpreting the evidence from a range of perspectives).

Collaboration in the Coalition

Although there is a strong emphasise on shared research understandings and practices across the Coalition, there are considerable variations between the schools in terms of the substantive concerns of their research, because these are expected to emerge out of each school's particular circumstances, interests and needs. For example, Groundwater-Smith (2006) offers case studies of research work undertaken in two of the schools. In doing so she illustrates not only the institutional differences between the schools, which have helped to determine the differing focus of their research activities, but also their shared commitment to the values of the Coalition, as demonstrated in the forms of research activities in which they chose to engage.

Therefore collaboration between the schools is more clearly focused on the processes of research. For example, when Groundwater-Smith and Mockler describe the Coalition in 2002, they note that the following joint activities have taken place (2002, p. 6):

- Teachers from each of the schools meet four times a year 'with different schools presenting brief research papers to their colleagues'.
- There is a Coalition web based community to support further discussion (although the authors suggest this is rarely used).
- Some teachers have presented formal conference papers and written journal articles.

More generally teachers within and across the group of schools, plus members of the University, act as facilitators and critical friends to each other. The authors also note the Coalition's intention of 'moving towards constructing knowledge, from evidence, which may be of use to others in the wider community' (ibid., p. 2); that is, beyond their immediate membership. An example of this, that has subsequently taken place, is a collaboration with the Australian Museum to explore how students learn in the setting of the museum (see Groundwater-Smith and Kelly, 2003).

Reflecting on the Coalition as a network of researching schools

Through the writings of Susan Groundwater-Smith and her colleagues, a sense of the narrative of the Coalition emerges in terms of how it has developed and grown. It therefore seems likely that there will be further changes in the future in response to new challenges and opportunities. Although these writings reveal a sense of optimism about the potential of this network to continue to bring about improvements in the lives of teachers and their schools, they also highlight a number of tensions that may threaten this work. In particular, there seems to be some unease about the possible erosion of the high level of trust amongst its members that is considered essential for the Coalition to work well.

These concerns include:

- 'the intensification of teachers' work' (Groundwater-Smith and Mockler, 2002, p. 10)
- 'the current political tensions between government and non-government schools' (ibid.)

- 'schooling is an uncertain environment and . . . schools are increasingly being placed into a competitive context' (Groundwater-Smith, 2002, p. 12)
- 'While the Coalition is not in receipt of external funding, it nevertheless would be inoperable if participating schools did not contribute teachers' times and resources to the work. Furthermore, it is dependent upon the goodwill and energy of those who convene the group and support it with expertise . . . However, the matter of convening and maintaining the group and writing of its considerable achievements counts for little in the academy' (Groundwater-Smith, 2006).

When the Coalition was still rather newly formed, Groundwater-Smith (2002) wrote, 'These are early days, but the possibilities are bounded only by the enthusiasm, energy and creativity of the schools themselves' (p. 12). However, it seems that the scope for such 'possibilities' is not fully in the control of the network, but is also partly determined by the actions of others, over whom the teachers in the Coalition's schools and the university may feel they have little authority.

THE SCHOOL-BASED RESEARCH CONSORTIA

For our final description of a network of researching schools we have chosen to focus on the School-Based Research Consortia initiative, in England. This is largely because it can be seen as a small-scale precursor of, and pilot for, the national Networked Learning Communities (NLC) programme. Like the NLCs, it comprised separate networks (or consortia) of schools working independently of one another, but with the understanding that opportunities for networking across and between them would be explored. Thus the Consortia provide a useful context for our research into the six NLCs, which are presented later in this book.

Who are the members of the School-Based Research Consortia?

The School-Based Research Consortia initiative took place from 1998 to 2001. It was partly supported by the Teacher Training Agency (TTA), a UK government body (now known as the Teacher Development Agency (TDA)) and partly by the Centre for British Teachers (CfBT), a private non-profit-making organisation. Four research consortia were established, each one based within a particular geographic area in England. In terms of institutional membership each consortium was expected to include a number of schools as well as at least one local authority (LA) and one institute of higher education. However, the actual numbers from each of these three sectors varied between the different consortia, as follows:

- Leeds School-Based Research Consortium comprised six primary schools, Leeds LA plus the University of Leeds.
- Manchester and Salford School-Based Research Consortium comprised eight primary schools, Manchester and Salford LAs, plus the Manchester Metropolitan University and the Manchester Victoria University.
- North-East Schools Consortium comprised six secondary schools, Newcastle, North Tyneside and Northumberland LAs, plus the University of Newcastle.
- Norwich Area Schools Consortium comprised seven secondary schools, including one special school for children designated as having emotional and behavioural difficulties, Norfolk LA plus the University of East Anglia.

Therefore, the total number of institutions involved in this initiative was twenty-seven schools, seven local authorities, five universities plus the TTA and CfBT.

In terms of the membership of key individuals, a teacher research co-ordinator (TRC) was established in every school in each consortium. Their responsibilities were dependent to some extent on where they worked but they were all expected to help to organise school based research activities and to attend consortium meetings. Each consortium was also allocated a 'link' person from the TTA. Other principal roles varied across the consortia. For example, members of the Manchester and Salford consortium appointed a 'consortium co-ordinator' from one of their participating universities; they also linked each TRC to a 'tutor', from either one of their universities or LAs. In the Norwich Area consortium, members appointed three 'consortium managers' from across different institutions (one headteacher, a member of the university and also one from the LA). In addition, each school was assigned a university 'mentor' to support the research work taking place.

Why be in the School-Based Research Consortia?

This initiative formed part of the TTA's programme for promoting teaching as a research and evidence based profession, with the intention of raising the achievements of students through the enhancement of teachers' research skills. This focus on school based practitioner research had two closely related purposes. The first concerned the development of understanding of the processes of such research, and the second concerned the development of knowledge regarding the substantive findings of that research. Inevitably, some members of the consortia chose to prioritise one purpose more than the other; furthermore, the balance between the two varied across and within institutions as well as over time.

Purposes, from the perspective of the funders of the Consortia

For the TTA and CfBT, the primary purpose of the consortia was to explore teachers' 'engagement in and with research' so as to improve students' learning. Indeed, this phrase is reiterated throughout the literature about the consortia and in particular in the writings emanating from the TTA itself (for example, TTA, 1998a, 1998b, 2000a and 2000b). As such it was particularly concerned with the processes of school-based research, including the kinds of research support, and the types of research evidence, that teachers find useful. In the annual reviews for this initiative, the following three overall aims were stated (see, for example, TTA, 2000b, p. 2):

1   Encourage teachers to 'engage' with research and evidence about pupils' achievements, for example, to use other people's research to inform their practice and/or to participate actively in research.
2   Increase the capacity for high quality, teacher focused classroom research by supporting teacher involvement in the development of research proposals for external funding.
3   Develop long-term, medium scale data sets that provide related quantitative and qualitative data about what teachers and pupils do and how that affects pupils' achievement.

Over the course of the initiative it became clear that the majority of the work taking place in the consortia focused on the first of these three aims rather than the other two (see Simons *et al.*, 2003, p. 354).

Purposes, from the perspectives of members of the four consortia

Within this broad framework, each consortium established its own set of purposes relating to school based research processes. For example, in its final summary to the TTA, the Leeds Consortium (2001) described its 'central objective' as being, 'to encourage the development of teachers as knowledgeable participants in educational research, directed towards the application of new and effective classroom techniques and strategies'. A further eight subsidiary aims were given, of which the following six have a particular emphasis on increasing the usefulness of research processes for teachers as well as supporting teachers when engaging in those processes. These were to:

•   'enhance teaching performance through exploration of evidence-based research and reflection on how best to incorporate it within chosen research foci'

- 'motivate teacher engagement in and with fresh research initiatives so as to develop into critical research users'
- 'improve understanding of the complexity of classroom phenomena ...'
- 'improve educational provision by strengthening the connections between school improvement planning ... and the practice and impact of specific research-based action'
- 'conduct research activities in a co-operative spirit of shared enterprise'
- 'disseminate information about research processes, pedagogical approaches, and results'.

Although these aims are specific to the Leeds consortium, it is possible to identify a number of common themes across the aims provided by all four consortia and, in particular, with regard to the processes for undertaking collaborative research as well as the dissemination and use of research findings.

At the same time, members of all four consortia had also chosen to join this initiative because they wanted to explore particular topics and areas of concern and interest in their schools. As would be expected, the substantive content of the research undertaken varied more widely across the consortia than the aims relating to research processes. The following is a summary of the main research topics undertaken in each consortium:

- Leeds: initially children's literacy and numeracy skills but later focusing on mental mathematics.
- Manchester and Salford: school improvement through literacy, numeracy and science but later also incorporating children's speaking and listening.
- Norwich Area: enhancing pedagogical skills to respond to the problem of student disaffection.
- North-East: improving critical thinking skills in classrooms.

Decisions about substantive issues were largely determined by the particular circumstances and perceived needs of the schools and other institutions that comprised each consortium. For example, the North-East consortium was built on an existing network of teachers who had already been collaborating with one of the LAs and the University of Newcastle, to develop the teaching and learning of thinking skills. In the Manchester and Salford consortium, the chosen focus was based on priorities that had been previously identified by school inspectors (Ofsted), regarding literacy, numeracy or science. They later agreed on a consortium-wide theme of speaking and listening, when all the schools decided that the children's language skills were affecting these three core areas of the curriculum.

In practice, members of all four consortia engaged in activities that pursued aims relating to both the processes as well as the substantive concerns of their research. For example, in the summary of the final report to the TTA, the Norwich Area Schools Consortium (2001) provided ten aims that had shaped their work. Some of these focused on the topic of the research undertaken, concerning student disaffection; for example, to 'implement changes designed to motivate and engage disaffected students in the learning process'. Others, however, related more generally to the research processes undertaken; for example, to 'guide teachers to familiarise themselves with relevant existing research literatures as an informative starting point for their own investigations'. To understand the balance of purposes between the processes of research and its substantive content it is necessary to take into account the different priorities of consortia members. For example, it seems likely that teachers and other members of schools in the Norwich Area consortium were more concerned with finding out how to motivate disaffected students than with how to undertake a literature review, whatever the connections might be between these two sets of activities. Similarly, some university members across the consortia chose to investigate the process of developing research relationships between themselves and teachers (see, for example, Baumfield (2001), North-East consortium; also Elliott (2002), Norwich Area consortium). This seems unlikely, however, to have been a particular research interest for many of the members teaching in the schools.

How do the School Based Research Consortia work?

In the same way in which there were a range of reasons why schools and other institutions chose to be members of the consortia, decisions about how they preferred to work together also varied. Indeed, these differences can be found not only between consortia but also within each consortium and indeed within individual schools. There were also shifts and developments at all levels across time. Therefore, identifying the key conditions, structures, processes and activities that have supported the research of the consortia members is not straightforward. Nevertheless, three areas appear to be particularly important when considering how this researching school network worked. These are:

1   engagement in and with a range of research processes, structures and activities
2   partnerships between schools and other institutions and
3   whole school, whole consortium and cross consortia learning.

Research processes, structures and activities

A number of research processes, structures and activities were common to all consortia, and were based on the requirements and expectations of the TTA and CfBT. First, all research had to be clearly focused on classroom pedagogy or teaching and learning processes, rather than on national policies or curriculum issues that were outside teachers' remit to change. Second, each school had to appoint a teacher as TRC and provide support for them to develop their role as both researcher and co-ordinator of research (for example, giving them time to fulfil their duties). Third, each consortium had to disseminate its findings. For example, each had to provide annual reports giving details of the consortium's learning in terms of both the processes and the substantive content of any research undertaken (see, for example, TTA, 2000a). Within these overall parameters each consortium chose to use a variety of research methods and approaches. These were partly determined by their appropriateness to the topics and interests being considered and partly by pragmatic and other context related factors. However, such diversity was also actively encouraged by the funding bodies, as it provided a range of opportunities across the consortia to gather evidence with regards to the kinds of research process that might be useful to teachers. The selection below illustrates some of the variety used in each consortium:

- Leeds: peer observation; reading and discussing published research materials; 'looking at learning', that is, close observation of children; sharing of understanding and progress across the team of TRCs
- Manchester and Salford: baseline assessment of teachers' attitudes to research; video observation of classroom techniques and pupil response; pupil 'logs'; consultation with outside experts on substantive issues; analysis of National Test results
- North-East: peer observation; video observations; peer coaching in both substantive issues and also research skills and techniques; professional dialogues
- Norwich Area: qualitative and quantitative data sets on classroom and school practices, plus teacher/student perceptions of such practices; case records of initiatives (using classroom and peer observation; pupil tracking; pupil questionnaires; teacher interviews).

Partnerships between schools and universities

As explained previously, membership of each consortium included not only schools but also at least one LA and one university. Over the three years of the initiative the changing relationships between these different institutions became, for some members, a focus of interest and concern. In particular, the nature of the research relationship developed between members of schools and universities was scrutinised (Baumfield, 2001; Cordingley *et al.*, 2002; Elliott, 2002). A number of key issues relating to these partnerships, including strengths and tensions, were identified:

- In each consortium, the university provided an administrative base for the research work. University staff also acted as research tutors and mentors, providing support to teachers in various forms: for example, training in research methods; guidance with literature reviews; co-researching in schools; practical support, such as arranging for the transcriptions of interviews and copying of videos; helping with the writing and dissemination of research findings.

- University (and sometimes LA) members also had a specific role in terms of supporting the developing research role of TRCs. Indeed, in an overview report for the TTA, at the end of the initiative academics are described as working with TRCs as they progress, with their help, from 'apprentices' to 'crafts people', and finally become 'coaches, quality assurers, co-ordinators and initiators' in their own right (Cordingley and Bell, 2002).

- Before the project started, a number of schools were already working with local universities, and all the schools had existing connections with their LAs. Where such relationships were already well established, there appeared to be greater potential to generate new ideas, probably because factors such as trust and local knowledge had already been secured. However, the long-term sustainability of such relationships was endangered by the competing demands on time and space embedded in institutional cultures, especially those relating to radically different forms of performance assessment. Adequate funding to support research relationships was therefore considered important.

- Although each consortium had its own particular organisational structure, there was an expectation that however such arrangements were made they would be premised on the notion of lateral representation from across all the institutions involved. However, and especially initially, this was not straightforward to achieve. Teachers, in particular, often held a hierarchical view of research, viewing the research of academics as 'better' than that undertaken by teachers. Although it was acknowledged that university members generally worked hard to be approachable and accessible, these differences were potential barriers to their collaboration with colleagues from schools.

Whole school, whole consortium and cross consortia learning

It was always a strong intention of the funding bodies that learning about research would take place at a number of different levels and within a series of interconnecting communities. These included not only small groups of teachers in individual schools, but also whole school, whole consortium and cross consortia learning. However, although there was an intention to identify possible patterns and structures (for example, the impact of school size, the relative importance of shared research topics, the role of universities and so forth), establishing how far such networked learning took place among consortia members remained uncertain. This is not a criticism of the work of the consortia but rather a reflection of the complexity of such processes and their role within the professional experiences of teachers, academics and LA advisers. Thus, it is possible, on the one hand, to describe the consortia over their three years' existence, as, 'Shifting from a loose confederation of separate if related concerns and interests to a complex, interlocking set of communities with a shared understanding of themselves as part of a single initiative' (Cordingley and Bell, 2002, p. 14), while, on the other hand, acknowledging that, 'The task of learning across boundaries formed the working environment, a research goal, a means to the end of improving teaching and learning – and a perpetual puzzle' (Cordingley *et al.*, 2002, p. 2). The last comment comes from a paper co-written by members from all four consortia, plus the project's overall manager. This 'perpetual puzzle' is, of course, not an enigma exclusive to these consortia: rather it poses a persistent challenge to any member of a researching school network.

Reflecting on the Consortia as a network of researching schools

The evaluation of the Consortia by Simons *et al.* (2003) has already been considered in Chapter 2. We return to it here to discuss a fundamental purpose of any network of researching schools. That is, how far did the Consortia initiative provide opportunities for teacher researchers to share their evidence and findings in ways that informed and transformed the practices of colleagues across the network? The authors identify a key concern with regard to this question, which relates to 'how the process of research itself was necessarily situated in teachers' own practices' (p. 350). They note that, in the early stages of the Consortia, many of the teacher researchers were uncertain about how far their research evidence would stand up to more traditional or academic measures of validity and reliability, and the implications that this had regarding the generalisability and, therefore, the usefulness of their findings:

> These teachers were interested in research as a systematic and transparent process, but also insistent about the situationally-bounded nature of their findings: as one put it 'what is credible for these pupils in this classroom in this school in this city'.
>
> (Simons *et al.*, 2003, p. 356)

The authors suggest that over time this dilemma was resolved in ways that made sense to teachers both in terms of the integrity of their research as well as its transferability to others:

> What the evaluation observed was essentially a three-stage process of generalising from individual data, each stage testing out relevance (to

the self, to colleagues and, eventually, to the consortium as a whole). It may be helpful to refer to these stages as the *personal*, the *collegial* and the *collective*, respectively'.

(ibid.)

This involved a shift away from notions of measurable 'evidence-based practice' (the original intentions of the TTA) towards a deeper understanding of 'practice-based evidence'.

- At the 'personal' stage, an individual teacher reflects on their research findings in ways that will inform their practice more generally. 'Generalisation takes the form of an insight, which is significant for the teacher in relation to a fundamental aspect of his work with learners. The insight looks set to resonate with practice from here on' (p. 357).
- At the 'collegial' stage, research takes place in groups 'in which the individual teacher has a degree of professional intimacy in relation to others . . . . The earlier stages of the consortia saw much work confined to these semi-private settings within schools . . . . Importantly, teachers' activities *do* produce evidence, but it is evidence that they find impossible to express in a conventional research codification' (ibid.).
- At the 'collective' stage, individual or groups of teachers are confident enough to work with colleagues from other schools in their consortium, and even at times across consortia. 'Now the research [assumes] more of the character of evidence as commonly recognised, as the collectivity explores its relevance for a wider range of settings' (ibid.).

However, Simons *et al.* note that even when evidence was gathered from across a number of schools, 'it does not come as freestanding pieces of knowledge but, in order to be viewed as evidence by the community, is bound up in the situation in which it is generated and re-generated' (p. 360):

> In fact, as freestanding information it is almost meaningless and the prospects for generalising from it severely limited. Our analysis of evaluation data suggests there is a need to appreciate the ways in which the results of research activity were shared-for-use by teachers in the Programme. The process is one that we term 'situated generalisation'.
>
> (Simons *et al.*, 2003, p. 378)

The authors conclude that there are three important factors that need to be considered when asking teachers to use the evidence of others:

> First, that teachers need to interpret and re-interpret what evidence means for them in the precise situation in which they are teaching. Second, that presentation of evidence needs to remain closely connected to the

situation in which it arose, not abstracted from it. Third, the collective interpretation and analysis of data by peers seems to act as a validity filter for acceptance in practice.

(ibid., p. 361)

Thus, this final point brings us back to the discussion in Chapter 2. That is, the success of the 'collective' (or networking) stage of research must take account of the affective and social aspects of teacher learning, and build on 'the confidence and trust that sharing teachers have in each other' (p. 359).

INTRODUCING OUR STUDY OF SIX NETWORKS OF RESEARCHING SCHOOLS

In the final section of this chapter we introduce our own study of six networks of researching schools. The background provided by the three networks – BASRC, the Coalition of Knowledge Building Schools and the School-Based Research consortia – helped us in the design and conduct of our research work. In particular, these accounts made clear to us the need to examine in detail the ways in which different members (not only across the networks but also within them) understood the concept of practitioner research and enquiry. It seemed likely that such variations would affect how research was undertaken as well as how its findings were used to develop practices in the schools. Related to this, we were also keen to explore the broader effects of practitioner research across network schools, including how far, and in what ways, it influenced school-wide decisions about classroom teaching and learning in each of the networks. Finally, it was evident that issues of sustainability in our case study networks could not be overlooked, not least because practitioner researchers in each of these three earlier accounts appeared to require considerable time and support to develop their skills, especially if their research was to be made properly useful to others in their network.

Networked Learning Communities

The networks which we studied were all part of the Networked Learning Communities (NLC) programme: a government funded research and development project, run under the auspices of the National College for School Leadership (NCSL). The programme took place between 2002 and 2006 and involved more than 1,500 schools (out of a total of some 24,000) from all sectors of the state educational system in England. Groups of schools were invited to apply to become networks, and those that were successful received some funding in the first three years to support their activities. Each network was expected to include a minimum of six schools and at least one other institutional member, usually a university or local authority. The NLC group also offered additional support, including regional and national meetings and conferences, publications and other materials plus the advice of a network 'facilitator'.

The director of the programme, David Jackson, described this initiative as being 'designed specifically to inform system learning and national policy' (Jackson, 2006, p. 6). It was also intended to provide practice evidence about:

- network design and implementation issues
- network size and type
- facilitation and leadership
- formation processes and growth states
- brokerage
- system support and
- incentivisation (ibid.).

The programme itself was organised according to six 'levels of learning': student learning, adult learning, leadership learning, organisational learning, school-to-school learning and network-to-network learning. All networks were also expected to build four key themes into their work so as to support learning across these six levels. Jackson describes these themes as 'non-negotiables'. They were:

i   moral purpose – a commitment to success for *all* children [. . .];
ii   shared leadership (for example, co-leadership);
iii   enquiry-based practice (evidence and data-driven learning); and
iv   adherence to a model of learning.

(ibid.)

Jackson goes on to argue that the model of learning (the fourth 'non-negotiable') 'provided a program-wide discipline and analytical template for what we called "networked learning"'. This model (see Figure 6.1) illustrates the three fields of knowledge with which practitioners were to engage when co-constructing knowledge: the emphasis on practitioners engaging in and with research is made explicit.

Our research questions and methods

Our study of six networks was undertaken as part of a larger research programme commissioned by the Networked Learning Community group. Their research strategy comprised a number of key questions, and our work contributed to addressing two of these: How are practitioner research and enquiry developed and sustained in networked learning communities? And, how do networked learning communities support schools to learn from

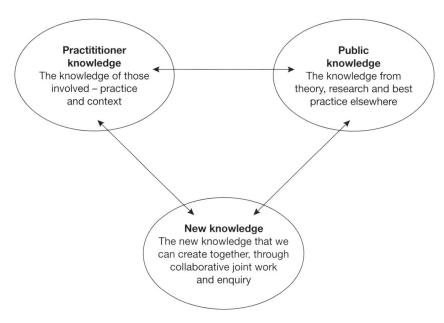

Figure 6.1 Three fields of knowledge (Jackson 2006)

research and evidence? It also aimed to inform a third research question: Are there particular kinds of learning process that are more likely to occur through school–school connections? Within this overall programme, our study set out to consider the following three research questions, each of which relates closely to key issues arising from the accounts of BASRC, the Coalition of Knowledge Building Schools and the School-Based Consortia, as already discussed in this chapter:

1   What is understood by research and enquiry?
   a   by different people who engage in this activity?
   b   what do people chose to do as research and enquiry?
   c   and why do they do it?
2   What is the impact or effect of research and enquiry on a school?
   a   how does it benefit a school or schools?
   b   and, how is it understood by those engaging in and promoting research and enquiry?
3   What sustains the effective use of research and enquiry in schools and networks? What are the implications for sustainability and organisational redesign in terms of: the organisational level; the leadership level; and the level of external support?

In consultation with members of the NLC group, six NLCs were selected because they were considered to be actively engaged in practitioner research and enquiry. Therefore, the case studies were expected to explore what was working well rather than examine how and why some networks were less successful in their research endeavours. Our sample of networks was also chosen because together they provided a spread across England and geographically in terms of urban and rural locations. They also represented a range of schools: from the primary and secondary sectors as well as from both mainstream and special school settings. The case studies took place during 2004–2005 and involved visiting each of the NLCs. During these visits we conducted interviews with groups and individuals, collected documentation and observed network and group sessions, plus lessons intended to demonstrate some of the effects of practitioner research on students' learning. Finally, a questionnaire was given to a sample of staff in each of the fifty-six schools. (Further details of the research undertaken in each network are available in the appendices.)

Chapter 7

Blackburn with Darwen leading into Networked Learning Community

Aligning, captaining and collaborating through research and enquiry

Colleen McLaughlin

INTRODUCTION

As the title suggests, the features of this network that have been focused on in this case study are the ways in which purposes and processes have been aligned to facilitate research and enquiry; the nature of the captaining of the team or the facilitation of the research and enquiry; and the process of collaboration, which have led to interesting and powerful practices of adult learning. The term alignment is being used in the sense that Gardner *et al.* (2001) employ it:

> A professional realm is healthiest when the values of the culture are in line with those of the domain, when the expectations of stakeholders match those of the field and when domain and field are themselves in sync. When these conditions exist, individual practitioners are free to operate at their best, morale is high and the professional realm flourishes. We term this a situation of *authentic alignment.*
>
> (Gardner *et al.*, 2001, p. 27)

KEY CHARACTERISTICS OF THE CONTEXT AND THE LEARNING COMMUNITY

Blackburn with Darwen is a town in the north west of England that became a unitary authority in 1998. According to the Local Education Authority's inspection (Ofsted) report of January 2001:

> the population is approximately 139,500 with a higher proportion in the age range 0–15 than found nationally. There are severely deprived areas

Table 7.1 Background to Blackburn with Darwen NLC

Total number of schools = nine secondary schools • The Local Education Authority mathematics consultant   is a co–leader and a facilitator of the network • HEI link lecturer from Manchester University
Approximate number of teachers = 800
Second cohort of Networked Learning Communities (2003 – 2007)

Some features of this network:
• initially focused on teaching and learning
   in mathematics
• strong involvement from the LEA
   mathematics consultants
• focused on action learning groups, individual
   learning initiatives and knowledge
   distribution tools
• listening to the learners' voices
• effective learning environments for pupil and
   professional learning

and the authority was ranked 26/310 on the 1999 index of Local Deprivation. Unemployment is above the national average. The proportion of pupils eligible for free school meals is above the average and the proportion of pupils from ethnic minority groups is high and mostly drawn from Pakistani and Indian descent.

(Ofsted, 2001)

This issue of its size and the particular features of the context are themes that run through the thinking and responses of the teachers and other professionals in this network.

The network itself consists of all of the nine secondary schools in the LEA. The network is co-led by an LEA consultant, a deputy head teacher and an LEA officer, with the head teachers driving the steering group. The primary focus was on the development of action learning or enquiry groups, very much within the context of mathematics. This subject focus is another important feature. These action learning groups were groups of teachers from across the schools exploring various aspects of learning within mathematics and science. Table 7.2 shows some of the topics of enquiry and action learning. The roots of the NLC were in the Secondary Maths Partnership, which had an existing structure and had been in operation for a year prior to its formation as an NLC in 2003. Clearly a lot had been learned for the work had evolved.

Table 7.2 Examples of topics of research and enquiry

- Raising the achievement of pupils who were below level 3 National Curriculum levels of attainment
- Transition from primary to secondary school with a focus on mathematics
- Improving pupil engagement in mathematics
- The use of different learning styles
- The use of video in mathematics lessons
- Research lessons on various topics including the use of graphical calculators
- The use of calculators in the classroom
- The use of information and communication technology (ICT) to enhance learning in mathematics

ALIGNMENT AND COLLABORATION

The group of enquirers shared many things, i.e. the locality, one LEA that was small, and the subject concerns. This was very important to them at all levels.

> This [NLC] is different because it's literally maths focused, on raising achievement in maths, whereas lots of the others are general, just education and learning in general. I prefer this one.
>
> (Teacher)

> This is a unitary authority and there are nine secondary schools. So . . . you've absolutely the perfect opportunity for setting up networks at all levels and fairly easily.
>
> (Head Teacher)

These connections were strengthened and supported by other important elements. The LEA consultant had instigated collaborative curriculum planning in mathematics, supported by meetings of heads of department and the meetings of the enquiry groups. The curriculum materials were pooled on a website that all the schools accessed. Latterly they have been using the website as a source of news, information sharing and problem solving. So there was a short history of collaboration, which the enquiry groups built on. This harnessing and alignment of purposes and structures is an important element in the work of this NLC. A head of department talking about his action learning illustrates this:

> I was more involved with the heads of department. We would tackle things together. It was as much an evaluation as a research thing. 'Can you let me know what you're planning?' 'We'll let you know what we are planning . . .' We found we got a lot more from that [collaboration].

A lot of being with other teachers who were helping you think about what's going on, as much as anything else.

(Head of Department)

Teachers talked a great deal about the importance of this collaboration and how they felt it was strengthened by talking to colleagues who knew the children in that locality and had experience of the sorts of challenges and conditions of work.

The thing that has been the most beneficial is the talking and communicating with other people.

(Head of Department)

The most important thing was the sharing of information and sort of having access to other people's experiences in school similar to ours and slightly different as well . . . The sharing of ideas with like-minded people.

(Teacher)

The teachers and the heads of department interviewed valued the collaboration very highly indeed, but there was some evidence that the national climate of competition between schools did not always fit easily with this. Teachers in one school had been asked to ensure that the school 'maintained the advantage', and one teacher reported, 'I know we're to be careful what we shares sometimes. We were told.' The political tensions of the national scene were mirrored in small ways in this network. However, the teachers did not find this an insurmountable difficulty, nor did it affect their desire for, and practice of, collaboration. What was valued as a focus and outcome of the work varied at different positions within the schools. The head teachers valued school improvement, the heads of faculty focused on curriculum development and the standards debate, and the teachers focused very much on classroom improvement and pupil learning. The network co-leader focused very much on pupil and adult learning.

RESEARCH, ENQUIRY AND PROFESSIONAL LEARNING

The original intention of setting up a mathematics group prior to the inception of the NLC was to value teachers as having important knowledge, which the LEA consultant felt was being underused. There was no intention initially to use research and enquiry as part of the process. However, the process of working towards producing a document at the end of an exploration of the use of lesson structures did not work. The idea of a written product as the end result was felt to be unsatisfactory because no one in the group was used to writing in that way, there was no accreditation for this work, it was pressurising, and there was a lack of fit with the audience of other mathematics teachers.

So in the second year of this group a different frame for writing up was used, and the group facilitators started to pay attention to evidence collection. In addition they provided support from two LEA mathematics advisors who acted as critical friends, and time was provided for these activities. The group of teachers involved met for three whole days over the year as they had done the previous year. The methods used were observation by peers or LEA consultants, personal journals and pupil questionnaires. The process was much more tightly focused, and the focus was on the question: How do we engage pupils in learning mathematics?

In the third year, the mathematics group had become an official NLC. The LEA consultant, John Westwell, said they were influenced in the year before this by the Networked Learning Communities' framework of the three fields of knowledge (NCSL, 2005), i.e. what is known – the knowledge from theory, research and best practice; what we know – the knowledge of those involved, i.e. what practitioners know; and new knowledge – the new knowledge that is created through collaborative work (see Figure 6.1, p. 111). This was used to shape the seminars in which the teachers engaged. So each seminar contained the following elements:

- something for the researchers to reflect on and talk about, and there were frameworks for this
- a presentation to the group with questions, points of clarification and comments
- something on research methods; this varied from identifying a focus for the research to the use of journals or writing up research
- a stimulus on the main topic of the work, the engagement of learners in mathematics; this was felt to be important because of the importance for teachers of having something to take away from the session such as a reading, a video or examples of others' research.

By the third year, the above pattern of working was seen as satisfactory, and the journal was seen as crucial. New researchers were inducted into the group by more experienced researchers. The pattern of the seminars was changed to one full day per year and three twilight sessions. In addition a second group was started, where the focus was on the use of research lessons, and the topic was the use of information and communication technology (ICT) in mathematics.

Research lessons are planned collaboratively by two or more colleagues [research partners] with the aim of solving a pedagogic problem, taking forward innovative practice or refining further ideas in development. The lessons are taught, observed and jointly analysed by the research partners. Participants will be involved in:

- the identification of a large problem or innovation of interest to them and their school
- the design, observation and analysis of a series of research lessons
- working with colleagues from other schools and networks.

(NCSL, 2005)

This new group had a strong agenda to learn about ICT and were not as strongly committed to researching their practice. They wanted to refine and develop practice as well as reflect on it. Key advantages of the research lesson framework were the manageability, i.e. there was limited and focused evidence collection; the final product, which was seen as valuable and clear; and the providing of value for time.

John Westwell, the facilitator of this group, had developed a model of professional learning which underpinned this work (see Figure 7.1). In this model the three elements of posing questions, taking action and reflecting are seen as the elements that constituted reflective practice. Most teachers were perceived to be doing this. Evidence collection was the element that made this action research or practitioner research and was described as having changed significantly how the practitioners viewed the classroom and teaching. The co-leader aimed to develop professional learning and not specifically to develop teacher researchers. There was also evidence that the different needs of different groups merited different emphasis and approach.

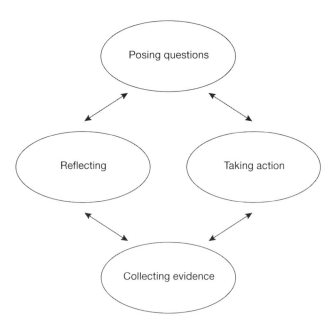

Figure 7.1 A model of professional learning

The importance of alignment of agendas emerged here too. Some teachers in the network were part of a national NLC teacher researcher group, and there were some tensions and conflicts of purpose between them and this second group. It was felt that the NLC national group focused on the network and the teachers wanted to focus on classrooms and lessons. However, the Blackburn with Darwen group had developed quite sophisticated and time efficient ways of working, as demonstrated in Box 7.1.

The teachers described all these elements in the learning process as powerful and important to them, along with collaboration. They saw the purposes as classroom improvement, subject development and professional learning. The conceptions of the purposes were varied. There was a strong emphasis on the sharing of practice between the schools and on this being undertaken in a way that matched the schools' agendas. The manageability was key or, as one teacher put it, 'tweaking v transforming'. Enquiry and sharing good

---

Box 7.1 Examples of some of the adult learning strategies used in the group sessions

- A clinic request form is used where each person writes down a request for some information on a problem they are having with mathematics software. Others consider whether they have a solution or know of someone or somewhere to go to find the solution.

A knowledge exchange process

Teachers complete and share in the group the following sentences:

- Have you heard that . . .? [news related to ICT in mathematics teaching, national bodies, free publications, funding streams]
- I have used and would recommend . . . [software, books/resources, websites]
- Something we do at our place . . . [organisation and access to hardware, classroom ICT resources, ways of disseminating and discussing ICT in the team]
- Would you like a copy of . . .? [sharing things you have produced in your own school, such as software files, resources, plans]
- Would you like to come to . . .? [invitations to observe teaching, see mathematics area and resources, attend mathematics professional learning activities]
- Can anybody help me . . .? [information, ideas, invitations]

practice were seen as very closely linked. Some also wanted to critique current policy and practice and emphasised the importance of teachers being able to shape the agenda for learning and enquiry. The agenda for this group was shaped very much by the network or the group as a whole, with much input by the LEA consultant. Most teachers were happy with this process, but there was some evidence that, as teachers became more experienced in the research and enquiry processes, they wanted more freedom and continuity of theme in their enquiry work. This dilemma between individual development, school improvement and national policy control is a difficult one.

In discussing the purposes and outcomes of the process, the teachers who had experienced the process said:

> It points you to things that you haven't actually thought of yourself . . .

> It's good because you put your work out, what you're doing . . .

> This gives us a chance to actually talk about education issues whereas I would say, being honest, that in your teaching training you don't really do much of that. You were given the right ideas on how to teach things but you didn't really discuss . . .

> It's making me aware of my own teaching for a start. You can always criticise what you're doing and look for ways to improve otherwise you just repeat old practice . . .

The teachers interviewed were largely very positive about the impact on them and of the benefits of collaboration. There was also awareness that not everyone in the schools felt similarly about collaborating in this way. This illustrates the need for the work to be constantly protected and developed. One teacher spoke of the attitudes of others in the school:

> It's pretty mixed if I'm being honest. I would say some people would say 'too time consuming, can't be bothered, don't want to know' . . . but again you've got a lot of open-minded people who are willing to give things a go.

SUPPORT FOR RESEARCH AND ENQUIRY

The teacher enquirers were very clear indeed about the necessary supports and the important elements in their development. They were adamant that they could not proceed without external support, and the image of a team and a captain was used to describe the central role of the LEA consultant, John Westwell. The key functions he performed were the provision of technical support for the research and enquiry, the co-ordination and arrangement of meetings and resources, the facilitation of the meetings, the seeking out and provision of access to external research and in-school support e.g. observation with feedback. Teachers felt very strongly that they could not provide these from within schools owing to pressure on time. Senior managers in schools supported this too:

> It's very good to have external support to smooth out all the difficulties, you know to sort out all the bits and pieces, of the admin and the setting up. If it's easy for people to do, they're more likely to do it . . . Anything that makes it easy – easy to use, easy to do, easy to report, anything at all like that is helpful.
>
> (Deputy Head)

Just providing money was perceived by senior managers as insufficient. The additional support of the LEA consultant was vital: he was able to harness the agendas and mediate between the heads of department, the head teachers and the teacher enquirers. He was able also to develop the sophisticated facilitation processes described above. He acted as 'a bridge' between the outside world and the network.

The greatest challenge for the network was the dissemination of research, enquiry and knowledge transfer between the teachers and the schools. This impinges on two of the three fields of knowledge being used as a framework, i.e. the area of what is already known and the creation and sharing of new knowledge. It was a double challenge in that the teachers found it difficult to access or use existing research as well as to write about or share their own research work.

The accessing of what was already known was the least developed aspect of the research and enquiry process. The majority of the teachers reported relying on subject association journals or the Internet and they talked of the need for writing to be brief and accessible in terms of language and style before they would read it. The strategy used by the LEA consultant was to include research articles or summaries of them as part of the framework of the meetings. (See the earlier section on Research, enquiry and professional learning.) This relied on the facilitator finding and processing the articles. The teachers said they would not have looked at these articles if this had not been processed by an external person. They found this strategy useful.

The other challenge was that of the dissemination of what the teachers had learned. One of the initial strategies adopted to address this problem was the writing up of the research and putting it on to a CD. Although the CD was an innovative and a useful tool, it was slow and the process had not been seen as successful in terms of sharing knowledge between the schools. Teachers valued highly the face-to-face sharing of knowledge and did not value other methods as highly. The other strategy being adopted was the appointment in February 2005 of a Network Communications Officer, whose main role was to manage the knowledge transfer across the network. She was clear that her main tasks were the 'monitoring and support of the network, building a portfolio of best practice in pupil voice work and acting as a bridge between theory and practice'. She felt that time was 'an issue with teachers. Time is of the biggest value for teachers'.

CONCLUDING REMARKS

This network is noteworthy for its alignment of purposes and processes. The collaboration of the mathematics departments was linked at many levels – the construction of a shared curriculum, the work of specific groups such as the heads of department and the teachers, and the research and enquiry work, which were linked to professional development and school agendas for development. This was planned and aided the research and enquiry work. The recent developments have also been in response to the needs of knowledge transfer and the development of research and enquiry. The fact that these processes meshed with the unitary nature of the LEA and enabled the local collaboration to feel significant and manageable is also a key feature.

Chapter 8

Bristol Opportunity Networked Learning Community

Learning to research, researching to learn

Kristine Black-Hawkins

Bristol Opportunity Network operated within a pre-existing Small Education Action Zone (EAZ), as part of the government's Excellence in Cities (EiC) initiative (DfES, 1999). The EAZ provided substantial financial support for a range of development work across the schools and these activities were complemented by the network; for example, the Director and Assistant Director of the EAZ were also the co-leaders for the network. Both were experienced teachers but, unlike other networks' co-leaders, they were released from other duties and were seconded full-time to the zone/network. The Director was head teacher of one of the network schools; she was highly knowledgeable about the area and had already established good working relationships with the other head teachers. The NLC funding was primarily used to promote and support practitioner research and enquiry through the establishment of a 'leading link' teacher in each school. Two of these teachers were also given extra responsibility as 'lead leading links', promoting research and enquiry across the group of schools. The opportunity zone was one of three EAZs within Bristol LA, which also supported its work. Finally, the zone/network had a number of important connections with two local universities; for example, the University of the West of England supported the development of student councils in each school and their associated Zone Student Parliament. Some research skills training for teachers had also been provided.

The eleven schools that formed the network are situated in the northern area of Bristol and are geographically reasonably close to one another. All ten of the primary schools are within the catchment area of the one secondary school, although some parents/carers choose not to send their children to this school. Furthermore, there are other primary schools close by that did not join the network. The network schools vary in terms of the socio-economic backgrounds of the student intake. In the bid to become an NLC, some schools were described as being 'affluent', whereas others were identified as having 'high social deprivation factors'; for example, it was noted that in one school over fifty per cent of students were eligible for free school meals. Just prior to the period of our case study, two schools, including the secondary, had been placed in 'special measures' following unsatisfactory Ofsted inspections,

Table 8.1 Background to Bristol Opportunity NLC

Total number of schools = eleven • one infants, one junior, eight junior mixed infant (JMI), one secondary • all mixed girls and boys • non–selective
Other links and partners: • Excellence in Cities initiative • Education in Action Zone • Bristol LA • University of Bristol • University of the West of England
Approximate number of teachers = 300
First cohort of Networked Learning Communities (funded for 2002–2005)
Some features of this network: • being part of an EAZ provided additional opportunities and resources not generally available to other networks, e.g. full-time, funded co-leaders • schools were geographically close to one another but varied in student intake • each school had established the post of a leading link teacher, which was key to research and enquiry activities • research and enquiry were focused on raising students' achievements through changing classroom practices

whereas, in contrast, others had received government achievement awards. The performance of children in the primary schools, as measured by national tests (Standard Assessment Tasks, commonly known as SATs) also varied significantly. For example, when the network was first formed the percentage of children, at age eleven, who attained level four or above ranged from thirty per cent to ninety-eight per cent (national average that year: English = seventy-five per cent; mathematics = seventy-three per cent; science = eighty per cent (DfES, 2002b)). See Table 8.1 for a summary of background details about the network.

PRACTITIONER RESEARCH AND ENQUIRY: SUPPORTING THE LEARNING OF CHILDREN AND TEACHERS

Understandings of research and enquiry in this network were partly shaped by its overall aims, and these in turn had been formed within the context of the EAZ's main concerns. In the zone's action plan to the DfES (2002a) three priorities were highlighted, all focusing on learning and with a strong emphasis on 'raising standards' in schools. These were:

- 'networked learning, powerful learning'
- 'collaborative learning'
- 'learning to lead'.

Expectations about the purpose of research and enquiry to be undertaken in the network were closely related to these and specifically concerned improving the classroom learning of both children and teachers. Or, in the words of one co-leader, research was about, 'Giving a better deal to children in the classroom [. . . and] getting the teachers to be better practitioners'. More specifically, this was also described in terms of raising children's achievement as measured by national tests (SATs).

Each school established the post of a 'leading link' teacher who was responsible for engaging in, promoting and supporting research and enquiry in their own schools and across the network. They were funded by the network and this provided them with weekly non-contact time to undertake their responsibilities, including regular opportunities to meet each other. As a group they focused on *Building Learning Power* (Claxton, 1999), which identifies four characteristics of successful learning ('reciprocity', 'reflectiveness', 'resilience' and 'resourcefulness'). Some leading link teachers used Claxton's work as a basis for their research and enquiry. As a group they explored ways of developing 'paired coaching', to support the learning of both children and teachers, and this also formed a research focus for some. However, whatever topics they chose, they were encouraged by their co-leaders to conceive of research and enquiry as a cycle requiring some form of baseline measurement, followed by a period of implementation of change and then re-testing to establish whether improvements had taken place. Finally, there was an expectation that research reports in the form of leaflets would be written and disseminated across the network and on its website.

Research and enquiry activities undertaken by individual teachers primarily concerned changing classroom practices, based on a need or problem that they had identified as being particularly important to children's learning in their own classrooms. As one teacher explained, 'To make it successful, it has to be something you want to do, it has to be something, for me, that's having a big impact for the children. . . . Something you believe in, that you're passionate about'.

The systematic gathering and analysis of evidence was central to their understanding of the research process:

> You need to have a baseline, you need to follow it through . . . having a methodology, maybe looking at other research that other people have done . . . It's a sense of achievement really when you are able to say . . . it's not just professional intuition . . . I've actually got the evidence . . . that rigour.

All teachers interviewed also talked about research and enquiry in terms of their professional development and, especially, the excitement of being learners themselves. One explained, 'I think that's a big part of research, learning from doing it'. Another described how being a leading link teacher, and engaging in research and enquiry, had reinvigorated his interest in his work and his sense of himself as a professional:

> Before, I was stuck in my classroom . . . . I did very few courses and things, so hardly ever got to see other people's classrooms. I love going to see other schools. It's been brilliant . . . really valuable, because we can get so closed in our own little world . . . it's so refreshing.

Headteachers were generally supportive of the research and enquiry activities taking place in their schools. Those who were most enthusiastic conceptualised the primary purpose of practitioner research more broadly as a means of bringing about whole school improvement by enhancing the learning of both children and teachers. Like the leading link teachers they also emphasised the importance of gathering robust evidence, especially if the research findings were then to influence teaching and learning across a number of classrooms in a school, and not just the practices taking place in one only:

> We need evidence and an outcome and I'd expect that. For example we had a piece of . . . research done by a teacher . . . She put her paper together explaining what she had done . . . how she set about it and what the outcomes were with hard data . . . We've really got to get the evidence that will prove that what we did had an impact. We can't just assume it did. We've got to make sure.

However, one head teacher viewed practitioner research and enquiry with some scepticism. She explained: 'Partly because I've got an older staff at the moment, actually interesting them in enquiry-based work is harder . . . It's the idea that . . . they're going to have to write something up at length.' She also noted that releasing a teacher to undertake research and enquiry or attend leading link meetings could cause problems with other staff in school. 'You get this, which we have had, particularly when [teacher] started, "Why are they going out every week?", "What are they doing?", "Why is that class having supply?".'

The emphasis on evidence, noted by teachers and some head teachers, was strongly reiterated by co-leaders. One co-leader explained this as, 'so that you know that it's made a difference'. However, with their network perspective, they also stressed that research findings should be presented in ways that could be shared with colleagues in the other network schools, as well as more generally in schools across the EAZ. Both co-leaders also conceived of practitioner research and enquiry as being a highly effective (even the 'best') form of professional development. One stated:

> You can train people . . . on courses, they can listen to things, they can see things, but actually when you identify something that needs to be addressed yourself, and develop strategies to address that issue and then evaluate that, it is far more powerful and more likely to be sustainable than just going on a course or a training session . . . Probably the best learning is where people have done it themselves.

RESEARCH AND ENQUIRY: STRENGTHENING SCHOOLS AS LEARNING COMMUNITIES

When asked about the value of practitioner research, all those interviewed referred to its effect on learning. This was described in terms of developing the learning of individuals (both children and staff) as well as strengthening classrooms and schools as learning communities. In response to being asked about the role of research in schools, one head teacher explained it as follows: 'It comes down to the ethos of the school, to what extent is the school a learning organisation. I expect young people to learn but . . . what you want to create is a place where everybody's learning.' Similarly, a leading link teacher argued that her engagement in research provided the children she taught with a positive model for learning:

> I can say to them [the children] I am researching, I am doing work, I am learning, especially in terms of learning to learn and Building Learning Power . . . I think that them being part of that learning process is only going to help really and is going to enhance their learning.

That research and enquiry support teachers' learners is a view shared by head teachers and co-leaders. One head teacher explained:

> I feel we are a learning school . . . that adults are learners as well as children . . . and the very best place to learn is actually in the classroom . . . where you need to learn and improve on practice. It's all to do with self-analysis, self-evaluation, being able to evaluate yourself. And, other colleagues to help evaluate for you.

In this way, teachers' research and enquiry were considered to have a broader impact than just within individuals' classrooms, because their findings could be used to support developments in teaching and learning across the school as a whole. For example, one teacher introduced the teaching of philosophy into her class and used this as a focus for her research, based on the knowledge, experience and expertise that she developed in doing so. By sharing her findings with colleagues in a staff meeting and also in more informal ways, such as working alongside colleagues with their classes, philosophy was gradually introduced throughout the school. In another school four teachers researched in collaboration on the teaching and learning of narrative writing. Their head teacher expected this research to contribute to the work of all teachers in the school: 'We're going to feedback to the rest of the staff on their [research . . .] and if we feel it's viable then we'll introduce it to the whole school'.

Research in this network had also helped to reduce the sense of isolation experienced by some teachers within their own classrooms and schools and had broadened their understanding of the experiences of their colleagues in other schools. It provided opportunities of sharing good practices, common concerns and problems; for example, in the leading link meetings. One teacher noted:

> It's been a real eye-opener, feeling part of that wider community which I never did before . . . It's been great being able to communicate and work with colleagues from very different types of schools . . . and the research that we've shared and has gone across the different schools has made that really obvious.

Or, as one head teacher argued, 'It's easy . . . to forget that a class teacher is really insular in their own classroom and you've got to give teachers opportunities to be aware of other practices in the school and in other schools'.

All interviewees identified similar intangible effects of research and enquiry on their schools. Teacher researchers described these in terms of increased motivation, confidence, interest, and sense of worth in their work. One head teacher noted the impact on the retention of staff. Another described research as providing a kind of 'buzz . . . And, it's nice to have that. It's that bit extra that you don't have otherwise'.

SUSTAINING RESEARCH AND ENQUIRY IN THE SCHOOLS AND ACROSS THE NETWORK

The following key features emerged from the case study in terms of supporting and sustaining the effective use of research and enquiry in this network:

- Membership of the EAZ provided existing support structures and substantially more funding than was available to NLCs more generally. These include the full-time appointments of Zone Director and Assistant Director, salaried administrative support and designated office space.

- The very active role of the co-leaders (Director and Assistant Director of the Zone) was crucial in supporting and promoting the practitioner research and enquiry of the leading link teachers. Seconding a head teacher to be the Director had worked very well, because she was very familiar with all the schools and was well respected amongst the head teachers and other staff.
- The role of the leading link teachers was essential in terms of co-ordinating research and enquiry within their schools and across the network. They were most effective when head teachers protected their time to engage in, support and promote research activities.
- The role of head teachers was also important in terms of providing direct practical and moral support for teacher researchers. The effects of research and enquiry seemed much more likely to be sustained when head teachers perceived them as being a means by which to inform their school's overall plans for improvement and influencing the practices of many teachers, rather than a series of 'one-off' projects relating to individual teachers only.
- The development of shared purposes through the *Building Learning Power* (Claxton, 2002) programme and paired 'coaching' had supported the sustainability of research and enquiry across the network.
- The nature of individual schools had also affected the sustainability of the effective use of research and enquiry. Introducing and developing research appeared to be more straightforward in the primary schools than in the secondary. This was partly to do with the scale and complexity of secondary schools, although it was likely that other circumstances may well have affected sustainability; for example, since the inception of the network the secondary school had had three different head teachers and has been put into, and come out of, 'special measures'.
- Co-leaders considered the external support from two local universities and the NLC group to have been important in terms of providing initial research training. NLC conferences and other events, plus their support materials, were also identified by some interviewees as being helpful.
- The network/zone website was extensive and regularly updated. This provided an important source of information for some members.

Chapter 9

Hartlepool Networked Learning Community

The journey of enquiry

Colleen McLaughlin

> Enquiry is a journey, a way of working, a mode of being, and a process of continuous learning. It can create new structural environments within which to operate. The schools that have been involved with enquiry driven improvement work over a period of time, gradually and progressively redesign themselves around the collaborative study of practice.
>
> (Jackson and Leo, 2003)

This notion of enquiry as a journey is a very central one in Hartlepool NLC and the phrase was often heard in conferences and featured in interviews. The notion of a journey and of learning were important and evident in the reported experience of those in this community. It will shape this case study, which will be framed around what the participants have learned, as it was one of the first NLCs 'to attempt this [enquiry] from scratch, without a history of enquiry or collaboration' (Network facilitator) (see Table 9.1).

HARTLEPOOL NLC

The following extract from an unpublished document produced in 2003 'as we started our journey' describes the setting and constituency of the NLC:

> The learning community of thirteen [primary] schools[1] is located in the town of Hartlepool on the North East Coast of England in an area of considerable socio-economic disadvantage. The network covers almost fifty per cent of the LEA as it is a small unitary authority. The community is based around a common and compelling learning focus. We have quite deliberately placed the emphasis on bottom up, inside-out improvement with a focus on re-professionalizing the work of teachers. We wish to move towards shared valued and aligned priorities.
>
> We have established collective enquiry as our central and most powerful vehicle for learning and are building our leadership capacity through a

Table 9.1 Background to Hartlepool NLC

Total number of schools = twelve • primary schools • all within Hartlepool and so geographically close
Approximate number of teachers = 160
First cohort of NLCs (2003–2005)
Some features of this network: • the focus is on teacher enquiry and cross school enquiry groups • the co-leaders are head teachers • the use of CPD time and resources is an interesting feature of the network • the higher education institute (HEI) link was not pursued in this network

major investment in our lead learners who are the vanguard of the enquiry process. We have an essentially optimistic and hopeful view of who we are and where we are headed. We aim to innovate our practice, find better ways of doing things and make our schools fantastic places to learn and work. We embarked on this enterprise convinced that we would find the unlocked and untapped potential in all our schools.

(Hartlepool Networked Learning Community, February 2003)

THE ENQUIRY GROUPS

The co-leaders had learned a great deal about how to facilitate and structure the enquiry groups. 'I think we could tell you how not to do it' (co-leader). The head teachers began with the help of an outside consultant, who identified fifteen common themes through undertaking an audit of skills through the head teachers. Groups of teachers were asked to align themselves to an enquiry group under each of these themes. This was later seen as counter-productive for the following reasons: the process was left too open-ended; groups were too large; the agenda was not one chosen by the teachers; the social cohesion of the group became a critical factor (and will be returned to later), and the process became unmanageable. So much had been learned about scale, sustainability and the architecture of the groups (Holmes, 2004).

The groups were reconstituted and teachers chose their own areas of interest. The head teacher steering group assigned funds to enquiry groups that were active. This was monitored closely and the principle of cross school groups was established firmly. Head teacher involvement was seen as 'unbelievably important' to the success of the enquiry groups, but the role assigned to head teachers was one of supporting not leading the groups. The democracy of the groups was very important to the co-leaders.

Table 9.2 The enquiry groups in 2005: topic and composition

Topics	No. of people in group
1 Breaking down barriers to learning	4
2 ICT across the curriculum	4
3 Stimulating writing	6
4 Teaching and learning	5
5 Language interaction in KS1	4
6 Leadership and management	3
7 Transforming learning	4
8 Child centred induction to smoother transition	6
9 Life long learning teaching skills of independent learning	2
10 Feeling safe and comfortable enough to make mistakes	3
11 Parental support 'knowing where the learner is right now'	2
12 Pupil self–esteem	5
13 Inspirational teaching that motivates, engages and connects prior knowledge	7
14 Motivating less able pupils	7
15 One group disbanded	4
Total	54
Total staff of the twelve schools	Approx. 160

Enquiry groups met in school time and resources were targeted at these meetings. In addition there were whole network meetings of enquirers and whole network staff conferences annually in allocated time. Groups consisted of all relevant staff, i.e. teachers, nursery nurses and teaching assistants. Table 9.2 shows the current enquiry groups and the number of staff in each group. The larger groups are composed of those who are in a National Curriculum key stage group or have a common role. For example the transition group examined the transition to and from the nursery (this later became expanded to examining key stages one and two).

WHAT IS ENQUIRY IN HARTLEPOOL NLC?

There were a range of activities and motivations for undertaking enquiry in the learning community. Teachers often struggled to define enquiry and were very keen to assert that what they were doing was not 'research'. In fact there were occasions when 'academic research' was polarised as something very far from what the teachers were undertaking. The work of the national NLC Group at the National College heavily influenced and helped the learning community. The three fields of knowledge (an NLC concept – see Figure 6.1, p. 111) were used often by the co-leaders. The following e-mail from co-leader to co-leaders encapsulates this:

Enquiry

1   is focused on professional activity, usually in the workplace itself

2   is intended to clarify aspects of that activity with a view to bringing about beneficial change and ultimately to improve student progress, achievement and development

3   may focus on both teaching and learning at the classroom level and supporting organisational conditions and changing management capacity

4   is based upon the exploration of three fields of knowledge and the interaction between them:

- practitioner knowledge: the knowledge that people bring to the table
- publicly available knowledge: the theory and knowledge that are publicly available to be drawn into learning environments
- the knowledge we create together – in community, through collaborative enquiry.

The enquirers held different and varied conceptions. For some it was closely tied to the national policy agendas: 'It was already kind of decided what our main initiative would be through Ofsted in school. So we came with like that in mind' (Teacher).

For others it was rooted in notions of social justice, pupil voice and passion: 'How dare we? How dare we assume that we know what's best for them when they haven't even been asked?' (Teacher).

The chance to engage with and ask students was very important. The dominant conception was that enquiry was about solving classroom problems and taking action: 'Because I wanted to find the answer to something. I wanted to find an answer to something that would have solved the problem I had with that class at that time' (Teacher).

For others it was an opportunity to introduce new initiatives that others had tried. An example was the development of circle time based on reading the work of Jenny Mosley (1998), implementing practices and then reflecting with colleagues.

The processes used to enquire in these different ways ranged from systematic enquiry, using research methods such as observation, questionnaires to parent and pupils, to reflective discussions with colleagues and others outside the schools, such as LEA consultants, sharing ideas and resources with colleagues and searching the Internet for resources. The enquiry embodied the characteristics quoted in the first co–leader definition of enquiry, i.e. focused on the classroom and classroom or school activity with a view to clarifying it and impacting on practice and policy.

CLOSE TO THE CLASSROOM: THE BENEFITS

The closeness to the classroom was the benefit for the enquirers. They distinguished this activity from other professional development opportunities by the control it gave them to address issues of importance to them in their classrooms and schools:

> You haven't got someone standing up there saying this is the team rule, this is what you need to do, blah, blah, blah. You can say right this is what I want to do and this is what we're going to look at and we're going to be producing at the end of it.
>
> (Enquirer)

> CPD is OK because you pick yourself, have some sort of choice but this is *me* starting with a question rather than being given a directive.
>
> (Enquirer)

For the enquirers, without exception, this was a highly motivating aspect. They talked of how it took them back to primary motivations for teaching:

> It's like the inspiration. You have the ideas and you know you want to do it but you get caught up in the everyday job and the children. And it removes you, it doesn't remove you from the children, but it lets you see the children and see what you are supposed to be doing.
>
> (Enquirer)

This also applied at head teacher level. Two of the co-leaders described involvement in the initiative as the 'best professional development I have had', and one said that it put 'the focus back on learning, which you tend to forget when you get in the office and the day to day job'. For many of the teachers it reduced their sense of isolation as professionals, and the collaborative element was seen as very important. For some the desire to go deeper into the enquiry process could also be frustrating. One of the head teacher co-leaders saw the closeness to the classroom as central to the work and that the next step was to develop leadership at this level. He talked about 'lead learners' as the key area for development.

IMPORTANT ELEMENTS OF THE PROCESS

The initial learning about the process of enquiry was that it had been too general and open-ended, lacking clarity of focus. The metaphor of the journey being important was also seen as a drawback in that it distracted from the need to clarify the enquiry. This was an area that the network felt they needed help with and where outside support would be valuable. The NLC national link person was highly valued and seen as an important bridge to the wider world of knowledge and learning. He realised this and often gave more of his time than was allotted to this role.

The social cohesion of the groups was a key factor. Groups that failed to start well soon collapsed, and the dynamic within the groups was key to their continuation. This was also noted by those not engaged in an enquiry group and affected their valuing of the activity. Where enquirers shared a common work focus such as a National Curriculum key stage or phase, such as those working in the nursery, they found it easier to have a shared sense of purpose. The capacity for primary teachers to work regularly across schools is unusual and the organisation of such cross school collaboration is a big task. It was also highly valued.

KNOWLEDGE USE AND KNOWLEDGE GENERATION

One of the areas reflected upon by many involved was whether the enquirers had drawn upon publicly available knowledge and how they had generated new knowledge. They had clearly brought their practitioner knowledge to the table and gained much from sharing it. The enquirers had found it difficult and time consuming to draw on wider research and knowledge. They had largely used the Internet or the expertise of others outside the school, such as LEA consultants. The Networked Learning Group played a key role here. Methods and tools such as 'learning walks' had been used widely and were seen as important. There is a need for such debate within learning communities and this was reflected upon by one of the NLC facilitators, who talked of the need to moderate the claims of the enquirers based on the enquiry that they had undertaken and the need for 'content knowledge'.

The issues of the basis of the knowledge being shared and generated, plus the status of the claims for the impact, are complex and they taxed this community in its development. Truthfulness and believability were key criteria for the judgement of findings, but it was acknowledged that there was a need to explore further the basis for the knowledge being generated and the impact it had had. Many talked of the need to have a bridge to the wider educational world or to have someone who could fulfil this function. The facilitators had been highly valued in this role but they saw the need for someone to mentor the process. One model posited was of using colleagues from higher education. The network had engaged initially with a university but this had been seen as unworkable owing largely to the finance required to do this. Some enquirers valued their contacts with higher education and regretted the lost connection. The university was seen as a potential resource for the technical training and support of research and enquiry, but it had not been used. It appeared that there was ignorance about the ways of working, pressures and agendas of the respective institutions.

SCHOOL-TO-SCHOOL LEARNING

The network had pooled the resource of time and used CPD time to meet as a whole network and to share the results of the enquiries and to also discuss, reflect or and plan the work of the network. This was valued and took the work of the enquiry groups beyond those immediately involved. However, as in other networks, the task of sharing what was learned is necessarily slow and, if it is to go beyond direct, face-to-face sharing, requires the network to find ways of writing or sharing the outcomes. The writing was difficult and the provision of a writing framework by the NLC facilitator was valued. Where schools had aligned the work to the groups already existing in schools, the school-to-school learning was more efficient and had a natural constituency.

The head teachers and teachers interviewed were clear that the schools and teachers in classrooms had learned a great deal and that it had affected practice at the level of the classroom and the school. The cross school collaboration was seen as a key factor. There were many examples of practice changing as a result of the network enquiries, e.g. the foundation stage group had decided to continue as part of ongoing practice to consult children and parents on the process and experience of transition as they had done as part of their enquiry.

> Primary school teachers don't necessarily have the time to go out and visit other places but this school was a failing school nine years ago. We've had to look outside the box and my staff now go into other schools as well and support them so there's a lot [of school to school learning] so the culture that we've now got has changed.
>
> (Head teacher and co-leader)

SUSTAINABILITY, SUPPORT AND LEADERSHIP FOR RESEARCH AND ENQUIRY

The co-leaders felt that they had learned a great deal about the process and they identified the following as key elements in sustaining research and enquiry: the involvement and commitment of the head teacher; resources to be clearly supporting the work of the enquirers and linked to processes of accountability, i.e. not giving schools money unless there was research activity; having external support that provided a bridge to the world of ideas, research and resources; aligning the enquiry to the central school tasks and structures; and having leadership capacity that was closely connected to the classroom. The £50,000 given to the network was important and for primary schools this amount of money was more significant than for secondary schools that have much larger budgets to draw on.

The leaders of the network were also aware of the tensions and difficulties in the process. They felt that at times there was a cultural tension in that the national climate was one of performance and accountability, whereas learning was about making mistakes, experimenting and critiquing. The development of a 'risk culture' was seen as an important element in the development of a learning community. The different agendas that leaders have to manage could be in tension and this is particularly important in areas such as Hartlepool where the head teachers are often managing very difficult contexts. One of the schools had been placed in 'special measures' after a national inspection and this did create a real anxiety within the network that perhaps it would place their much-valued work at risk.

The leaders of the network were clear that this work demanded capacity of different sorts: the capacity to meet the demands of the work of collaborative enquiry, i.e. the organisational demands, which are considerable; the capacity to facilitate research and enquiry; and leadership capacity. The leaders acknowledged how demanding the work of leading a network was and that they needed as a next step to develop leadership at different levels and to distribute it. They were in some agreement that head teachers did not have the capacity over a long period to carry the leadership alone. They had valued and needed the work of the external facilitator. An example of the leadership dilemmas is exemplified here:

> It has got to the point now where I'm thinking there's more work here, there's more from yesterday's conference, people have got interests, they want to do this, they want to do that and actually yeah this is brilliant but I don't want my school to suffer or me personally to suffer when most of my time is being pushed towards network and not the school. So I think there's a capacity issue as far as leadership's concerned at the moment, which we'll have to discuss.
>
> (Co-leader)

Timescales were also an issue that needed managing. The time it takes to conduct an enquiry, reflect, discuss and then write up or disseminate face to face an enquiry did not always match externally imposed deadlines or the pace of school practice. Dissemination and communication of the outcomes of the research were a clear challenge. So the challenges of research and enquiry were very evident but they were not reasons in the view of this network for not undertaking this work, but rather developmental challenges to be met in the next stage of the journey.

Note

1   One of the schools dropped out later.

Chapter 10

Cambridge SUPER Networked Learning Community

A Schools–University Partnership for Educational Research

Colleen McLaughlin

INTRODUCTION

SUPER is a network of which we are still currently members, and thus we are particularly aware not only of its strengths but also of its limitations. Our involvement means that the portrayal of this network must be different from the others as our perspectives are different. It has also been the subject of a book that acts as a partner to this one (*Researching Schools*, McLaughlin *et al.*, 2006). The case study will draw on that work but with a particular focus on the research undertaken in the network schools, rather than the wider issues of schools–university partnerships. It will also refer to the activities of the network up until 2005, so that it covers the same period of time as the other five networks in this book.

At the time of the research, in terms of institutional membership, there were nine organisations in SUPER, all based in East Anglia, England. These comprised eight secondary/upper schools and the Faculty of Education, University of Cambridge. Together this constituted a population of approximately eight hundred teachers and ten thousand students, all of whom potentially could be both the researchers and the researched. The schools are diverse and geographically distant. They are seen as successful schools by common public measures of education: for example, some were Beacon schools. Unlike many of the schools in the other networks described in this book, the SUPER schools could not generally be described as working in challenging circumstances.

THE HISTORY AND AIMS OF SUPER

SUPER was set up in 1997 with the interest and support of Professors Donald McIntyre and David Hargreaves at the Faculty, arising from a range of existing associations they had with a small number of local head teachers. Its primary purpose was to examine whether, and if so how, the Faculty and a group of schools could work effectively as a partnership so as to serve the research interests of all members. In addition Professor McIntyre in 1999 highlighted two related aims of the project in an application for research funding: to support practitioner research taking place in and between the schools and to research the processes and conditions necessary for such research to flourish.

From this the following overall shared purposes were developed:

1   to explore the conditions and effects of schools and a university working together to generate and to make use of educational research
2   to engage with and in school based practitioner research
3   and, in doing so, to address the following questions:
   •   What kinds of research are useful, why and to whom?
   •   How can a school develop a research culture? And what does this mean?
   •   What kinds of networking structure, process, activity and relationship help to develop and sustain research within and between the institutions?

To support this work, within and across the schools, each school appointed a member of staff to take on the role of teacher research co-ordinator (TRC).

SUPER was a 'network' that derived from the enthusiasm of the head teachers or other members of their senior management teams. This was reflected in the working of the network primarily as meetings of, and agreements among, the TRC and the University critical friends, complemented to a lesser extent by the student voice co-ordinators' (SVCs') meetings, with other activity being largely school-specific and highly autonomous within the schools. As it was conceived primarily as a partnership between the schools and the University, very diverse activities were conducted within the schools with the support of the University. Other network or partnership level activities occurred, such as residential meetings and conferences, but the core activities were school-specific, apart from TRC meetings. There was an early attempt to conduct a common research project in all the schools but this was found to be unsatisfactory in that it did not meet the more specific needs of the schools. Latterly there have been some partnership level research projects.

During the period from 2002 to 2005 when SUPER was funded as an NLC, three interconnected and shared research themes were chosen by the TRCs, head teachers and members of the faculty. These were the focus for the practitioner research:

•   independence in learning, for students and staff
•   the development of student voice in learning and in the use of evidence
•   learning about leadership.

They were constructed to be deliberately broad so as to provide teachers, students and schools with opportunities to research specific areas that were relevant and of interest to them, rather than imposed by others. This openness also allowed scope for connections to be made across the network. (The role of SVC was established in each school as a direct result of the second research focus/theme.)

The research undertaken was highly varied within and between the schools and took place in various arenas. It can be generally categorised thus:

- individual teacher research: initiated by an individual or a general school question (by far the largest category in terms of research work being undertaken)
- subject and departmental research: school or university initiated, individual or collaborative, within or across schools
- more thematic and collaborative research across the schools, initiated by a school, individual or university
- student-undertaken research on a topic initiated either by a teacher or university colleague or by the students themselves.

THE INTERNAL STRUCTURES OF SUPER

There were key individuals in each of the schools who were required to fulfil particular roles and responsibilities to support both research and networking activities. These were:

1 TRCs: expected to co-ordinate and support research generally in their schools and network with each other and with the Faculty
2 SVCs: expected to co-ordinate and support research in their schools around issues of student voice and meet across the network and with the Faculty
3 Head teachers: expected to support the management of research in schools and to network actively with each other and with members of the Faculty.

There were also the following key roles within the Faculty:

- critical friends (one per school): expected to support research in the schools and also to undertake their own investigations into the nature and development of the research and the networking taking place in the school
- network manager: expected to co-ordinate networking activities as well as be a critical friend
- network research officer: expected to research the SUPER network as a whole and also be a critical friend

VIEWS OF RESEARCH IN THE NETWORK SCHOOLS

Purposes

Members of the schools had different conceptions of and practices in research: some had high hopes. A hope of a few was that evidence-informed practice would provide a quick fix in terms of addressing classroom concerns. Therefore, timescales had to be adjusted and tempered. Another view was of research as central to informing curriculum development, much as Lawrence Stenhouse had discussed (Stenhouse, 1975). A common thread was the emphasis on the capacity of research to support professional development and this was seen by some as its prime purpose. There was considerable assent among many schools that research had to be focused on teaching, learning and school improvement. They were not interested in knowledge creation per se but only in relation to making a difference to the classrooms and students in their schools. This is exemplified by the then head teacher of one school:

> I'm not here just to be a research department. I'm not in that business, these kids are too important. I want to be certain that they get direct benefit in a learning sense that values them and makes them feel part of it all.

Conceptions

The understandings of what is research ranged over a wide territory. Some activities perceived as 'research' in some of the schools were considered as something else (development, sharing practice, consultation and so forth) in other schools in the partnership. Just as there were variations between schools in terms of how research was conceived, so there was variation among members within the schools. Not all teachers saw undertaking research as part of their role. However, some teachers not only embraced research, but also considered it to be either an essential part of their professional work, or a desirable extra, special activity that kept them engaged in the job. Where the schools were successful at involving many teachers and keeping them involved, it was based on the belief that research *was*, or at least *could be*, a core activity for a teacher. Other teachers were happy to undertake research for a while, perhaps through the BPRS scheme, but saw this as a special, 'one-off' activity rather than a part of their developing professionalism.

WHAT KINDS OF RESEARCH KNOWLEDGE WERE FOUND TO BE USEFUL AND VALUED?

Classroom action research was the form of knowledge creation that seemed to be the most common and the easiest to undertake. It was where many of the schools focused their early efforts. The teachers involved saw this form of research as profitable and relevant. Research was used to assist the reflection on practice and decision making at different levels of the schools: individual teachers making decisions in their own classrooms; departments reflecting upon practice and making decisions at departmental level; and in some cases research being used to inform whole school policy on aspects of teaching and learning.

There were a few examples of collaborative research across the partnership. Early on in the partnership, some teachers from each of the schools collaborated on a Thinking Skills project. However, this came to be seen as limiting to individual schools' particular agendas and thus wider themes were adopted as umbrellas for research: these were the three research foci mentioned earlier. There were also examples of collaborative research projects with university colleagues: for example, the Technology Integrated Pedagogic Strategies (TIPS) project.

Valuing and accessing the knowledge of students

The engagement with students' knowledge was seen as very powerful and useful. In two of the schools this came to be viewed as the most important form of research work and took precedence over teacher research. It also often involved the development of students as researchers.

KNOWLEDGE CREATION AND DISSEMINATION

The majority of the teachers who chose to engage in research activities considered the development of their own knowledge and understanding, about their own practice, in their own classrooms, to be the primary purpose of doing so. They were not driven to write for a wider public audience, although some did and found it professionally interesting and confidence building. For example, BPRS required that teachers wrote up their work to a set framework. It was also debatable whether many of the teachers considered it necessary to share their research findings even with the 'village' of their own school community; that is, many saw themselves as the only audience for the research. In the schools where dissemination and working with departmental or other colleagues were built into the research model, they often found the shift from working for themselves, with the support of a critical friend, to working with colleagues a challenging one. The degree to which the teachers could be said to be members of a community of critical discourse varied considerably. There were a range of settings in which teachers worked: some were members of research groups that, often with the support of the critical friend from the university, debated the processes and outcomes of their research work; others worked on their own, with critical friends and TRCs supporting them; others, again, chose to work completely alone. The majority of the teachers who undertook research valued opportunities to work in groups and to share their findings with other interested colleagues, although the extent to which this was able to happen varied among the schools.

Dissemination

There were limited opportunities created across the partnership to share the findings of research being undertaken in the schools. There was an annual Teaching and Learning conference where all those engaged in research in the schools were invited to share and hear of each other's projects. However, releasing all these staff was very demanding of schools' resources. The partnership also had a website on which accounts of research, known as SUPER sheets, were posted, although this proved to be less popular as a form of communication than had been anticipated. Within the schools various strategies were employed to disseminate the research. In some there was a harnessing of the existing forms of communication and the development of new ones to this end. The range of strategies included regular research sections in staff bulletins, specific research reports, the development of research sections on school websites (e.g. www.sohamcollege.org.uk/knowledge creation) and staff presentations at schools' professional development days.

Engaging with the issues of research quality

The idea of critical discourse is that through such debates the quality of the work will be examined and the quality enhanced. Within the partnership schools there were some limited examples of practitioners wrestling with this question. In one school they engaged with it over time and proposed three criteria for their research:

> The validation of the knowledge was seen as coming from three sources. It was a triangle of teacher experience and reflection; data on pupil outcomes; and data on the pupils' experience and attitudes. This was seen as giving it credibility.
>
> (TRC)

These criteria are different from the conventional ones used to validate academic knowledge. They are criteria for judging and learning about the effectiveness of teaching practices. They are persuasive to this end but they indicate a shift from validating knowledge to validating practices of teaching.

HOW WAS PRACTITIONER RESEARCH DEVELOPED AND SUSTAINED?

Development was visible: developments in thinking as well as developments in practice. It was dynamic, and the principle of gradualism was also visible. Many of the leaders of the activity within the schools saw that they needed to move slowly to develop a research culture (Ebbutt, 2002) and that this often began with the involvement of a few enthusiastic volunteers and then moved to a more sustained engagement with research either through departments or through themes. In some schools the process materialised more quickly than in others. The process of acquiring knowledge through research and disseminating or translating that into action is a longer one than the school research leaders anticipated:

> One way of seeing the differences between the research cultures of the schools that I have described is to view them as a series of developmental stages along an evolutionary path. The implication of this observation is that should schools wish to develop to the point of embracing an embedded research culture, they will need to evolve through the prior stages: 'no culture of research', 'emergent research culture', 'established research culture,' to 'established-embedded research culture'.
>
> (Ebbutt, 2002, p. 138)

The original aims of SUPER were to work together in partnership but initially there was an emphasis on the partnership with the university. This was highly valued and was the primary impetus for the formation of SUPER. The developments then can be seen at different levels: the development of the school as a researching school; the development of the network of schools; and the development of schools–university partnerships. The schools valued their connections with each other, and much sharing of research outcomes as well as ideas for developing the use of, and engagement with, research occurred at the TRC and other meetings. However, initially the focus on developing a research culture and practice within the schools absorbed much of the energy. When the partnership went into the NLC programme certain developments occurred and enhanced smaller processes that had been occurring. So meetings of head teachers received more emphasis and happened more frequently. The development of the work across the schools also took time, and many mechanisms were used to enhance it: the introduction of a website; the use of SUPER sheets to share research findings; annual teaching and learning conferences where researchers shared their findings; and an annual residential where planning and reviewing the work of the network took place. The network was characterised by participants at one of these residential meetings as being like a wheel with a hub and spokes: that is, the university was the hub and the schools were the spokes. What was also at the hub of the work was the schools' own research agendas, and the loose coupling seemed to suit the schools well.

Alignment

Gardner et al.'s (2006) concept of alignment proved useful in exploring an aspect of the development of a research culture and practice:

In alignment, all of the various interest groups basically call for the same kinds of performances . . . 'Good work' is most likely to occur when four forces all point in the same direction. When professional standards, peer behavior, internal values and social values all tell us to do the same thing, there is no problem.

(Gardner *et al.*, 2006, p. 19)

Two key processes seemed important. First was that the values and beliefs in the nature of the enterprise were shared between the leaders of research and the wider groups. Second was the notion of harnessing forces to support the processes and not allowing major forces to inhibit the work. In one school the structures and processes of management and communication were all shifted to support the process of teacher research, so there was a flow to the activity. The school allocated finance and allotted curriculum time to departments. The work done fed into the teaching and learning policy of the school. In this school those engaged in research had to battle with the impressive enough problems of the research itself rather than the problems of time, resources and space. In other schools BPRS was cited as a significant element. It could be seen as a force for alignment providing status, structure, and finance to buy time and resources. In the absence of BPRS many of the schools in these cases went on to provide these listed elements from their own resources. The subject department seemed to be an undervalued force here.

Structures and support

Even when school management favoured a research culture and encouraged teacher research, *and* made resources available to teachers to support research, this did not ensure widespread research activity. It seemed that part of establishing and maintaining a research culture entailed providing structures that support staff in their research. These structures went beyond rhetoric and even the availability of funding. All schools had a commitment to developing research cultures and had, albeit limited, funding available for staff to undertake research. The level of research activity was variable, both across schools and within some schools across time.

Three roles emerged as important over time. They were the roles of the TRC, the critical friend and the SVC. The TRC was seen as pivotal. The SVC role was seen as more suited for an enthusiast than a senior manager. However, at one school it was decided to make student voice part of a senior management role, and this was seen as an important and effective commitment to such work in that school. The critical friend role was constantly cited as important in bringing resources from beyond the school, supporting individuals or groups of researchers, providing research training and expertise and bringing an external dispassionate and different perspective to the work. Giving critical constructive feedback to the school about the research endeavours of its members was also highly valued. Furthermore, in many of the schools the subject department was an organising structure and this was a fit with normal collaborative structures that many schools found useful.

IMPACT ON TEACHERS AND STUDENTS

Claims for the impact of the SUPER endeavour are hard to make as it is hard to isolate any direct effects in such complex organisations. However, staff in many of the schools did see the research activity as contributing directly to students' achievement and school improvement. The teacher researchers spoke strongly of the impact on their sense of professional identity, sense of autonomy, motivation and professional regeneration. Many of the school leaders supported and underlined this. One head teacher considered teacher research as a key strategy for the retention of staff.

There were examples within the schools of major and minor changes in practice as a result of teacher research. The degree to which the schools embedded the changed practices varied from making it a central plank of school policy on teaching and learning to listening to the outcomes of the research work but not necessarily supporting its institutionalisation, which may or may not be appropriate. In one school, for example, the teacher researchers were given allocated school finance to hold a position as a researcher within a department for a year. During this year they undertook a research project within their own classroom and then extended it to other departmental colleagues to test the findings. The results of this process were then fed into the teaching and learning policy within the school. In another school, the teachers chose their focus and worked individually on their projects, sharing them with colleagues at staff meetings and conferences. They demonstrate the multiplicity of purposes and variety of practices that occurred under the umbrella of engaging in research as a school.

Chapter 11

South West London Networked Learning Community

Collaborating in action research

Kristine Black-Hawkins

Membership of this network comprised one junior and five (previously six) secondary schools, all within the London Borough of Hounslow. The over-arching purpose of the network was the improvement of students' academic achievements through the development of higher-order thinking skills, with a particular emphasis on teaching and learning within the science curriculum. The primary means of realising this aim had been through the provision of opportunities for teachers to engage collaboratively in research and enquiry activities that focused on the development of their classroom practices. Funding from the NLC had largely been used to support this work, including the dissemination of research findings as well as the sharing of associated teaching and learning materials with all teachers across the network via a CD-ROM.

Schools in this LA had not necessarily had a strong history of working together, although since the borough became part of the Excellence in Cities initiative (DfES, 1999) there had been greater opportunities and incentives for collaboration. An example of this was the establishment of an LA co-ordinator to support 'gifted and talented' students, across a group of fourteen schools. The postholder was also one of the two co-leaders of the NLC; the other was an assistant head teacher in one of the network schools. Both had considerable experience of supporting teachers' professional development and between them had taught in a number of different schools within the LA. The network also developed links with a member of the academic staff from St Mary's University College, London, who provided research skills training for the teacher researchers. Finally, a critical friend from the Institute of Education, University of London, had offered advice on, and evaluation of, the network's activities.

The LA has 'a low socio-economic profile in many areas' (NLC bid), although some parts are more affluent than others. Although the six schools that formed the network are all relatively close to each other geographically, there are important variations among them. The most obvious distinction is that only one is a junior school: the network was originally for secondary schools only. However, the NLC bid also noted that, across the LA, progress

Table 11.1 Background details of South West London NLC

Total number of schools = six
• five (previously six) secondary, plus one junior
• some single sex, some mixed girls and boys
• some faith based schools, some non-denominational

Other links and partners:
• Excellence in Cities, including 'Gifted and Talented' network
• London Borough of Hounslow LA
• St Mary's University College, London
• external critical friend

Approximate number of teachers = six hundred

First cohort of NLCs (funded for 2002–2005)

Some features of this network:
• schools were geographically close to one another but varied in student intake
• research and enquiry were undertaken in the form of collaborative (paired) action research
• research and enquiry were focused on 'raising standards' through improving classroom practices, with an emphasis on science and foundation subjects
• research capacity in the schools was to be built through a teacher coaching scheme

in primary science was generally better than at secondary level. The later inclusion of a junior school in the network therefore provided opportunities for the secondary teachers to benefit from the experiences of their primary colleagues. Among the five secondary schools there are significant differences in student intake. Two of the schools are for girls only and three are co-educational; one is Church of England, four are non-denominational. In one school, over seventy per cent of students are classified as being of ethnic minority descent, whereas in another the figure is eighteen per cent, with student intake being predominantly white. Examination results also vary, and local perceptions are that some schools are 'better' than others; certainly some are more popular with parents/carers. When the network was first formed, students achieving five or more GCSEs at grade C or above in the five schools ranged from twenty-eight per cent to sixty-five per cent (LA average = 49.5 per cent; national average = 51.6 per cent; DfES, 2002b). See Table 11.1 for further background details about the network.

DEVELOPING TEACHING AND LEARNING THROUGH PLANNED COLLABORATIVE RESEARCH AND ENQUIRY

From its inception the primary function of this network was the development of collaborative practitioner research and enquiry. However, the nature of

Table 11.2 Key purposes of research in South West London NLC

- The teaching and learning of science
- The development of students' higher-order thinking skills
- Teacher collaboration within the same school, across different curriculum areas
- Teacher collaboration within the network, across different schools
- The development of leadership skills and qualities in the teacher researchers

the research that took place was clearly shaped by previously identified concerns about teaching and learning across the network and within the LA more generally. Research in this network therefore particularly focused on bringing about improvements in the areas noted in Table 11.2.

The focus on science was especially relevant to the network's overall approach to research. In the bid to become a NLC, concerns about science teaching were described as follows:

> There is a widespread pattern of underachievement in science. This has been exacerbated by the impact of the recruitment crisis and the turbulence of staff which has resulted. Science teachers, in particular, are now having to take on the training and support of temporary and overseas trained colleagues.

Practitioner research was seen as having the potential not only to support the recruitment and retention of science teachers but also to provide much needed professional development for those in post but with limited experience of science teaching in the UK. Furthermore, by building in opportunities to research collaboratively with teachers from other subject areas and different schools, but always with a sharp focus on thinking skills, the intention was to improve students' learning across the curriculum.

Although these may seem a highly ambitious set of expectations for practitioner research, a carefully staged programme was devised to support the work of cross-curricular research (see Table 11.3).

Table 11.3 Programme for practitioner research in South West London NLC

Year	Number of researchers ... at each school	... in the network
1	×1 science teacher + ×1 foundation subject teacher	2 × 6 = 12
2	×2 science teachers + ×2 foundation subject teachers	4 × 6 = 24
3	×4 science teachers + ×4 foundation subject teachers	8 × 6 = 48
4 →	continue to expand ...	????

This gradual process was seen as important: as one co-leader explained, they were 'starting from scratch . . . no history of research in the schools'. In the first year, therefore, there were to be two teachers (one science and one foundation subject) working together on a research project in which they had a common interest, question or concern. They were to be provided with research skills training and support from St Mary's University College, London. In the second year, the original pair of teachers were to induct two more colleagues into the research process, so that there would be four practitioner researchers in each of the schools. In the following and subsequent years the numbers of teachers engaging in research would increase further, building on the developing knowledge and expertise in the schools, including opportunities for cross network research. An important intention here was also to develop qualities of leadership in experienced teacher researchers as they supported others in their schools.

While this programme provided a framework for the research, in terms of numbers of teachers involved as well as expectations about collaborative working practices, it was also sufficiently flexible to support and encourage a wide variety of research activities to take place. Table 11.4 provides some examples of the topics of research carried out by teachers in year one.

All these topics fitted into the network's theme of developing students' higher-order thinking skills. Beyond that, teacher researchers were strongly encouraged to identify problems, interests or needs that focused on their own classroom experiences. This 'ownership' of the focus was considered to be very important to the development of the research. One of the co-leaders explained:

> [We] start from . . . the teachers' needs . . . 'What are the gifts, what are the challenges, what are the passions that this particular person has

Table 11.4 Research topics undertaken in the first year of the South West London NLC

- 'Adding value to learning': the usefulness etc. of homework to students (science and geography)
- 'The mind's inner eye – independent learning by reflection': students reflecting on their learning and learning style (science and history)
- 'Altered images – reflecting changing perceptions by pupils of themselves as learners' (science and geography)
- 'Investigation into transition between KS4 and KS5': Developing strategies to raise 'added value' in exam results (science and French)
- 'Road maps and signposts – drawing independent conclusions': developing organisational structures that pupils can use to organise their own thinking (science and history)
- 'The question tree – fruitful questioning beyond the question mark': Developing higher-order thinking skills for children and staff, based on Bloom's taxonomy (two class teachers, junior school)

got? And, how can we harness these to move the school on?' . . . If you allow people to do that which they're passionate about they will do it much better . . . if you employ people who are questioning about their own practice, the nature of the school in which they are, their work will throw up questions that they want to find answers to. And if you enable them to identify and then chase those questions, you are . . . naturally then answering the school's problems because the problems that they are interested in have evolved from the school.

Within these parameters there was a general agreement among those members of the network who were interviewed that the methodological framework that they used was an action research model. This had been shaped by the research training provided by St Mary's College, in conjunction with the co-leaders. For practitioners, action research was seen as a pragmatic and robust response to their classroom concerns: a process involving the identification of a professional problem or interest, the implementation of a programme of change and the evaluation of the effects of doing so. This understanding is illustrated by the following comments from two of the teachers:

> At the beginning I associated action research with something very academic . . . that you might do at university . . . that required lots of data collection . . . to do with producing an end piece which was reams of paper or a big thesis . . . Now I just think of action research as enquiry, as doing what I do anyway as a teacher, being reflective about the kind of practice I use in my classroom, about the way in which I teach the children, but just making it a bit more evidenced based.
>
> You obviously have to have something to measure. In terms of . . . classroom practices it's seeing whether this thing that you're looking at has any impact on your class . . . If I use this in my classroom will it improve the things that I'm trying to improve? . . . So for us it was thinking skills . . . what tools can we use to improve thinking skills?

As might be expected, members of senior management teams viewed action research as contributing both to the professional development of individual teachers and also more broadly to the school as a whole. Such purposes are evident in the two statements below.

> There has been thinking and reading and understanding of what we're doing . . . As an outcome of this, [name] and [name] are more reflective teachers . . . I think anything that will move people's thinking towards not just the difficulties and the problems but the possibilities . . . It's that reflective learner which is what we're all meant to be as teachers but in reality very few people are.

Action research ... challenges what I think we often get in teaching which is: This is what happens in my classroom therefore I know it to be true' ... We've tried within the school to encourage the staff to be critical, not destructively critical, but to ask difficult questions ... in a constructive manner. We don't see it as challenging. We see it as part of a healthy school.

PUTTING THE PROGRAMME INTO PRACTICE: SUCCESSES AND CHALLENGES

The programme for research (Table 11.3) was more effectively implemented in some schools than in others. One co-leader noted that, as collaboration was expected from the start, the original pairing of researchers proved to be 'crucial'. That is, it worked particularly well when the teachers were mutually supportive and encouraging: keen to learn together and share ideas, methods and materials. She also highlighted two key characteristics of those researchers most likely to persuade further colleagues to engage in and/or with research. These were to be 'passionate advocates' of practitioner enquiry and to be highly respected by other staff in terms of 'classroom credibility'.

All interviewees involved in the first year of the programme greatly appreciated the research training provided at cross-network meetings. These were co-ordinated by a member of staff from St Mary's College who was particularly valued for her support and guidance. An assistant head teacher from one school described her as being 'an absolute star'. The following comment by a year one researcher is also typical: 'She was really influential ... really good at talking us through the process ... making sure that we had all those different elements incorporated in our projects ... giving us the confidence.'

From year two onwards the amount of research training provided was reduced because new researchers were expected to be supported within their schools by year one 'mentors'. However, this approach encountered some important and unanticipated difficulties. Most notably, its success was largely dependent on the first pair of teachers remaining involved in the research programme so that they could provide the induction for colleagues. In a number of schools some of these key staff left, others stayed but withdrew from the research. In one school, for example, the year one researchers dropped out of the programme because of other pressures on their time and were not able to support their new year two colleagues. Instead of being part of a group of four, the latter found themselves in the same position as year one researchers a year earlier, but without the training programme provided by the HEI. Such circumstances also brought about other tensions across the network when researchers from years one and two from different schools came together for meetings. One of the year one teachers expressed her concerns as follows:

We found it hard in the second year. In the first year it was fine. There were only two researchers from every school and everyone was very eager but in the second year when we had two more researchers come aboard from each school it was really hard to integrate them . . . At the beginning we all had the same starting point: we were all brand new, didn't know anything about action research. In second year . . . we wanted to move on . . . but we'd taken on some new second year researchers as well, so do we start from the beginning?

Indeed, the staged process (Table 11.3) was only being fully implemented at the junior school: that is, developing from two, to four, to eight practitioner researchers over the first three years. Interestingly, at this school the original model had been expanded so that *all* teachers were expected to be involved in action research activities.

The co-leaders summarised the main practical difficulties facing the schools as being:

- establishing a common research strand, across each pair of teachers
- inducting or coaching new researchers, for example, from year one to year two
- the specific, and often challenging, circumstances of some schools, particularly staff shortages
- key teachers moving to other schools so that, even if excellent research has taken place, it becomes difficult to sustain

Some teachers identified an additional problem regarding attendance at network meetings. They articulated a strong commitment regarding not leaving their classes unless they were appropriately staffed, and this had not always been straightforward for those schools where it was less easy to ensure suitable 'supply cover'. Furthermore, irregular attendance at meetings was considered to affect the continuity of the shared work across the network.

The success of the research undertaken in individual schools had partly been determined by the level of support it was given by head teachers and their senior management teams. Particularly important was the provision, by head teachers, of opportunities for researchers to share their findings with colleagues in ways that were likely to make a difference to classroom practices across the school. One of the head teachers explained:

Where the head teacher has clearly made a commitment, a real, real commitment, then it's been more successful. It goes without saying . . . Because then it is going to be in the School Development Plan . . . It is going to have a profile within the school. . . . Where those heads have teaching and learning at the heart of their school and driving their school, you've got more effective action research going on.

(Head teacher)

Head teachers had also had an important role to play in terms of their involvement in the network's steering group, which had overseen planning, including the financing of the research activities.

In some schools it had been possible to be a highly enthusiastic and competent researcher and yet have a limited impact on the teaching and learning taking place outside one's own classroom. One co-leader argued that head teachers had to 'make time and space for [research] to happen'. At the same time, she acknowledged that this had not always been straight-forward: there were 'competing priorities for management [who] therefore intellectually understand but cannot always support in terms of giving time'. She described one head teacher who was keen to participate but because of 'challenging circumstances and shortage of teachers [was . . .] struggling to maintain momentum'. By year three, this school only had three teacher researchers in place rather than eight as planned.

More generally, interviewees (co-leaders, teachers and senior staff in schools) referred to the importance of the culture of a school in terms of providing a suitable environment in which practitioner research could flourish. However, the notion of a causal relationship between a school's culture and school based research was seen as problematic. Some argued that those schools most in need of the benefits of being involved in such work might also be the least likely to have the capacity to do so, not only in terms of time and resources but also with regard to the leadership skills of their management teams. So whereas one person noted, 'We need to engender a culture of enquiry in the schools', another described a primary purpose of the network as being to 'Create a culture of innovation, creativity, risk-taking'.

SUSTAINING RESEARCH AND ENQUIRY IN THE SCHOOLS AND THE NETWORK

The following are some of the key ways in which the effective use of research and enquiry in this network had been supported and sustained:

- The sharp focus on teachers' own classroom interests and problems had helped to sustain the research activities in some schools. Making a difference to the learning experiences of students had remained a central concern of the researchers.
- Although the development of paired researchers had encountered some difficulties in some schools, where it had been successful it had worked very well, providing mutual support, encouragement and intellectual rigour, which together enhanced the quality of the research undertaken.
- In some schools the role of research mentor/coach had provided important opportunities to develop the leadership qualities of teachers who were not necessarily part of the established school management structures.

This, in turn, had enhanced job satisfaction and might have also contributed to the retention of such staff.

- The research training provided by the HEI had been crucial to the success of research activities, offering useful technical skills and knowledge to teachers as well as developing their confidence. It had also allowed a shared language and understanding across the group of researchers, thus supporting their learning as a network.
- The role of the co-leaders had been important in supporting the research. They had guided and promoted the work of individual researchers as well as maintained communications across the network, research training and other associated activities. In particular, they co-ordinated the production of a CD-ROM to provide access to the research for all teachers in the network and not just those directly involved.

Chapter 12

Surrey LIFE Networked Learning Community

Learning (and research) is for everyone

Kristine Black-Hawkins

Membership of this network comprised all ten of the special schools, within Surrey's LA, that are designated for children and young people identified as having severe learning difficulties (SLD). Some of these schools also offer specialist provision for students with other associated disabilities; for example, profound and multiple learning difficulties (PMLD) and/or students identified as having autistic spectrum disorders (ASD). Eight are all-age schools, and two schools cater for secondary students only; together they provide education for children and young people aged two to nineteen years old, from nursery through to further education (FE). The acronym LIFE stands for Learning and Inclusion For Everyone. This refers to the network's overall aim to support the learning of *all* children and young people in Surrey identified as having SLD. Thus, an intended focus was to develop outreach work from the special schools to children and young people in local mainstream schools and colleges. The network originally planned to work with the University of Kingston and Surrey LA; however, circumstances, such as staffing changes in those organisations, meant that such collaboration was minimal. Some members of the network found especially helpful the support provided by the NLC group, as is evident in their attendance at NLC meetings and use of their materials.

Relationships between the ten schools were described, by those interviewed, as being good and are certainly not constrained by the kinds of competitiveness that sometimes existed between mainstream schools in other networks. More than twenty years before Surrey LIFE was established, the head teachers of these special schools had formed a consortium that continues to meet regularly to discuss common concerns and to share ideas. Over the years, comfortable working relationships developed, and new head teachers were welcomed into the group. The consortium then became the steering group for the network, and all co-leaders were selected from its head teacher membership.

However, there had been fewer opportunities for other staff to meet together across the schools or to share resources. Two practical reasons hindered such activities. First, the ten schools are spread out across the county of Surrey: travelling between them can take considerable time, not least because of traffic congestion. Second, staff–student ratios are critical in special school settings. Releasing teachers from the classroom is not straightforward, and the use of supply teachers requires very careful management. Furthermore, a distinctive feature of Surrey LIFE is that there are more teaching assistants (TAs) than teachers working in its schools. Not only is it difficult to release TAs from the classroom, but also they mainly work school hours only, and so after-school meetings are unsustainable.

Surrey LIFE was part of the second cohort of NLCs, formed in September 2003. Evidence for this case study was gathered when it had been operating for just over a year. Because the network had had little support from external institutions (apart from the NLC group) it had been almost entirely reliant on its own members to provide research skills training and to organise structures to support research and enquiry activities in and across the schools. The steering group, understandably, had taken some time to put into place such arrangements, not least because the headteachers were keen to ensure that any changes would be sustainable after the network funding ended. Therefore, the emphasis of this case study report is on what might be learnt when a network of schools, with common interests and shared histories, sets out to *develop* collaborative practitioner research and enquiry. See Table 12.1 for further background details about the network.

Table 12.1 Background to Surrey LIFE NLC

Total number of schools = ten
• eight all age, two secondary/FE only (including ages from two to nineteen years)
• all mixed girls and boys
• all special schools, for children and young people designated as having SLD and other associated disabilities
Other links and partners:
• Surrey LA
• University of Kingston

Approximate number of teachers = two hundred and fifty

Approximate number of teaching assistants = four hundred

Second cohort of NLCs (funded for 2003–2006)

Some features of this network:
• the head teachers from all ten schools had worked together as a consortium for over twenty years before the NLC was formed
• the head teachers took responsibility for the network's key roles as co-leaders and members of its steering group
• each school had established a 'research co-ordinator'
• the majority of the staff in the schools are TAs and they were actively encouraged to be involved in the network
• activities to encourage 'pupil voice' in these special schools posed particular challenges for teachers because of the communication and other learning difficulties of the pupils

ESTABLISHING STRUCTURES TO DEVELOP RESEARCH AND ENQUIRY

In addition to the steering group, referred to above, the following research related groups and activities were introduced. Some had become more firmly established than others during the period of our case study visits.

- research co-ordinators' group
- teacher research group for student voice
- assistants' group
- learning walks.

All included a strong focus on school-to-school learning. Their intention was to draw on and to share a range of colleagues' experiences from across the network.

The research co-ordinators' group

Although this was the last of the groups to be formed, it seemed likely to be particularly important in determining the use of research and enquiry in the schools and across the network. Therefore understandings of research and enquiry among its members are also likely to be influential to this work. Its first formal meeting was in March 2005, some eighteen months after the network had started. It comprised one teacher from each of the ten schools plus two of the head teachers who were particularly keen to support practitioner research and enquiry. During this first meeting a general discussion took place about the role of the research co-ordinator, and the following key elements were identified and recorded (see Table 12.2).

A further discussion took place about the nature and purposes of practitioner research and enquiry in the context of Surrey LIFE. There emerged a high level of agreement amongst the group. Table 12.3 provides a summary of the key points recorded.

Table 12.2 Role of the research co-ordinator

- have an oversight of research in own school
- have an oversight of literature resources
- link with CPD co-ordinator
- set up [school] systems and structures for sharing and giving feedback
- attend LIFE research co-ordinator meetings and training sessions
- contribute to LIFE website
- develop research plan [for own school and for network]
- develop research links with other networks/mainstream schools
- bid for funding

Table 12.3 Research and enquiry are . . .

- tools to formalise what we are doing: more focused, disciplined and structured, involving rigour in what we do, looking at things more deeply
- asking questions, getting answers and doing something about it
- staff working together in a collaborative way: sharing and developing ideas; sharing results
- having the space and confidence to try things out, take risks
- adding the knowledge and research from outside our own schools

One of the head teacher members of this group described her understanding of practitioner research in terms of 'action research' focusing on school and classroom based issues:

> It's not traditional research in the sense of . . . data collection . . . to see if that group's better than this group. It's really more I've got this idea or . . . problem about what's not working right and I've really got to look at it . . . in that more structured rigorous way, having the time and the focus to read up about it, see what other people are doing.

The teacher research group for pupil voice

The pupil voice group was established early on in the network and then met regularly. It comprised one teacher from each of the schools, plus one of the head teachers. Its work was considered to be highly important by some, especially as many children and young people in Surrey LIFE experience different kinds of communication difficulty. One member of staff noted, 'Our students are done to all the time and it's very hard to get a pupil voice'. Providing a range of appropriate means by which the voices of students can be heard was challenging for staff, and a number of creative approaches had been developed, such as using photographs, signing and symbols. Across the network two particular aspects of this work were emphasised: first, the development of student councils and, second, greater student involvement in annual reviews and also the associated Individual Education Plans (IEPs). (These relate to the statutory requirements and procedures for students with Statements of Special Educational Needs.)

Up until the period of the case study, members of the group had concentrated on learning from each other's experiences and sharing classroom expertise, strategies and techniques. There was clear evidence that they considered these types of activity to be useful and that they had strengthened professional dialogue between teachers from different schools.

> You hear about . . . a new idea or technique. Well, let's try this or let's try that, finding out in that kind of way . . . We'll discuss it and then

we all go away and implement something and then obviously with our findings we come back and . . . we discuss again.

The steering group's intention that pupil voice work should also be research focused, as noted in its name, had not at that stage been realised. However, it was hoped that the developing role of the research co-ordinators in each school would support this proposed shift in emphasis.

Assistants' group

As the majority of staff in the network's schools were TAs rather than teachers this was a potentially important group. From the start, and in contrast to many other networks, TAs had been given the opportunity to participate in the work taking place in Surrey LIFE. The group had, however, encountered some difficulties in terms of its members having sufficient time, first, to attend network meetings and, second, to exchange what they had learnt with colleagues in their own schools. A number of approaches had been introduced to help to alleviate this: for example, the group were producing a network booklet to help disseminate their work. Within their own schools, some TAs had tried out 'job-swapping' and others had organised a series of highly focused but brief (say, 15 minutes) observations of colleagues. As with pupil voice, this group had concentrated initially on sharing classroom expertise, strategies and techniques, rather than engaging in research and enquiry *per se*.

Learning walks

The network had set up a extensive programme of 'learning walks': an idea based on the work of Lauren Resnick and introduced in Surrey LIFE by an NLC facilitator. The focus of these activities had been the role of the TAs. Schools had formed pairs and arranged reciprocal visits involving one member of the senior management team, a teacher and a TA from each school. Immediately after each visit, a head teacher from a third school joined this trio to lead a discussion about what has been observed. From this, three ideas were identified by each visitor to become planned developments to try out in their own school.

Responses to the learning walks had generally been positive. They had helped to increase some members' sense of being part of a network as well as having generated excitement and interest about learning from others. One TA described her enthusiasm for visiting other schools:

I'd love to be able to go and see all the schools . . . It's hard in school because you're always rushing around so it is nice when you out of school without [your] children around . . . It helps because [TAs in other schools] can say we tried that and it didn't work for us and we can say it's not working too bad for us.

Other staff had been less supportive of the scheme. One head teacher maintained its value largely depended on which schools you worked at and which school you visited. She argued that her staff 'can't really learn anything from some schools'. Some teachers suggested that the walks, rather than providing them with new ideas, simply affirmed their existing practices: 'Shows us how good we are'. The process of identifying three developments had also encountered some difficulties in terms of its practical application. One head teacher explained:

> They are all so excited but nobody knows what anyone's doing . . . It wasn't until . . . the other week and I said to [another head teacher] 'Do you know what they're up to? What are people doing?' We hadn't shared it at all . . . their targets [. . . don't] necessarily fit into any of the school plans.

THE PURPOSE OF RESEARCH AND ITS BENEFITS TO SCHOOLS

The groups and activities described above contributed to the development of some network members' understanding of the purposes of research and enquiry. They had also brought some benefits to the schools. It was interesting to note that, in Surrey LIFE, a wide range of members considered themselves as being engaged in research activities, including head teachers, teachers and TAs. They described their work in terms of being 'exciting', 'motivating' and 'rewarding'. This sense of democratic involvement was different from that found in many other NLCs, where it was predominantly teachers only who undertook research and enquiry.

All those interviewed and observed talked about the reason for their involvement in terms of improving teaching and learning in their classrooms and schools. This view was certainly reiterated throughout all six of our NLC case studies, but for Surrey LIFE this particularly related to their working in special education and specifically in schools designated for children and young people identified as having SLDs. They considered much of the professional development currently available for teachers, as well as published research, to be inappropriate to their students and schools. As one teacher noted, 'When it gets to severe learning difficulties, it gets more and more specialist'. Another indicated: 'In a special school . . . pupils will not respond to something that's not going to work for them, so we have to change, we have to adapt'.

Engaging in research and enquiry, and sharing their findings with others in the network, seemed really important for some of its members. A research co-ordinator in one of the schools explained her frustration when she first implemented the national literacy strategy a few years ago, because available support materials were designed for mainstream classes and were unsuitable for her students. This, however, gave her the impetus to undertake her own research as part of a Masters degree. She went on to explain: '[Now] I think that I am a much, much better literacy teacher for doing it . . . it gave me the chance to reflect and write . . . and get it all clear in my mind'. The same teacher described her current enthusiasm about taking on the role of research co-ordinator for her school and being part of a network in which research took place. She hoped that doing so would provide a pool of relevant and useful research knowledge on which she could then draw.

> I'm really excited because I know that whoever I meet [in the research co-ordinators' group] is going to be doing something that is probably relevant to me as a teacher in such a specialist area of education . . . Everyone coming together as . . . a network of people means that there will be discussion across the schools.

The purpose of research and enquiry in terms of bringing about school-to-school learning as well as alleviating the isolation of special schools was evident from teachers, TAs and head teachers throughout this case study. Some argued that engaging in research helped to reduce their separateness from the mainstream, not only in practical ways, but also in terms of how they were valued as professionals. As one head teacher explained, 'I've always wanted people to do . . . research to prove that we're part of the profession and we're worth something'.

INITIATING AND SUSTAINING THE DEVELOPMENT OF RESEARCH AND ENQUIRY IN THE SCHOOLS AND ACROSS THE NETWORK

Discussing how the effective use of research and enquiry was being sustained in Surrey LIFE is not straightforward, as its work was very much at a development stage. Nevertheless, the following points may provide some useful guidance about a group of schools coming together to set up collaborative practitioner research:

• The long-standing relationship between the head teachers was a real strength of this network in terms of their knowledge about each other's schools and their willingness to work together. Their commitment as a group to the network was indicated in their formulation and full membership of the network steering group, including their decision that all three co-leaders should be head teachers.

- The determination of the steering group to be mindful of sustainability, from the beginning of Surrey LIFE, was likely to be a strength when developing practitioner research and enquiry. Initial activities had been focused on establishing structures (such as, the role of research co-ordinators and the pupil voice and TA groups) rather than on short-term research projects. However, the issue of attendance for teachers and especially TAs remained unresolved in some schools, and this may continue to hamper longer-term sustainability.

- Another early decision, likely to effect the sustainability of research and enquiry in the network, was the involvement of a wide range of staff in each of the schools. Head teachers, teachers and TAs had all had opportunities to engage in network activities and these different perspectives were likely to strengthen the work undertaken.

- The early focus on school-to-school learning, through the sharing of resources and ideas, provided important opportunities for networking among members of the schools and this may well help to build a strong foundation for future across-school collaborative research and enquiry.

- The role of the NLC group had been important in terms of providing resources to support research and enquiry through meetings, events and materials. However, the provision of research support by an external institution also seemed necessary so as to supplement the knowledge and experience that already existed in the schools.

Chapter 13

Researching in networks

The views of practitioners

Andrew Townsend

INTRODUCTION

The research that underpins this book utilised a variety of methods to collect data. These included: questionnaires, interviews, observations and examinations of network documentation that, together, gave a detailed picture of how each participating network had approached enquiry and the effect that these differing approaches had on the subsequent recognition, creation and use of knowledge by network members. This chapter is principally concerned with an exploration of data from the questionnaire completed by all participants and is structured around the following themes:

* the characteristics of networked enquiry
* the nature of enquiry and enquirers
* the processes of enquiry
* changes resulting from enquiry
* implications for practice and for networking.

Before the issues above are explored, the design and use of the questionnaire element of this research are described.

INVESTIGATING NETWORKS OF ENQUIRY

Enquiry was just one of the aspects of networking identified by the Networked Learning Group at the NCSL. In this context the term enquiry was used to describe a variety of approaches to developing practice including:

* collaborative action research
* teachers conducting research commissioned by the NCSL
* collaborative teaching developments
* school visits, where groups of practitioners would observe the practice of colleagues in the network

The networks discussed in this book all adopted the first of these forms of enquiry, namely an approach most closely related to practitioner action research (Winter, 1989). This was also the most fundamental to the design of the NLCs, being described as one of the basic principles underlying the creation of the networks in the first place (Jackson, 2002b). Questionnaires were completed by a mixture of network members, not all of whom were active in enquiry. This allowed a comparison of the views of network members who had actively engaged with those who had been involved in other elements of network activities. Indeed the design of the questionnaire was made with these sorts of comparison in mind, and had three sections dealing with:

*   section one: an exploration of respondent characteristics, including years of experience, management positions held and nature of school.
*   section two: the conduct of enquiry; this section was only completed by active enquirers and asked respondents to describe the dimensions of their work, such as the focus of their change, their motivations for becoming involved in enquiry etc.
*   section three: attitudes to enquiry; this final section had a series of opposing statements investigating different attitudes towards enquiry. Respondents identified their own view on a five point rating scale (Cohen et al., 2000, pp. 252–4). This section, like section one, was completed by all participants.

Questionnaires were completed by a total of 650 respondents, across all six of the networks, of whom 345 identified themselves as being active enquirers (55.5 per cent). This questionnaire used a variety of question types, including dichotomous (yes/no), multiple choice, rating scales and open-ended questions providing participants with the options to make further comment on their responses. Tests suggested that responses to this questionnaire were sufficiently reliable to justify a statistical analysis, and so an analysis was conducted around the themes identified above.[1] The most interesting outcomes of this analysis are discussed below. The first of these deals with the nature of enquirers and enquiry.

THE CHARACTERISTIC OF ENQUIRY IN THESE NETWORKS

Each of the networks studied had different reasons for working together; they incorporated different sorts of school and had varied foci for development. Some, such as the Blackburn with Darwen network, were constructed purely of one type of school, in this case secondary schools, whereas others were mixed, serving a range of pupil ages. Of these networks, Surrey LIFE had the widest range of pupil ages, although this network was unique as it was

Table 13.1 Network membership by responsibility

Network	SUPER	Surrey LIFE	Bristol	Hartlepool	SW London	Blackburn
Class teacher	181	47	26	109	27	32
Deputy head teacher	9	5	4	8	3	4
Head teacher	2	6	1	5	1	0
Key stage co-ordinator	28	9	3	12	1	3
Subject co-ordinator/ head of department	62	36	16	49	10	15
Pastoral responsibility	50	1	2	23	7	5
TA	0	78	3	1	1	0
Learning support teacher	6	5	2	2	0	2
Other responsibilities	33	20	0	20	10	8

composed entirely of schools serving only pupils who had been identified as having special educational needs.

The nature of involvement in the enquiry elements of these networks also varied. In some networks enquiry was targeted at particular groups, such as teachers of a particular subject or at people with specific responsibilities in schools, learning assistants, for example. The breakdown of responsibility by network is shown in Table 13.1. It should be noted that some network members had multiple roles, especially those from small schools (including many of the primary schools) and so would have completed more than one response for this questionnaire item.

THE NATURE OF ENQUIRY AND ENQUIRERS

Respondents had a range of different positions and responsibilities within their schools. The largest group of respondents by responsibility was, perhaps unsurprisingly, of class teachers (406), whereas the smallest was of head teachers (fifteen). It is interesting to note that a far higher proportion of head teachers identified themselves as being active in the enquiry dimension of their network (eighty per cent), in comparison with respondents who had other responsibilities. However, as noted, the actual number of head teachers who completed a questionnaire was very small and precludes a more detailed examination of the interaction of leadership and enquiry here.

Section one of the questionnaire allowed a comparison of the numbers of respondents from each area of responsibility who identified themselves as enquirers; this is shown in Table 13.2. Of all of the areas recorded, only TAs had an involvement in enquiry of less than fifty per cent, but even in this case the sample still had an appreciable proportion of enquirers (of the seventy-eight respondents who identified themselves as TAs thirty-three, or

Table 13.2 Percentage of active enquirers by school responsibility

	Enquirers (%)
Class teacher	57.64
TA	42.31
Deputy head teacher	66.67
Head teacher	80.00
Key stage co-ordinator	63.64
Subject co-ordinator/head of department	66.67
Pastoral responsibility	52.44
Learning support teacher	56.25
Other responsibilities	65.91

fourty-two per cent, identified themselves as being active enquirers). Nevertheless, the spread of respondents across all categories does reflect the diversity of the different types of network studied and also indicates a similarly broad range of participation in enquiry within these networks.

People who identified themselves as being active enquirers were also asked to describe the nature of their work and to relate it to alternative forms of enquiry. This included the option of saying that none of the listed alternatives adequately described their work. Responses to this question are shown in Figure 13.1. Only five of the 345 responses (1.4 per cent) stated that the forms of enquiry listed failed to relate to their work, and so we can be reasonably confident that the terms used had relevance to the enquirers who completed these questionnaires.

Of these different options, three seemed to be most commonly related to the work of these enquirers, one relating to reflective practice, the other two to different levels of enquiry, whole school or individual classroom. Indeed, counted together, thirty-two per cent of respondents related their work to the term enquiry in some form (school or classroom based), almost double the number who identified themselves as being engaged in reflective practice. It would appear then that, despite the justification of networks being strongly related to the history and traditions of action research (Jackson, 2002b), the majority of network participants thought of themselves as being enquirers and reflective practitioners rather than any form of researcher. This might seem in some respects a purely semantic question, and yet the terms used to define the work of these networks was emphasised by network personnel.

The term enquiry seems to have formed a prominent part in the construction and justification for these networks. The introduction to one conference, attended by members of the research team, defined the network as being the supporting collaborative structure for the generation of practitioner-relevant knowledge through enquiry. In this case, enquiry was defined as being a process of knowledge generation, conducted by practitioners and contrasted

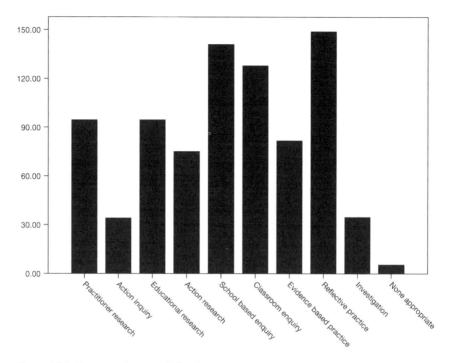

Figure 13.1 How enquiry was defined

against an academic form of research that was seen as being less relevant to practice. Of the responses from the networks in question, more than two-thirds of the enquirers (sixty-seven per cent) identified their work as being related to either classroom or school based enquiry. Although it is perhaps unsurprising that so many associated their work with the same terms utilised by the network in documentation and events, it is interesting to note that one third of enquirers saw their work in a different light.

This raises issues of how networked enquiry is defined and advocated. Adopting a limited definition of enquiry could restrict the potential of the network to reflect the full diversity of interests of their members. Indeed, as one-third of enquirers did not associate themselves with the view of enquiry described above, there is a danger that the adoption of a restricted definition of networked enquiry could create an exclusive movement and could make barriers that need not exist, especially if enquiry is defined by the exclusion of other approaches, in this case academic research. It therefore seems important for people engaging in networked enquiry to consider how inclusive their network should be, to decide how flexible a definition of enquiry they should advocate, and to decide, at the same time as deciding who will be a part of the network, who will be (or will feel) excluded.

Enquirers in these networks were also asked to select from a number of different options describing the focus of their enquiry work; the responses to this question are shown in Figure 13.2. Once again very few respondents were unable to associate with one of the options provided, suggesting that the themes had relevance to network members.

Of the options provided, one, of enquiry for pupil classroom learning, was considerably more popular than any other. This focus is in accord with the largest single group of active enquirers in these networks, class teachers; indeed one-third of people who completed a questionnaire chose this theme as best describing the focus of their enquiries (216 of 655). Far fewer identified the second most popular response (122), of whole school issues; and only a very limited number identified their work with issues either around school management or of working with parents. This highlights the clear focus on pupil learning that was created in these networks; indeed, impact on pupil learning was one of the measures used by the Networked Learning Group to investigate the success, and prolonged funding, of each network (NCSL, 2002b).

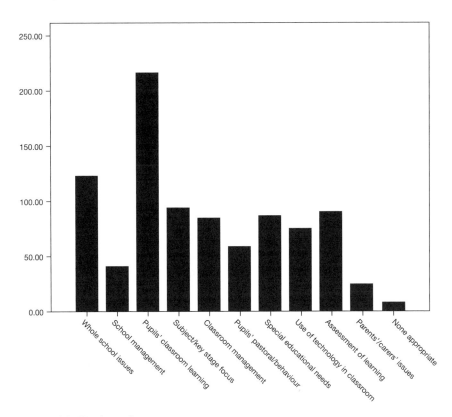

Figure 13.2 The focus for enquiry

This interest in factors that might influence pupil learning is also evident in the issues that most motivated network members to become actively involved in enquiry (see Figure 13.3). Of the reasons identified, the most common were concerned with making improvements in practice and in pupils' learning. Secondary to this were interests in supporting school improvement as a whole, and in identifying best practice. With much lower responses for other items, such as enquiring for social justice, the main motivating factors seem to have been developing practices to improve pupil performance. This, seen in conjunction with the most common focus of pupil learning, highlights the nature of these networks: being principally focused on the conduct and impact of classroom practice.

The large proportion of respondents for whom pupil learning in classrooms was the principle concern and whose main role was of classroom teaching does raise questions about the purpose of enquiry. Although the focus on classrooms, practice and pupil learning are all entirely complementary, it is worth considering why less attention was paid to other issues, such as those concerning pastoral care for children or pupil behaviour. One factor for this might be because enquirers saw implications for pupil learning in all elements of their work; however, the large number of responses were to a very specific

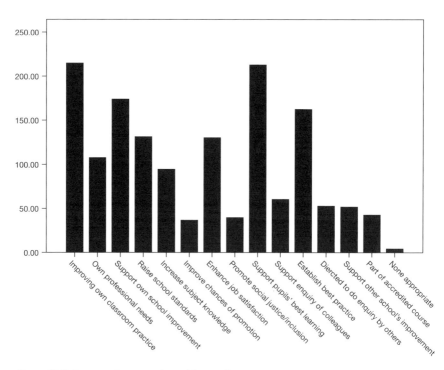

Figure 13.3 Reasons for engaging with enquiry

location for that focus, of pupil learning in classrooms. It is also possible that as the Networked Learning Group had identified this as one of the performance measures of networks this was given greater prominence than other possible enquiry foci. The small number of enquirers who identified management issues as a focus is consistent with the smaller number of enquirers who came from management positions. But even bearing this in mind, the figure is very low in comparison with other foci, and yet there seems no reason why enquiry should not play a role in the provision of pastoral care or in management and leadership. The focus on pupil learning is both welcome and desirable, but it is also worth asking what other forms of development could be enhanced through enquiry and considering whether more explicit attempts should be made to champion practitioner enquiry as a mechanism for developing other forms or locations of practice.

These responses all help to build a picture of networks of enquiry clearly focused on classroom practices, with aspirations for improving those practices to enhance pupil learning and subsequent performance, a focus that is entirely consistent with much of the history of action research in education, at least in the UK context (Elliott, 1991; Koshy, 2005; Stenhouse, 1975), and also with the recent history of the terms enquiry and inquiry (see, for example, Street and Temperley, 2005). In addition to exploring the focus for, and motivations of, enquirers, section two of the questionnaire also sought to identify what strategies and processes had been adopted as a part of this networked approach to enquiry.

THE PROCESS OF ENQUIRY

Section two of the questionnaire explored the nature of the enquiry process adopted by networks and so was only completed by respondents who identified themselves as active enquirers. This included a question identifying who had supported enquiry work; the responses to this question are shown in Figure 13.4. These suggest that, despite the aspirations of networks to provide cross school collaborative structures to support knowledge creation through enquiry, the main source of support identified by enquirers came from within their own schools.

Although the support for enquiry was mainly derived from within institutions and not from across the network, enquirers still felt that there was a benefit to collaborative enquiry. The final section of the questionnaire asked respondents to identify their views of enquiry on a rating scale between two opposing positions. One of these questions asked respondents to identify whether they thought collaborative or individual enquiry was of more benefit. The results of this question are shown in Figure 13.5, which shows the number of responses to each point on the rating scale, one indicating that enquirers preferred working entirely alone up to five indicating a preference for enquiring

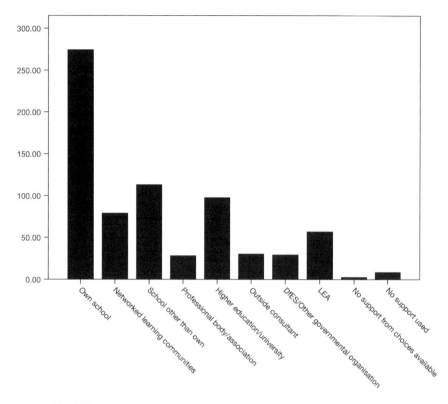

Figure 13.4 Who has supported enquiry

entirely collaboratively. The distribution of these responses is strongly towards the right of the graph, in other words, the feeling of enquirers in these networks was that collaborative enquiry was more beneficial than individual enquiry.

Enquirers were also asked to identify with whom they had shared the outcomes of their work. The results of this question are shown in Figure 13.6. The most striking feature of the results for this question are that, although networks aspired to create collaborative groups across different schools, enquiry outcomes were shared more often within rather than between schools. Indeed the four most common responses to this question all referred to sharing enquiry within the enquirer's own school. This sharing was with, in order of frequency: other teaching colleagues, senior management, curriculum or subject teams and, lastly, with pupils. The next two most common responses were both aspects of networking, namely sharing with other schools in the network and with the Networked Learning Group themselves.

In addition to saying with whom they had shared their work, enquirers were also asked to indicate how their work had been shared. The result for

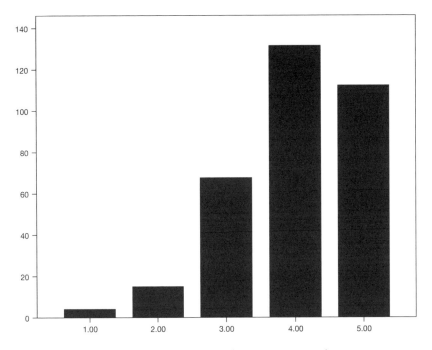

Figure 13.5 Enquiring collaboratively more useful than enquiring alone

this question, shown in Figure 13.7, provides some indication of why this sharing was so much based around individual schools, despite the aspirations for school-to-school collaboration. The three most common forms of sharing were all with colleagues from within the enquirers' own schools, most commonly through informal conversation, then through more formal conversations, and, third most popular, through sharing written reports.

These results might seem surprising, as all these enquirers were supposedly active members of a network of schools and had expressed their interest in collaborative enquiry. However, they can also be considered in a different light, related to the initial construction of these networks. The funding each network received was, in part, concerned with the numbers of schools forming the network and in receiving the consent of headteachers as representatives of those schools. This established structures of networks based around clusters of schools committing to work together over a period of time, and so the initial structure of a network was defined as a collective of institutions. This raises questions about the nature of networking and whether networks are networks of individuals or networks of schools and might seem to be a crucial blow to the aspirations to create cross school collaborative enquiry groups. However, this does not necessarily need to be the case, as

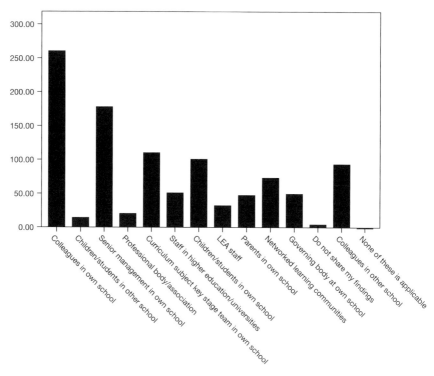

Figure 13.6 Who the outcomes of enquiry were shared with

networks may well have elements of both individual and institutional networking, and different forms of collaboration could exist within and between schools.

Although it may be an apparent contradiction that, of all of the sources of support in these networks, the most commonly received by enquirers was from their own school, this does not necessarily mean that this was unrelated to the network. Indeed these responses might suggest that an effective form of network arrangement is to bring together institutions with a common purpose shared throughout the network, and to bring together groups of individuals from different schools, who can remain a part of a wider network but who can collaborate on and support each other's work within their institutions. If networking is indeed intended to bridge gaps between schools then the mechanisms that are put in place across networks would benefit from taking into account existing approaches to sharing practice already present within members' schools. Although it would be a challenge to replicate the informal nature of interactions within schools, when asked which method was of most benefit to sharing practice, the enquirers participating in this research chose informal sharing with colleagues as the preferred approach.

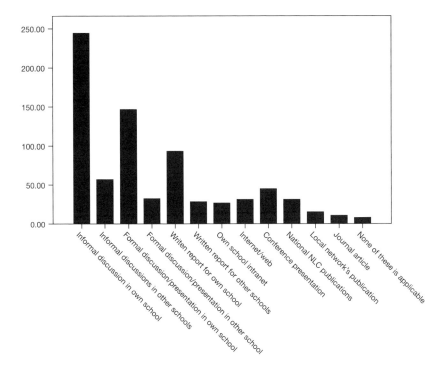

Figure 13.7 How the outcomes of enquiry were shared

The challenge for networking is therefore to build upon these preferences and to try to find formal and informal ways in which learning from enquiry can be shared through networks.

CHANGES RESULTING FROM ENQUIRY

The final section of the questionnaire asked participants to identify their own views with those of a series of opposing statements. One of these questions dealt with the extent to which participants felt that their classroom practices had changed as a result of enquiry. The opposing statements used in this question are shown in Figure 13.8.

Responses of four or five indicate that the respondent feels that their views more closely match the right hand statement, i.e. that there has been a substantial change in classroom practices resulting from enquiry. The actual responses made by active enquirers from these networks are shown in Figure 13.9. The pattern of these responses is strongly skewed to the right, indicating

Figure 13.8 Opposing statements about change from enquiry

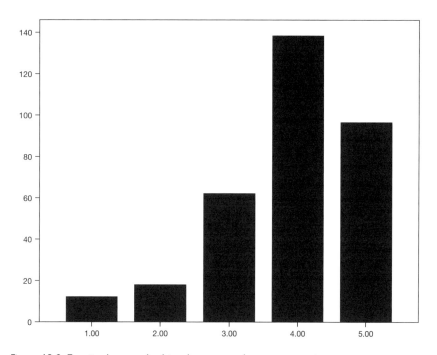

Figure 13.9 Enquiry has resulted in changes to classroom practice

that the majority of respondents felt that there had been substantial changes in their classroom practice resulting from enquiry[2].

Seen in conjunction with the clear focus of these networks on classroom practices, identified above, this would seem to suggest that enquirers have realised their aims, namely that engaging in enquiry has led to changes in classroom practices. However, this, in the eyes of respondents, has not necessarily led to an associated improvement in pupil performance. Figure 13.10 shows the views of enquirers concerning whether their work had resulted in improvements in pupil test results and, although the majority feel that there had been some improvement, when seen in comparison with Figure 13.9, above, enquirers seem to have less confidence of improvements in pupil test results than in having made changes to their practice.

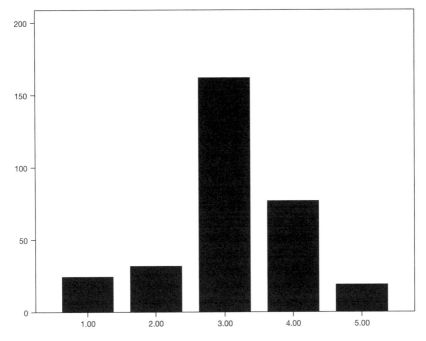

Figure 13.10 Enquiry has resulted in improvements in pupil performance in national tests

There could have been a number of reasons for this, such as a recognition by enquirers that change does not necessarily mean improvement (although it would be surprising if the changes implemented by enquirers were not intended to improve practices) or that the term improvement requires a broader definition than one purely associated with pupil performance in tests. However, this difference in the strength of views of enquirers, between changes to classroom practice and improved pupil test results, does suggest that interactions between enquiry and change are more complex than an assumed process of incremental improvement based upon the outcomes of successive or shared enquiry and focused on technical elements of educational practice leading to change that can be measured using standardised national tests.

It would also seem that, in these networks, the changes made to classroom practice as a result of engaging in enquiry have not been limited to the enquirers' own practice, as participants were asked whether they had learnt from the experiences of their colleagues. The two statements from this question referring to learning from others' experience of enquiry are shown in Figure 13.11.

The responses of active enquirers to this question are shown in Figure 13.12. The pattern of these responses is skewed to the right, towards the

Figure 13.11 Opposing statements concerning transfer of knowledge

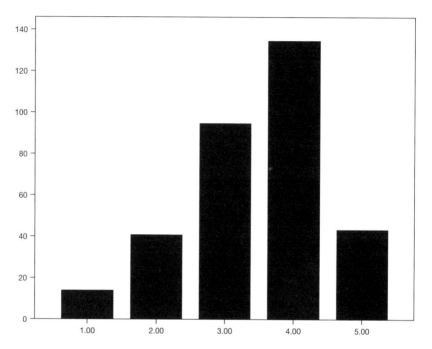

Figure 13.12 Degree of knowledge transfer from enquiry, enquiry active responses only

side indicating that changes have been made to classroom practices from findings generated from other people's enquiries[3].

Although, at first sight, this response seems quite positive, indicating that enquirers felt that there had been some changes in their own practice based around the findings of colleagues, a closer examination of these opposing statements suggests, even more strongly, that there has been a transfer of learning from enquiry. In this case it is only the small group of individuals who indicated one on the questionnaire (4.3 per cent of responses) who felt that their practices had not changed at all as a result of others' enquiries.

As the final section of the questionnaire was completed by all respondents, not just those actively involved in enquiry, it is also possible to explore the extent to which the practices of non-enquirers have changed as a result of

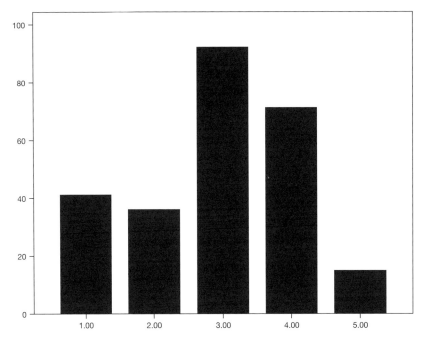

Figure 13.13 Degree of knowledge transfer from enquiry, non-enquiry responses only

enquiries conducted by their fellow network members. Figure 13.13 shows the distribution of the responses of non-enquirers to the same question shown in Figure 13.12. Once again these results appear slightly skewed, although less so than respondents who identified themselves as enquirers[4].

The visual difference between these graphs was further investigated using statistical tests that compared the mean responses of the two groups[5]. The results of this comparison of means, along with comparison of responses from two other questions, are shown in Table 13.3.

Table 13.3 Difference in the mean responses of enquirers and non-enquirers

	Overall mean	Enquirers, mean	Non-enquirers' mean	Difference
My practice has changed from colleagues' enquiry findings	3.2459	3.4681	2.9333	0.53
Enquiry supports more practitioner reflection	4.0162	4.2538	3.7192	0.53
Engaging in enquiry is useful form of staff development	3.8471	4.0631	3.5672	0.50

As the mean value for enquirers is higher than that for non-enquirers, this confirms that they feel that they have learnt more from others' enquiry. Although the graphs and table above suggest some transfer of learning between network members, they do not indicate whether this transfer is within or between network schools. When seen in conjunction with Figures 13.4–13.6, it seems most likely that this transfer for knowledge would have come about as a result of informal sharing of practices within schools.

The other two questions that seemed to elicit the greatest difference in responses from enquirers and non-enquirers dealt with relationships between enquiry, reflective practice and professional development, shown in Table 13.3. Enquirers were more convinced of the potential benefits of enquiry to their professional development and in the link between enquiry and reflective practice. The actual distribution of responses to the question concerning reflection and enquiry underline the strength of this perceived connection (see Figure 13.14), with all responses to this question made at level two or higher, in other words no one who completed a questionnaire thought that enquiry had no effect on practitioner reflection.

These relationships between practitioner enquiry, professional development and reflective practice, have both been described by advocates of action research (Campbell *et al.*, 2004; Leitch and Day, 2000). The exact nature

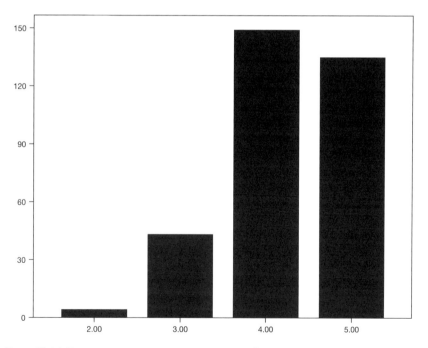

Figure 13.14 Enquiry supports more practitioner reflection, enquirers only

of these relationships is uncertain but it does seem that, in both cases, network members who had actively engaged in enquiry perceived this relationship more strongly than their network colleagues, although it is not clear from this whether these views predated or are a result of involvement in enquiry. Nevertheless there is a clear connection between the major themes of this analysis, of a focus on developing classroom practices through enquiry, enhancing reflection on practice and leading to professional development.

There is less conviction about improving pupil test results but, taken together, the implication seems to be that networked enquiry has provided a vehicle through which the knowledge and understanding of particular contexts have been enhanced and that this has led to changes in practice that, although not necessarily directly related to pupil test performance, have had implications for colleagues.

IMPLICATIONS FOR PRACTICE AND FOR NETWORKING

This chapter has raised a number of issues that have come from the questionnaire completed by a large number of network members. The views reported by participants in this research have emphasised the focus of networks and networked enquiry on classroom practice, intended to improve pupil learning, and the close relationships between reflective practice, professional development and networked enquiry. However, despite being convinced of changes being made to classroom practices and to enquiry increasing the degree of reflection on practice, network members were less convinced about the influence that this has had on pupil performance. In addition, despite the focus on networking and network structures, the predominant form of support seemed to have been provided through the schools that formed these networks. And so, as well as considering how networks can support enquiry, questions could also be asked about how schools need to engage with the network as a whole.

Throughout this chapter the main discussion has been focused on the majority of respondents' views. It should be noted that, in almost all cases, the responses to each question covered the entire spread of responses, even if the bulk were skewed to one side. This raises an interesting consideration of its own. Despite the views reported by network members that were mostly positive about the conduct of enquiry and the resulting effects on practice, there were always some who had chosen to become involved in the network and to engage positively in enquiry, but who had not become convinced of any benefit from that involvement. This challenges the tendency to generalise the views of network members based on observations of the majority position. The network and the enquiry elements may have been of benefit to the majority of people participating in this research, but for some it seems, at best, to have been insignificant, at worst counter-productive. As a result any attempt to view networks and networking as being entirely positive should be speculative and should recognise that, although many may benefit, a few may not, and so it is the obligation of leaders or advocates of networking in general and networked enquiry specifically to consider how this work might relate to all members of affected schools, and how the conduct of the network might take account of those views, regardless of their being in the minority.

Despite concerns about generalising from diverse populations, this analysis has highlighted the potential that networked enquiry can offer to be a significant force to achieve change that is relevant to people who have the most knowledge of the context for that change. It has also highlighted critical questions, derived from the views of active enquirers, about how this process relates to networks and how the conduct and outcomes of this work can best be supported.

Notes

1   Dichotomous responses provided a Kuder–Richardson coefficient of 0.9306, considerably above the 0.7 threshold for reliable responses. A Chronbach's alpha test of multiple responses returned an alpha value of 0.9047, once again well above the 0.7 threshold.
2   A calculation of skewness returns a value of -0.943, i.e. strongly skewed to the right.
3   An analysis of the skewness of this distribution shows a figure of -0.507, in other words strongly skewed to the right.
4   In this case the skewness value was -0.287, still indicating that results were skewed to the right, but far less so than in Figure 13.3.
5   Differences in means were tested using an independent samples t-test; for all three of these questions the differences in means was significant; $p < 0.001$.

Chapter 14

Key questions arising from studies of researching schools

Colleen McLaughlin

INTRODUCTION

In this chapter we will delineate some key questions raised by the descriptions of networks that have preceded it. In Chapter 5, questions were raised from an examination of the literature on teachers' learning through collaboration, researching schools and researching networks. This chapter will explore the questions emerging from studies of the practice of networks of researching schools.

THE PURPOSES OF RESEARCH WITHIN NETWORKS

The practitioners within these networks of researching schools espoused different purposes for the use of research and varied conceptions of it. In this chapter we will use the term research to cover a wide range of terms, i.e. enquiry, inquiry and research. However, many did not use the word research and preferred other terms – these were not mere whims, for embedded within these terms were important conceptions for these groups. Figure 14.1 shows how some practitioners described their research work within the sample of NLCs studied.

Within the BASRC network the stated aims involved adopting 'a cycle of inquiry', very similar to the action research cycle, as well as working on a notion of sharing best practice and engaging with data to inform school improvement. There were suggestions and hopes that the research network would help to 'engage in a systematic and sustainable improvement process' (BASRC, 2007), advance social justice and develop the engagement with school based research. Within the Coalition of Knowledge Creating Schools the idea of identifying and sharing best practice was explicitly rejected. The Coalition of Knowledge Creating Schools does not look for 'that elusive, indeed we would argue impossible, goal "best practice"' (Groundwater-Smith and Mockler, 2002, p. 2), arguing that doing so contradicts their conceptualisation of evidence as needing to be understood in the 'lived life of the school'

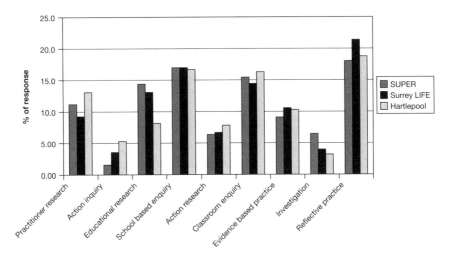

Figure 14.1 How enquirers in different networks viewed their research

(ibid., p.5). Instead they seek, 'The on-going improvement of the work of [the] schools through the systematic and public collection and discussion of evidence regarding teaching and learning within the lived life of the school'.

The TTA School-Based Research Consortium aimed to facilitate teachers 'cngagement in and with research' and so improve students' learning. They aimed to encourage teachers to do school based research but also to develop externally funded research projects for work across the network and to develop the use and interrogation of data within schools. Within the UK NLC programme research was embraced as a core and non-negotiable element of the work of knowledge creation, although enquiry was the preferred term:

> Enquiry is a fundamental tenet of the networked learning communities. When networks 'need to know', the members are prepared to routinely investigate their work. Enquiry is the process for systematically and intentionally exploring and considering information from research, from experts and from each other, in support of decision making and problem solving. Enquiry involves thinking about, reflecting on and challenging individual and collective experiences, in order to come to a deepened understanding of beliefs and practices.
>
> (Earl and Katz, 2005, p. 6)

This definition reflected a widely used model of learning in the NLC programme, known as the 'three fields of knowledge'. The three fields of knowledge were: what we know, that is the knowledge of practitioners; what is known, the knowledge from theory, research and best practice; and new knowledge, the new knowledge created in networks and schools (see also Figure 6.1):

> At the heart of the networked learning models we draw upon in our work lies a recognition of the importance of the social construction of learning, the role of enquiry processes in applying learning in practice, and the need to draw equally upon three fields of knowledge. Within this model of learning, the fields of knowledge are utilised in a dynamic relationship with one another through network-based activity, application and study within classrooms.
>
> (Networked Learning Communities, 2005, p. 3)

In these quotations and in the other case studies we see a multiplicity of purposes for research in networks of schools, ranging from the intentions to research classroom practice in schools and networks, through exemplifying best practice and sharing it, to larger claims for knowledge creation that might inform system change on a larger scale. All statements of purpose in some way included the aim of developing teachers as professionals. These different conceptions of the purposes of networked practitioner research are not mutually exclusive but they are very different in scale, scope and as modes of knowledge creation. The first set of questions, then, is about the purposes of research in networks of schools. Does it matter what the purposes are for networks of researching schools? What differences do different claims and purposes make to the processes and resources required and claims for the outcomes?

The conceptions of purpose seem to mirror the contexts of the different practitioners. The different daily working agendas of people in different positions within the educational sphere appeared to influence their perceptions of the prime purposes of the research. For example, Chapter 13 reports that classroom teachers in the NLCs described tended to emphasise engagement with pupils and learning and teaching processes, as did the researchers in the TTA consortium; heads of department tended to emphasise the use of data to examine standards and address accountability concerns; head teachers tended to focus on measurable outcomes and showed concern about accountability to external bodies, although this was not necessarily the case. Those working in networks of schools in difficult or challenging circumstances were clearly influenced by the aims of their work in these contexts and the pressures upon them. This is not surprising. It does however raise the question: how do we engage with the multiple and overlapping purposes of practitioner research in networks? A connected question might be: does it matter that there are multiple purposes and in what ways does it matter?

NETWORKING FOR PROFESSIONAL DEVELOPMENT

The two aspects that are perceived to make a contribution to professional development in networks are the collaborative element and the collaborative engagement with research. The benefits are there to be seen in these studies of practice. In Chapter 13 the teachers involved in collaborative enquiry reported this as a highly valued process of learning, and they also reported learning a great deal from the findings of those enquiries. Andrew Townsend concludes in Chapter 13, '. . . there is a clear connection between the major themes of this analysis, of a focus on developing classroom practices through enquiry, enhancing reflection on practice and leading to professional development', although he also cautions that this is not the case for all and for some collaborative enquiry is seen as destructive. Copland (2002, p. 5) described the 'cycle of inquiry' as the 'engine of BASRC's theory of social change' and McLaughlin and Zarrow (2001, p. 87) reported that the results of the enquiry process had led to new understandings about practice in schools and classrooms. It is clear in these studies that the research process and, in some cases, the outcomes were highly valued by individuals and schools. We also see some examples of collaboration being fitted to the normal processes of teachers' working lives, e.g. in subject groups or phase groups across schools and that this has an ease of fit. This raises questions around the forms of collaboration within networks rather than within schools. In Chapter 5 the question of whether collaboration in networks was different to collaboration in schools or had increased benefits is one that is relevant here too, as most of the dissemination of learning took place within schools. This question of sharing knowledge will be returned to in the final section. The demands of collaboration across schools are considerable and place considerable demands on the management and use of time, for example. There is a useful study of conflict in schools (Achinstein, 2002), and the issue of conflict and collaboration within networks would seem to be an area that is under-researched and one that merits further attention.

NETWORKING FOR SCHOOL IMPROVEMENT

All the networks of schools hoped to improve schools; however, there were significant differences in how they saw the role of research within that process and how they measured whether it had met its aim of contributing to teacher and pupil learning. In BASRC and the NLC, the measure was students' attainment scores. This was shown to be complex and difficult to ascertain. What is the most appropriate way to assess school improvement through research and how do you measure networks for school improvement? The complexity of measuring the connection to research is clearly there at school level, never mind at network level. Engaging in collaborative research is something that benefits teachers' well-being as well as their learning and professional problem solving, so are these not sufficient grounds for measuring the impact on school improvement?

The other area of interest here is the resources allocated to, and seen as necessary to, support networks for school improvement. They ranged in these studies from one hundred million dollars to no funding at all; from a large infrastructure around the network to sustain and service it, to one person supporting the work of the network; and from large scale district work to collections of interested schools. However, the majority of networks did have some form of external resource, and in four cases they included higher education personnel. Other partners were local district personnel or other governmental organisations such as the NCSL. The question of the capacity of a network of schools to undertake research without external support is therefore raised. What might be the most useful forms of external support and what might be the most useful tasks for those supporting school networks to undertake? The earlier discussions about the working conditions of teachers (see Chapters 2, 3 and 5) might indicate that this need for external support might be related to schools' capacity to undertake these sorts of activity. The tasks that external agents seemed to engage in across these network studies were facilitating the dissemination of research; providing access to external knowledge about education; facilitating communication between schools; and organising network level activities.

The final difference to focus on here is the voluntary or prescribed nature of the research. In these networks it is largely a matter of teachers volunteering to undertake research, although the boundaries between them are not so clear in all cases. There is, however, a notion of development within school cultures too. So the question arises of how choice relates to the development of networks that use research for school improvement. This is an important question now as in the UK, for example, schools are being required to be in networks.

NETWORKING FOR KNOWLEDGE CREATION

The production of knowledge, including new knowledge that would be publicly shared, was an explicit aim of the NLC programme and the TTA Consortium, which intended to submit proposals for externally funded research and to develop the use of data in schools. The Coalition of Knowledge Creating Schools clearly has this as a prime aim. BASRC too aimed to engage in assessing and creating knowledge for the reform of schools. This seems to be the most challenging aspect of the work and yet it is the central claim for many who advocate networks as transformative (Hargreaves 1999; 2003b). The type of research that seemed to engage teachers in the network studies is school based research focused on and aimed at colleagues, rather than the generation of knowledge for a wider educational public. Indeed, even where this is engaged with, it is very demanding and seems to require much additional support. The dissemination of knowledge within networks proved to be a significant challenge, and the questionnaire data in Chapter 13 suggests that teacher researchers wanted to share with colleagues and learned a great deal from this. They also preferred face-to-face methods of dissemination, which were undertaken largely in their schools rather than across schools. The questions that arise from the issues of sharing and learning from each other, as well as the wider knowledge base, are many and complex. They include: what are the optimum conditions for knowledge sharing and creation in schools and networks? What is shared and how are matters of quality judged? What do teachers see as useful knowledge, and which forms of knowledge dissemination do they prefer?

What counts as quality in networked practitioner research?

In these studies of networks the nature of practitioner research and the grounds for claims about the knowledge generated are important topics. The practitioners in the NLCs studied used different discourses to talk about their research. There was evidence that these discourses drove the processes used to undertake the research and the ways in which the research work was measured or seen to have achieved its purposes. The different discourses used were:

- a standards discourse that emphasised pupil outcomes
- a discourse of professional development that emphasised collegiality and collaboration
- a discourse of professional learning about classroom and school practice, which included the discourse of sharing 'best practice'
- a discourse of knowledge creation, evidence collection and research
- a discourse of social justice and democracy.

There was also some evidence of real and potential tensions between these different discourses and their underlying criteria for judgements of quality. Clearly the long-term aim of practitioner research is the improvement of students' educational experience and learning. However, how that is measured and judged may differ according to the purpose and the expected timescale for impact. If the prime purpose of research is the development of practitioner collaboration and learning, very different success criteria will be applied from those if the conception of practitioner research is as a process that will result in gains in pupil achievement scores. There was evidence in these case descriptions that managing the tension between experimentation and risk taking that research-informed development requires did not always easily sit alongside a climate of performance, short-term timescales and accountability.

These different conceptions are very different in their scale and the criteria to be used. There were particular issues around the generation of knowledge. Many practitioners and networks aimed to share their research findings across the network. Others aimed to share and generate knowledge within a particular group. There was nervousness about the use of the word research and whether the work being undertaken should aim to be disseminated beyond the local group. So a further questions is: how can we develop the different criteria for judging the different purposes of practitioner research within networks of schools?

Susan Groundwater-Smith (2002) and Simons *et al.* (2003) have engaged with this matter. Groundwater-Smith argues for 'a forensic rather than an adversarial notion of evidence' (pp. 4–5) and includes in this three tests: is it ethical? has it been triangulated? and has it been intersubjectively verified? These tests are similar to the test that a school in SUPER applied to its school based research. Simons *et al.* (ibid.) distinguish between the personal, the collegial and the collective levels of research and the different tests that might be applied to these levels. So a key question is how do we judge the research generated in networks, and are the tests the same as we might apply to research for different purposes within schools?

What was found to be useful?

The majority of those engaged in research engaged in the action research model of research or other similar problem-solving models of research and found these the most useful. Their focus was the shared or individual problems and practice in the classroom. Engagement with the theory and current research knowledge was not seen as a useful or easy activity by the majority of those engaged in research activities. Given the nature of the claims for networking practitioner research and for networks to generate new knowledge available to the wider educational community, this is an important issue. However, there was also evidence of development here, i.e. those who engaged in research came to value the research others within and outside of the networks. This echoes the findings of others in other areas (Brown, 2005; Ratcliffe *et al.*, 2005; Simons *et al.*, 2003). Accessing the work of others was a significant challenge for those working in schools, and outside agents played an important role here. So the question of how to support and develop access to, and the use of, educational research and thinking is an important one if the wider purposes of networking practitioner research are to be met.

Part 3

Looking to the future

Chapter 15

Networks of researching schools

A way forward?

In this final chapter, we aim to consider the potential value of the idea of networks of researching schools and to identify some of the conditions that would be necessary for this idea to be useful in practice. In doing so, we shall take account of the questions raised in Chapters 5 and 14, and also of the evidence about particular research networks that we have presented in Chapters 6–13.

We shall approach this task from three different perspectives. First, we shall consider some of the more or less ambitious purposes for which research networks might be developed, the realism of such purposes and the conditions necessary for networks to be able in practice to realise such purposes. What would it take, we shall ask, for networks of schools to be fit for these purposes?

Second, we shall examine some of the tensions and challenges that networks of researching schools have to face and some of the possible growth points available to them.

Finally, our third perspective on the realism of a research networks project, and on the conditions for its usefulness, is to consider who would have to do what in order for it to succeed. What new roles, responsibilities and obligations would government, schools, teachers and others have to accept before the potential of research networks of schools could be realised?

PURPOSES OF NETWORKS OF RESEARCH SCHOOLS

This section is concerned with three main themes:

- For what purposes might networks of research schools be created and sustained?
- To what extent have these purposes been pursued in the networks studied?
- Under what conditions might these various purposes be most fruitfully pursued?

Possible purposes of research networks

In considering this, we still find it useful to identify, on one hand, the purposes of engaging in research and, on the other, the purposes of networking. The three purposes of school based research that we distinguished in Chapter 2 are also possible purposes of research networks of schools:

1   *Teachers' professional development*: The long established and strong tradition of collaborative practitioner research has been most effectively directed towards the purpose of engaging individual teachers in critically examining aspects of their own practice and in exploring ways in which their practice can be improved. Often, although not always, teachers have engaged in such research with the support of groups within their own schools, sharing ideas and giving each other both practical help and emotional support. A relatively modest purpose for school research networks can be to facilitate the development of such mutually supportive groups on a broader basis, which could perhaps be both more prestigious and a source of more novel and more stimulating ideas.

2   *School improvement*: We found in Chapter 2 that the primary purpose with which individual schools set out to engage in research was for their own improvement. It seems likely therefore that networks of researching schools are formed for the same purpose, with the intention that schools' improvement through engaging in research can be enhanced as a result of the increased resources, stimuli and support that the networks can offer.

3   *Knowledge creation*: A more ambitious purpose for researching schools was seen to be that they should aim to contribute to validated public knowledge about good practice, although it was noted that clear examples of schools unambiguously espousing this purpose were hard to find. However, even in articulating his vision of knowledge creating schools, Hargreaves (1999) suggested that a more credible scenario was that *networks* of researching schools might be able to pursue this purpose successfully. Hargreaves (2003b) reiterated this belief even more strongly:

> Because a federation is so much larger than an individual school, it can prioritise a shared topic for knowledge creation and have a much more sophisticated design, both for sharing the innovative workload, so each school undertakes a limited and variable amount of activity, and for testing it more rigorously than is ever possible in a single secondary school or department.
>
> (Hargreaves, 2003b, p. 40)

Three purposes of *networking* can also be distinguished:

1   *Mutual support and sharing of ideas*: The most basic purpose of networking among schools is that they should share helpful ideas and, in

various ways, be mutually supportive. This purpose seems appropriately complementary to the undertaking of research either for the professional development of individual teachers or for the more ambitious purpose of whole school improvement. Again, this would seem to be a relatively modest purpose with which to engage in networking.

2   *Engagement in joint research work*: This purpose of networking is clearly implicit in the suggestion that knowledge creation is likely to be more viable within networks than in individual schools. Thus Hargreaves (2003b, p. 40), for example, in pursuing this argument, suggests a number of ways in which schools might jointly design their research:

   • several schools might test different solutions to a common problem, to check which solutions are most effective;
   • several schools might test the same innovations, but do so in contrasting circumstances to check if the innovation works in spite of such differences;
   • several specialist schools of the same specialism might take different aspects of a common innovation, so that at a later stage each school contributes one element of an overall innovation that would have been too large for a single school to test;
   • several schools might agree to engage in a randomised controlled trial on a problem that needs to be solved but at present there is no reason to prefer one solution over another.

3   *Sharing of good practice*: As the problem of dissemination of the findings of research into good practice has been stubbornly resistant to solution, this third and most ambitious purpose of networking would be especially valuable if networks that had done joint research then set out to share validated good practice. Hargreaves (2003b) notes that, 'unfortunately our knowledge of how (the sharing of good practice) might be done is frighteningly slight' (p. 44), and he goes on to explain the difficulties:

> Knowledge transfer among teachers is often difficult to achieve . . . [because] the way in which it is implemented or applied in practice often depends on tacit knowledge . . . So *best practice has to be demonstrated,* not just explained, and its replication by another practitioner has to be practised through trial and error; this entails *creatively adapting* the innovation that is being transferred. The donor and the recipient in the transfer process need to spend some time together if the transfer is to be successful . . . The innovation transfer works when the knowledge involved remains embodied and contextualised in a working relationship that is co-creative for both participants.
>
> (Hargreaves, 2003b, p. 50)

He also outlines Szulanski's (2003, p. 51) hypothesis that the difficulty of knowledge transfer increases when:

   • it is not clear how or why the new practice works

- the donor is not motivated to share fully
- the donor is not credible in the eyes of the recipient
- the recipient is not motivated to accept the innovation
- the recipient's organisation is barren ground for new ideas
- the relationship between donor and recipient lacks respect and intimacy.

Thus the sharing of good practice might seem to be a purpose for which networks of researching schools would be especially useful and are especially needed, but also a very ambitious purpose.

To what extent have these purposes been pursued in the networks studied?

Many people in all the networks we have studied valued their membership of the networks because it reduced their sense of isolation in their own classrooms and schools. The basic networking purpose of providing mutual support of various kinds, including the exchange of ideas, was identified in all the networks as important. A second common purpose was that of learning through enquiry, broadly conceived, and of the professional development to which this led. In all networks, furthermore, there were people who were able to report the benefits of these purposes having been effectively realised. The most striking common feature of all the networks was their shared pursuit of these most basic purposes.

Beyond that, the networks varied considerably in their purposes. In particular, there was across the networks a spectrum from those that emphasised their learning from teachers' researching of their own practices to those that emphasised their learning from sharing ideas with other schools in their network. Thus in several of the networks (e.g. Bay Area Schools, Coalition of Knowledge Building Schools, SUPER, South West London), the primary purpose was focused on schools' active promotion of research by their own teachers, with relatively little interest in learning from the research conducted in other schools nor indeed from these other schools' teaching practices more generally. The felt value of these networks was in their sense of solidarity, their shared values, their shared understandings of research and of how it should inform practice, and their learning from each other about the processes of research. The shared infrastructure was also valued, including the externally provided organisational frameworks, guidance on research methods and, in some cases, financial resources. For such networks, networking among the schools was important, but probably no more important than the bilateral relationship between each school and the centre, which was commonly although not necessarily university based.

In contrast, there were networks in which 'research' was of minor importance. It might even be rejected as a term, usually in favour of the more diffuse 'enquiry', as in the Hartlepool NLC; or it might not be explicitly rejected as an idea, but just be slow to get off the ground, as in the Surrey LIFE NLC. In such networks, it was learning directly through the process of networking that seemed to be the primary purpose, with an emphasis on exchanging ideas about good practice through, for example, face-to-face meetings, observation and 'learning walks', and also on reflecting about schools' and teachers' own practices in the light of what they learned from other schools. Without the complication of the extra dimension of 'research', such networks exemplify the possibilities of learning through networking at its most straightforward. But of course, without that extra dimension, learning through networking depends directly on the belief that the schools with which one is networking have something to teach one.

In a few of the networks studied, there seem to have been clear efforts made to learn both from researching and from networking and for the two processes to be interrelated, but even where this purpose was actively pursued, doing so does not appear to have been easy. For the TTA's research consortia, for example, 'the task of learning across boundaries formed the working environment, a research goal, a means to the end of improving teaching and learning and a perpetual puzzle' (Cordingley et al., 2002). Perhaps the most persuasive account of combining these two kinds of learning comes from the Blackburn with Darwen NLC, where mathematics teachers from different schools seemed effectively to share with each other their ongoing enquiries into classroom teaching. It may be important therefore to examine the distinctive nature of that network.

For all the networks, school improvement was explicitly and unambiguously a central purpose, and, in so far as school improvement can plausibly be claimed to follow automatically from the reflection, learning and professional development of teachers in these schools, it was clear that the work of the networks was deliberately directed towards the realisation of this purpose. If, however, it is argued that school improvement depends not only on individual teachers' professional development but also on co-ordinated developments across whole schools, or at least within coherent parts of schools, then the evidence about the deliberate development of networks for the pursuit of school improvement is much more sparse. We noted of the Blackburn with Darwen NLC that, 'the head teachers valued school improvement, the heads of faculty focused on curriculum development and the standards debate, and the teachers focused very much on classroom improvement and pupil learning'. Such different perspectives from staff in different positions are to be expected and can be valuable if they are mutually complementary. Similarly, schools and networks might ideally be expected to have different but complementary perspectives: it is surely the task of individual schools to plan for their own improvement, whereas the role of networks is to offer learning facilities that help the individual schools in undertaking that task. We had some evidence of individual schools using the resources of networks to pursue their own diverse school improvement plans. What was less in evidence were well developed conceptions of how research networks might best be developed for the specific purpose of helping with school improvement.

Knowledge creation in the sense that participants should develop new knowledge was certainly a purpose of all the networks, but did they espouse a purpose of contributing to validated public knowledge about good practice? The largest and best endowed of the networks, the BASRC, possibly had such a purpose, in that it was committed to dissemination beyond and within the network through publications. More generally, the answer is even less certain; but perhaps that is because the question is not clear enough. As emerged in Chapter 2, the Mode Two type of research espoused explicitly by Hargreaves (1999), and implicitly by many school based researchers, suggests a type of dissemination that relies more on personal involvement and interpersonal contact than on written publications, and several of the networks (e.g. the TTA School-Based Research Consortia; Blackburn with Darwen NLC) not only valued the knowledge generated by their research but also seemed to value dissemination of it in just that way. In some cases, too, there seemed to be a commitment, albeit sometimes rather tentative, to validation of the 'situated generalisations' generated (Simons *et al.*, 2003) through, for example, forms of triangulation.

Although we may therefore conclude that several of the networks pursued the purpose of creating validated public knowledge of the Mode Two type, there is very limited evidence of them using what might be seen as the distinctive potential strengths of networks for powerful research designs. In some networks, schools did plan their research jointly, using what we would see as entirely appropriate research designs, such as multiple case studies; and their members collaborated in data gathering and analysis, by observing each other's teaching and analysing each other's research journals. But, while appropriate, such designs and methods would arguably have been just as appropriate for research within individual schools, and did not make use of the distinctive characteristics of networks in ways such as those exemplified by Hargreaves (2003a, 2003b).

Finally, teachers who did joint research in their networks showed clear recognition of the problems of sharing good practice, even when such good practice was established. Insistent as they were about the 'situationally-bounded nature of their findings' (Simons *et al.*, 2003), they were extremely cautious about sharing them widely. They were in no doubt that face-to-face interaction between teachers who had established a trusting relationship was much the best way in which to share good practice. Their attitudes reflected very clearly the conclusion reached by Fielding *et al.* (2005) that 'a relationships model of practice transfer may be at least as relevant as a content-driven model'. Nonetheless, there was very limited evidence of extensive resources being invested by the networks in this demanding task of sharing validated good practice, through for example working together in classrooms. No doubt that was partly because this task only became meaningful towards the end of research projects, when there might be little time or other resources to spare. Also, however, one is left with the impression that, although the sharing of knowledge about good practice was highly valued, the emphasis on undertaking manageable tasks ('tweaking rather than transforming', as one of the Blackburn with Darwen NLC teachers put it) meant that the investment of large amounts of time in sharing particular validated practices seemed inappropriate. This is in sharp contrast to Hargreaves' (2003b) argument that the primary function of networking should be to replace teachers' personal 'tinkering' by providing the vehicle for transformation: 'Transformation means that such covert personalised, micro-innovation is no longer adequate to the task facing schools, which will now need to create and sustain an explicit climate of experimentation and planned innovation . . .' (p. 34).

Under what conditions might these various purposes be most fruitfully pursued?

What have we learned about the conditions that are important for the sensible pursuit of these purposes?

Research networking for professional development; mutual support and sharing of ideas

There is little doubt that membership of a researching schools network can contribute to teachers' professional development. Certainly the conditions that are conducive to such development work seem to align closely to certain processes, assumptions and values associated with school networks. It seems important that such networks should be voluntary, flexible and able to establish supportive, non-hierarchical relationships in which high levels of trust and openness are generated among members. The nature of these relationships is reinforced if the network has a key purpose focused on collaborative learning about classroom practices and/or specific curriculum areas. Teachers recognise the benefits of contributing to such networks because doing so allows them to draw on the collective knowledge, skills and experience of the other members. These opportunities for sharing ideas, problems and materials are seen as having direct relevance to their daily professional lives. Ensuring that such conditions are created and maintained in networks is clearly a very important leadership task.

One notable difficulty of such networks relates however to the nature of the relationships among its members and its possible impact on the quality of their learning. This is that, precisely because they provide opportunities for shared professional discourse based on trust, members may over time become too comfortable about the status quo, thus creating a culture within the network in which assumptions are rarely challenged and risk taking is avoided. Genuine collaboration among teachers, as Achinstein (2002) demonstrated, does tend to lead to productive conflict, but it is an easy temptation to avoid such conflict. These concerns may be addressed by ensuring that the network has a fluid membership and permeable boundaries, but it may be difficult in such a network to maintain the necessary high level of trust. One solution to this dilemma may be to maintain a stable network but to involve an external critical friend, who has the demanding role of maintaining trust while providing challenge. The value of this role is discussed later in terms of the involvement of university members in networks.

The dangers of complacency are likely to be further reduced when professional development is sought, both through networking and through disciplined research. As noted earlier, there was some tendency in the networks we studied for learning and professional development to rely either on the challenge of ideas from other schools or on within-school research. The combination of both of these kinds of challenge may be especially helpful, although such a combination tended to occur only where there was strong leadership of the network from people not associated with any particular schools. For purposes of professional development, however, collaborative research need not be directed towards the generation of public knowledge but may instead, in the tradition of Lawrence Stenhouse, be directed towards improvements in the practice of the teachers engaged in the research.

Research networking for school improvement

Our studies of networks of researching schools suggest that many networks consider whole school improvement to be a primary purpose of their work. Particular conditions likely to support such work, as well as the nature of the difficulties that might be encountered, are closely related to the different ways in which such networks are conceived and organised. For example, there is a clear distinction between networks in which members primarily set out to collaborate on joint research and those in which members mainly come together to develop their research skills and expertise. The first approach requires each school not only to focus on research topics that relate to its own development plans, but also to co-ordinate these decisions so that they contribute to the planned development of all the schools. This is a more demanding process, especially if it also includes a necessary responsiveness to the views of the individual teachers conducting the research. Issues of scale can be important here: networks with fewer schools may be able to reach consensus more easily, whereas those comprising smaller schools (for example primary or special schools) or focused on smaller units, such as same-subject departments, may have greater commonality of interests or concerns. Meanwhile, the second approach, based on research processes, seems more straightforward but has the disadvantage of not necessarily generating research evidence that can usefully be shared to support whole school improvement across schools.

There would seem to be other necessary conditions to ensure that research networks contribute effectively to school improvement. In particular, there is a need for a strong commitment and clear planning by senior management to ensure that research findings arising from the network are used to contribute significantly to changes in school practice rather than only at the level of individual teachers. (The institutional responsibilities of school leaders are discussed in more detail later.) Also, if the overall intention of a network is to bring about whole school improvement, it is imperative that the research undertaken should be robust in its design and conduct. Although the quality of research undertaken by any teacher is always important, new issues arise when the findings of the research are to be used to determine policies and practices across a number of schools and therefore must be based on highly reliable and validated evidence. It has to be said, however, that neither of these issues seemed to arise as significant concerns in any of the networks we studied. There was evidence that a few individual schools were confronting questions about the conditions necessary for their network research activities to contribute to school improvement; but there appeared to be a striking absence of debate at network level about what these conditions might be, far less how they could be put in place. As yet, it seems that, although school improvement is a common aspiration of research networks, there has been relatively little planning for its realisation.

A further potential tension arises from the promotion of research networks by government agencies. If school improvement is primarily understood in terms of gains in students' scores on national standardised tests, and becomes entangled with notions of performance, accountability and competition between schools, this can very easily undermine the high levels of trust and interdependence on which network relationships rely. It may also inhibit desirable kinds of collaborative research activity that benefit from risk taking and experimentation.

Research networking for knowledge creation and the sharing of good practice

Identifying the conditions required to support research networks that have the primary purposes of creating, validating and sharing knowledge about good practice has not been straightforward. This is mainly because, in practice, such networks have yet to be properly established. It is Hargreaves (1999; 2003a, 2003b) who has put forward the vision of such an approach and he has made a persuasive case for the advantages to be gained from doing so. As we have outlined earlier in this chapter, this would involve all schools disciplining themselves to contribute in agreed ways to the implementation of joint research plans, leading to the identification of excellent practice and the subsequent investment of substantial resources in the sharing of such good practice.

If the advantages of this are so clearly apparent, the question then to be addressed is why such networks have yet to be properly established. Perhaps the answer is that the conditions for this type of network are not currently available. As previously noted, it can prove difficult for schools to plan for and to engage in joint research; only a minority of the networks that we studied even seemed to attempt to do so. A second difficulty is the sharp contrast between Hargreaves' insistence on the need for rigorous and high-quality school based research and Jackson's notion, as Director of the Network Learning Communities organisation, that some kind of unspecified 'good enough' research would do; and it is certainly tempting for teachers to see notions of academic rigour as not particularly relevant to their concerns. A third difficulty is the very limited recognition of the great complexity of the task of transferring research findings from one school to another, or even from one teacher to another (Fielding *et al.*, 2005; Hargreaves, 2003a, 2003b; Simons *et al.*, 2003).

The conditions necessary to overcome these three difficulties are demanding. Schools would need to surrender to the research networks that they join much more authority than they currently do. Teachers would need to have a much fuller understanding of educational research and a greater commitment to valuing research for the development of good practice. And everyone involved – government, schools and individual teachers – would need to be persuaded, as they are far from being at present, of the value of devoting substantial time and resources to the complex task of sharing validated good practice among teachers. More generally, the changes required would depend upon all concerned being persuaded of the need for fundamental changes to the institutional structure and culture of schools. At present that seems a very distant dream.

TENSIONS, CHALLENGES AND GROWTH POINTS OF NETWORKS OF RESEARCHING SCHOOLS

In this section we shall explore the tensions, challenges and potential growth points for those engaged in networks of researching schools. We shall draw on the questions and findings that emerged both from the literature and the studies of cases that have gone before. We will organise our discussions under three major headings: teacher learning, school improvement and knowledge creation.

Teacher learning

Arguments for the promotion of networks of schools that have focused on the use of and engagement with research have built upon the work on collaborative teacher learning. The argument has been that the isolation created by teachers' working conditions and traditional ways of working will be reduced and all will benefit from some form of joint working with colleagues, either within or outside the school walls (Hargreaves, 2004; Hopkins, 2000). The seminal work by Lortie (1975) on the isolation of individual teachers has become extended and linked up to work on social capital, thus leading to the notion of networks of collaborating practitioners (Hargreaves, 2004). The literature and the studies of networks show that by and large teachers reported considerable personal, social and professional benefits from reflecting and researching alongside others. They reported that the collaborative element was productive and highly valued. Collaboration was seen as a potentially potent form of professional learning and development; it extended the view of the teacher's professional role and was intellectually stimulating and refreshing as a mode of working. Therefore, it is possible to say that collaborative teacher learning in networks of schools is a potentially potent source of development for teachers', schools' and pupils' learning.

However, there are other important factors to be considered, and the taken-for-granted nature of the benefits of collaboration has been questioned. First is the issue of scale; second are the forms of collaboration with the resulting implications for the ease of collaboration; and third are the necessary conditions for collaboration. The increased scale of moving to collaboration between practitioners across schools is a considerable one. The greater scale of collaboration necessarily involves different forms of collaboration and different questions to be asked.

We saw earlier how collaboration within schools involved facing certain challenges: normal working conditions can leave little time for joint working; collaboration can present significant emotional challenges for teachers accustomed to working alone; and it necessitates a capacity to deal with conflicts that were previously avoided. As we increase the scale, it is reasonable to hypothesise that the demands increase and that these challenges and new ones will present themselves.

However, the studies of collaborative teacher learning suggested that there are certain potential growth points. A major one is the closeness of fit to the classroom. The studies of NLCs showed how those involved valued the ability to form and shape the agenda for research and learning, focusing mainly on the problems they encountered in their classrooms or the shared professional challenges within subject areas or particular phases of the school's work. The description of networks as 'dignifying and giving shape to the process and content of educators' experiences, the daily-ness of their work, which is often invisible to outsiders yet binds insiders together', (Lieberman, 1999) seems to be a claim that fits well with our understandings of, and the claims for, the work of networks of practitioners. We note that it is smaller in scale than some other claims for networks (Hargreaves, 2004; Hopkins, 2000). It also seems to accord with the findings of Lieberman and McLaughlin

(1992) about individual schools that, 'the level of community that is closest to the classroom is the most salient for teachers and thus most able to influence their practice and career experiences' (p. 94). This chimes with Little's (1982) study and her suggestion that a shared language is helpful, as is frequency of contact. So the question of *who* collaborates with *whom* is one that needs careful consideration, and we would suggest that some shared experiences, some shared language and common purpose are very important. It also raises the issue of the forms of collaborative teacher learning.

When considering *who* collaborates with *whom*, it may be useful to distinguish between different forms of collaboration within networks for different purposes. A challenge is to link these different groups up and enhance communication between them. If a valid hypothesis is that it is most powerful to keep research closely connected to the classroom, then it might follow that the groups of collaborators should be small and should share some characteristics of practice or interests that will enable them to engage in focused and explicit enquiry. The problems of sharing craft knowledge will be lessened, but not necessarily removed. Research and case descriptions support this in so far as there are clear examples of the beneficial impact of shared purposes and interests in certain groups (e.g. the mathematics group in Blackburn with Darwen). Building on and developing existing structures, such as subject departments, would seem to have potential for growth. These units might form the closest and most intense groups of teacher learning within and between schools. They might also provide the vehicle for development. One of the factors that emerged from the literature and from our studies is the developmental nature of 'the capacity and disposition to dig deeply into matters of practice' (Little, 2002a, p. 918). Focusing on small groups who have the opportunity to engage over time and develop shared understanding, as well as the necessary social and emotional aspects of collaboration, may enhance the development of teacher learning within schools and networks. Little (2005, p. 21) has suggested that it is important to focus on the *level of practice* and that 'revising materials of instruction' is an example of such a focus on the level of practice and is a potential starting point for developing professional learning about practice. Such tasks can of course be very fruitfully undertaken through joint research.

However, there are other profitable forms of collaboration that involve teacher learning. These may take the form of sharing the outcomes of research through network meetings and conferences, which would be a less frequent form of collaboration and less demanding. These may go a long way towards supporting a research culture and to enhancing the use of research in teachers' learning. Networks of schools can involve a range of different activities for teacher learning and they can engage different groups at different times. Shared purposes need to be at a general level and agreed, but there needs also to be flexibility and a range of activities for teacher learning.

School improvement

As we have stated, considerable claims have been made both for networks and for school based knowledge creating research as vehicles for schools improvement. McCarthy *et al.* (2004, p. 61) argued that 'networking between schools is increasingly recognised as the key driver of school improvement'. Others (Hargreaves, 2004; Hopkins, 2000) have supported this claim. The studies of those engaged in research within schools and networks have suggested that the benefits are that capacity can be improved through the pooling of resources but also that, with increased capacity, come increased demands and that some external resources are necessary. All of the networks described in our case studies were reliant on some form of external help, either from a local authority representative, a higher education partner or a national group such as the NCSL. Whether this was a part of an initial start up and would decrease as development took place is debatable. Other networks described in other countries and in the UK seemed to need external support. Increased finance for the schools themselves was in most cases one important element for the networks described, and particularly for the primary schools involved, where the capacity to spread resources is not as strong as within large secondary schools. A second element that seemed helpful was having an organisational 'hub' for the network, not located in any of the schools. A third element that seemed necessary was the provision of research expertise. This included research training and consultancy, but many external agents were also seen as a bridge to the world of research knowledge and ideas. Teachers wanted research knowledge and found it hard to access it. In many of the NLCs the practitioners talked of their lack of capacity to find and then read and research it in the form of journal articles or other academic reports. There are initiatives that aim to address this issue, e.g. the research of the month on the General Teaching Council website in the UK or the work of BASRC in the US.

We hypothesised in Chapter 2 that there were some necessary conditions for corporate engagement of teachers in research towards school improvement. These were:

- it depends upon an integrated strategy of which it is one element;
- it depends upon the overall commitment of senior management to this strategy;
- it depends upon the effective co-ordination of overall school development planning with research projects voluntarily undertaken by individuals and groups;
- it depends upon active, informed and sensitive support from university departments of education;
- it is necessary to engage with claims for the nature and quality of the research;

- it depends upon the provision by senior managers of significant resources, especially of time, to facilitate both the research and its effective use;
- it depends upon the long-term commitment of the school, including its governing body.

These hypothesised conditions have much in common with the elements identified in Chapters 3 and 4 as key to the support of collaborative learning in networks. However there are also some tensions within them. First is the tension between coherence and the 'messy nature' of networks. The problems of co-ordinating overall school development planning with research projects voluntarily undertaken by groups of teachers inevitably become much greater when these groups are networks from several schools. The benefits of a network's work for the schools involved depend in large measure on that work being explicitly valued by each school's management and on deliberate planning of support for the work and of opportunities for it to be influential within the school. But a delicate balance needs to be struck between this and the equally important need for networks to have a high degree of autonomy in the direction of their own work. These conditions make considerable demands on leadership within schools and networks, which will be explored further in the final section of this chapter.

We noted that several of the research networks that we studied, which were much valued by their members, did not have common research agendas across schools but instead collaborated in terms of their common interest in research processes. In such networks, each school can pursue its own research agenda, and in such circumstances it is probably easier for internal school coherence to be achieved. Furthermore, some of the effort at the network level can be devoted to sharing the outcomes of individual schools' research. It may be appropriate for networks to have mixed economies, with some within-school research being negotiated with school managers, whereas other research projects at the network level are more loosely related to individual school plans.

Knowledge creation

We can say less about this area than about others, as we have found few research networks that were committed to the creation of validated public knowledge for use beyond, or even across, their network. The major tension therefore is between the realities of research networks as they are and visions of research networks as they might be, especially the vision articulated by Hargreaves (1999, 2003a, 2003b). This is not a tension between contrasting levels of sensitivity to schools as they are, as Hargreaves' vision is firmly grounded in a very good understanding of the realities of classroom teaching, but rather a tension between modest and highly ambitious aspirations for research networks. The networks we have studied have necessarily been concerned with doing what they have found possible within the limits both of the resources available to them and of the kinds of professional knowledge and value that those involved have developed. In contrast, Hargreaves' vision stems from a righteous impatience with the limited achievements of existing school systems and on a powerful argument about much greater possible achievements, based on informed understandings of cutting edge activities in other professions.

One important thing that the actual school networks have in common with Hargreaves' vision is a strong sense of the inadequacy of academic research into teaching and learning. Although there is an openness to whatever help such research can provide, there is a common understanding that research should be able to offer more than academic research has yet been able to offer. Furthermore, Hargreaves' idea that Mode Two research is what is needed to fill the gap is consistent with the evidence from networks that, for research findings to be valued, not only do they need to be seen to have contextual relevance, but also there need to be interpersonal relationships between the teachers doing the research and those who might use it. There are however big gaps in other respects: Hargreaves' ambition for networked based research to transform the quality of practice is premised on the need for highly rigorous research, the identification of, and subsequent focus on, a limited number of very powerful ideas, and a heavy investment in the complex task of sharing good practice; and, in all these respects, current practice (and, it must be said, current policy) is very different.

Where then are the growth points, if any? They are to be found less in networks than in individual schools in which senior management not only sees research as a valuable process for engaging teachers in reflection on their practice but also recognises that significant school improvement will occur only if the research that teachers do is rigorous, so that it produces clear and valid findings about good practice, and if there is then sufficient investment in the sharing of good practice. The challenging tasks of developing the necessary professional culture in such schools and, equally important, of attracting and allocating the necessary resources to engaging in and using research, may lead their head teachers to seek alliances with other like-minded schools. As yet, however, moves in this direction seem not only rare but also quite timid. For that to change, there will need to be radical shifts in the policy environment.

SUPPORTING THE SUCCESS OF NETWORKS OF RESEARCHING SCHOOLS

In this section we reflect on who might have responsibility for supporting the demanding work of networks of researching schools. We consider the three main groups that have emerged from our studies: head teachers and their schools, members of universities and government. We examine the nature of their roles and how these might need to change to provide the conditions necessary for such work. We also reflect on the possible implications of doing so with regard to other obligations to their organisations.

The roles and responsibilities of headteachers and their schools

It is self-evident that head teachers, and schools as institutions, have a primary obligation to provide their students with the best learning experiences possible. Thus, if a school joins a research network, it is imperative that both the researching and networking activities of members of that school should unambiguously contribute to this fundamental intention. Within these parameters, we have identified three key areas of responsibility for headteachers and schools. These are:

- developing a culture that supports research and network activities
- planning for researching and for networking
- providing resources and opportunities for researching and networking.

All three are, of course, closely interconnected.

Developing a culture that supports research and network activities

Our findings from across the networks we studied suggest that head teachers are crucial in developing the cultures of their schools, which promote high levels of social capital among members. Research and network activities require collaborative relationships based on trust and creativity, rather than privacy that can lead to suspicion and complacency. If these are not established between members within individual schools then it may be less straightforward to develop them institutionally across a network of schools. Not only must head teachers, and others who lead research and network activities, make explicit their full commitment to the work, they must also must find ways to ensure that all members are encouraged (although not coerced) to contribute to it. A range of opportunities need to be made available to avoid marginalising those who are initially least enthusiastic. For example, if some members choose not to be researchers, then their views could be sought, or their experiences used, as forms of research evidence. In particular, leaders need to listen to the voices of members who may be less often heard: for example, staff who are new, disillusioned or work in a support role; students and parents/carers, including those who are perceived as being diffident, difficult or non-conforming.

Furthermore, developing a school culture conducive to researching and networking requires that the work is also shared among members in terms of leadership roles. All the studies reported in this book emphasise the importance of doing this. It seems necessary in practical terms, because doing so spreads the workload and provides greater continuity when key school and network staff leave. Perhaps more importantly, it also helps to build a broader base of skills and expertise within individual schools and across networks, so contributing to the collaborative nature of the work.

Head teachers also have a collective responsibility for the overall development of the culture of the network, for example, by ensuring good working relationships with the other head teachers. If a network is underpinned by values based on competitiveness between the schools, then relationships that are reliant upon high levels of trust and interdependence are unlikely to be sustained. Networks that are part of larger educational systems that are predicated on notions of performance, accountability and competition will require their head teachers to be especially attentive to these concerns.

Planning for researching and for networking

Head teachers and schools also have to take responsibility for planning their research and network activities so that the costs of undertaking them are outweighed by the benefits of doing so. The majority of the schools in our studies saw their involvement in the networks as contributing to their overall school improvement. However, this seems to require schools to make the work integral to their overall development planning structures, rather than viewing it as an interesting but 'added on' activity. If the research is to be undertaken collaboratively across the network, then decisions about research topics that support individual schools' own development plans need to be co-ordinated so that they contribute to the development plans of all the schools. Furthermore, planning is also essential to ensure that the research findings arising from the network are used to bring about significant changes in practice at the level of the school rather than only at the level of individual teacher researchers. Finally, it is imperative that head teachers put checks into place to monitor the quality of the research undertaken. This is particularly important when findings are used not only to change the practices of individual teachers but also to determine policies and practices across the whole school, or even possibly the network.

Providing resources and opportunities for researching and networking

The funding made available to the different networks in our studies varied tremendously, from those that received considerable sums to those that were almost entirely self-financing. Nevertheless, there were teachers in all of them who gave up their own time to carry out the work. Government agencies clearly have a role to play here, and this will be discussed later. However, if head teachers elect to join a network, then they also have an obligation to make available adequate resources so that researching and networking are not reliant on the goodwill of their teachers alone. There is also evidence to suggest that teachers who are given time to undertake the work see this as a validation of its worth in the school.

Providing resources is not only about funding but also about using opportunities to draw on existing resources to help research and networking to take place, in particular those resources that facilitate long-term collaboration between teachers and others within a school and across the network. Head teachers might choose to redirect time and money already allocated to professional development, specifically to the work of the network. They might also encourage staff to make good use of structures, such as curriculum departments in secondary schools, or year groups in primary schools, as spaces in which research can effectively take place. In all of our studies of networks, teachers emphasised the importance of meeting face-to-face with network colleagues. Head teachers therefore have a responsibility for allowing this to happen in ways that are not disruptive of students' learning. For example, they might make creative changes to school structures, perhaps reconfiguring how lessons and timetables are organised across the school.

The roles and responsibilities of universities

The majority of the school networks reported in this book also included members of universities (and sometimes other external organisations such as LAs), whose role was to assist practitioners in their research activities. A range of support was offered such as: the provision of research training and materials; acting as a research critical friend to schools; and the management and co-ordination of network activities. Furthermore, the involvement of universities in networks was generally highly valued by the teachers and leaders in the schools. In particular, their support was considered important because it enhanced the quality of the research undertaken by providing essential research skills, as well as an external, and sometimes challenging, perspective on the work. In addition, network members welcomed the opportunity to have greater access to the 'expert' knowledge and 'cutting edge' research taking place in universities, especially if it was closely related to the substantive topics that concerned their research. Therefore, if networks of researching schools are to succeed in the future, it seems necessary that teachers and schools should be given adequate access to research expertise, training and resources. Furthermore, our studies would suggest that members of universities are well placed to offer these forms of support.

There are, nevertheless, fundamental differences between the natures of schools and universities as organisations and the roles of teachers and academics within them, which shape members' understanding of educational research. These different perspectives may prove challenging for networks. It seems important, therefore, that members from both sets of institutions are able to acknowledge and value the distinct but complementary contributions they each can make to the research process. It will also be helpful if they can recognise and be sympathetic to the differing demands and expectations of school and university life, and their impact on the processes of research. We have identified the following distinctions (see also McIntyre and Black-Hawkins, 2006):

- *The population to be served*: Schools and networks are primarily concerned with knowledge that will benefit their own students, whereas universities are concerned with a wider and more abstractly defined population.
- *The context of knowledge use*: Similarly, schools and networks are interested in undertaking research that is useful in their own specific and distinctive context, whereas universities are interested in more generally useful knowledge.
- *The process of dissemination*: Teachers prefer to disseminate their findings through local face-to-face meetings and the sharing of practice, whereas academics are obliged to disseminate their findings and conclusions primarily through written publications.
- *Criteria for quality control*: Schools tend to evaluate their research activities in terms of professional credibility and demonstrable relevance to current practices, rather than the robustness of methodologies. University researchers, however, know that their work will be judged primarily in terms of its academic rigour and only thereafter in terms of wider criteria.
- *Process rather than product*: Schools and networks generally consider the process of teachers and students engaging in research to be at least as beneficial to them as the actual findings, whereas the value of research for academics is almost entirely in the contribution that the findings make to educational knowledge.
- *Time-scale*: For the teachers, the usefulness of research findings depends on the immediacy of their availability, including their contribution to the learning of students currently in the network schools. However, for university researchers, the speed with which knowledge becomes available is much less important than the transparent rigour of its evidence-based conclusions.

These institutional distinctions between schools and universities need not necessarily cause conflict. However, networks are more likely to be successful when there is a shared understanding of these differences, an acceptance of the appropriateness of one another's concerns, a readiness to be helpful wherever possible and a recognition that each side has much to learn from the other. Members of universities must take responsibility to help to develop and nurture relationships with their colleagues in schools that are based on mutual support, respect and trust. Although their role is critical in terms of ensuring the robust nature of research in the network, members of universities should offer support in ways that are properly useful to the practices of teachers and schools, and that will not be construed by schools as either patronising or hierarchical towards teachers and their research efforts.

Finally, because a fundamental obligation of academics is to engage in their own research, they must find ways of doing so that allow them to collaborate with networks, but not jeopardise their own institutional responsibilities. There are a number of ways in which this can happen. For example, they can draw on the network to provide opportunities to develop long-standing and close relationships with its schools, which can then become rewarding sites for their research. Doing so could also allow university staff to engage in collaborative research work with members of these schools. University staff might also choose to research the actual processes of the network of which they are members. As we have indicated throughout this book, understandings of how school networks function and also how researching schools work remains underdeveloped. Thus there continues to be a real need for careful and detailed examination of the consequences, benefits and costs of bringing these two elements together. This book is, itself, a contribution to this work.

The roles and responsibilities of government

Because of the demanding nature of the work required of networks of researching schools, it may be that they would be more successful in their endeavours if they were to receive governmental support. In our studies of networks we identified very different levels of governmental involvement, from those in which there was no direct association, to others in which small and also large amounts of funding were provided. There are two clear means by which a government could support future networks: first by providing additional resources; and, second, by making changes to school systems so that they become more conducive to the nature of the work. The first of these appears relatively straightforward, whereas the second requires a more radical transformation of the status quo. However, neither are unproblematic and both are dependent on the explicit trust of government in the professional judgements of teachers.

It is apparent in all of the studies in this book that good quality research and networking both take time to happen and to develop. There are therefore clear cost implications for schools, which a government could help to alleviate. However, it might be argued that direct government sponsorship would be counterproductive if it militated against the voluntary and shifting nature of network membership, or if it brought with it demands about the nature and direction of the work, which in turn stifled experimentation and creativity. This suggests that any such funding might be most effective if schools and networks were allowed to use it independently of governmental controls. At the same time, governments must fulfil their obligations to all children and young people in schools, and to tax payers more generally. Therefore, it seems unlikely that any government would be prepared to make substantial funding available to teachers, schools and networks (or indeed universities), without expecting some form of accountability for monies spent. Currently schools are often judged in terms of raising standards according to gains made over time in students' scores on national standardised tests. However, if this criterion were applied to networks, it might well inhibit the types of collaborative research activity that benefit from creative risk-taking. An emphasis on performance might also injure the development of trust in the relationships between the schools. New forms of accountability would therefore need to be established, which would provide more appropriate evidence that funds were being properly used.

Governments may also support networks by ensuring that the conditions under which teachers work and schools operate are conducive to the types of activity in which networks wish to engage. Schools are demanding places for teachers, and their working experiences are generally so intense that most consider engaging in researching and networking activities as less immediately important than their primary obligation to support students' learning. If governments wish to encourage research networks then they must take responsibility for bringing about fundamental changes to the working practices of teachers and also to the institutional structures of schools. Currently, there is little flexibility in the routines of school life: teachers still generally work in classrooms isolated from their colleagues and teach according to prescribed curricula. A loosening of these constraints would allow greater opportunities for creative and collaborative approaches to research. If all teachers in networks were given, say, 5 hours every week for professional development work, this could provide the time, space, commitment and energy required for the work to be undertaken seriously. There are, of course, not only significant funding implications in these suggestions but also educational ones. In a climate of control and authority, these shifts in power, from government to teachers and schools, seem somewhat improbable.

A WAY FORWARD?

We began this book by noting that improving schools through facilitating learning by teachers from and through research in networks was in its infancy. What can we conclude might be a way forward for these infants? It is clear that there has been much very valuable and varied activity in networks of practitioner researchers. There has been much advocacy and a range of claims for networks for a range of purposes. In looking at a way forward, the concepts of maximal and minimal aspirations seem useful. They can be applied to the two dimensions of networking and research. The implications of adopting a maximal or a minimal notion are very different both in scale and scope.

A maximal view of networks is encapsulated in some of the claims of Hargreaves (2003a, 2003b), who argued that networks could go far beyond the local and specific. He argued that large-scale networks of schools could provide a critical and effective means by which radical innovation could take place in schools, thereby bringing about a systemic transformation of UK education organisational structures. A minimal notion of networks is captured in terms such as partnerships or 'responsible communities of practice' working 'for the development and authentic improvement of schools to be based upon systematic practitioner inquiry undertaken as a collegial activity embedded within the culture of the school' (Groundwater-Smith and Dadds, 2004). Here the scale is smaller and the emphasis is on networks of schools working on their own agendas and creating local, situated knowledge shared primarily within the school but also across the schools. The evidence is there to suggest that, given the current conditions in schools, the capacity for this loose coupling or minimal conception of networks is a feasible one. Claims for the maximal notion of networks are necessarily more speculative, and their validity has yet to be demonstrated.

The second dimension is that of research and knowledge creation in networks of schools. A maximal concept of research is that networks of schools:

> can prioritise a shared topic for knowledge creation and have a much more sophisticated design, both for sharing the innovative workload, so that each school undertakes a limited and variable amount of activity, and for testing it more rigorously than is ever possible in a single . . . school or department . . . generating a far more robust evidence base . . . in a far shorter time.
>
> (Hargreaves, 2003b, p. 40)

The evidence we have examined suggests that this too is a task that has not yet been achieved in practice and that it requires significant external resources, as well as a significant shift in the way teachers and schools operate. It is still not an aim that is embedded in the aspirations or practices of teacher researchers or of researching schools. There is no evidence of networks of schools having the capacity or desire to work on co-ordinated research projects, although this has been an aim of networks we have explored such as the TTA, BASRC and SUPER networks and to a lesser extent the NLC networks. The minimal notion is of schools as learning communities where the results of the research process may lead to 'new understandings about practice in their school and classroom' (McLaughlin and Zarrow, 2001, p.87) and where sharing of these outcomes can inform the understanding of others in the network. The minimal notion seems to be closer to the agendas and practices of teachers and managers in schools. Although we should not underestimate what can be achieved with partnerships of schools and other organisations, such as local authorities or university departments of education, school improvement by this means will be slow and sporadic. The way forward must surely be to start from the fairly modest agendas and practices of teachers and schools embodied in current research networks, but actively to use these networks both to understand the problems and possibilities of more ambitious plans and gradually to develop them into more far-reaching schemes.

Finally, networks of researching schools can make a real difference to the quality of schooling if and only if there is a strong and intelligent policy commitment to supporting them. There are certainly indications in England currently that the national government sees networking as a valuable way forward. However, the value of networking, and of research networking in particular, will depend on a much more significant allocation of resources to the development, exploration and provision of this very new way of working. It will depend also on a much more thoughtful accountability climate in which the articulation, rigorous testing and sharing of good practices by teachers are encouraged as never before.

Appendix I

Research methods, data collection and research instruments

The questionnaire

QUESTIONNAIRE DESIGN

This questionnaire was designed to explore the perceptions and application of enquiry within case study networks and is constructed with three sections. Section 1 identified the basic descriptors of respondents, including their gender, years of teaching experience, the nature of their responsibilities within schools and the age of pupils for whom they had responsibility. This section enabled the responses of different groups within the entire sample to be compared, including: enquirers and non-enquirers; different networks; different years of experience; and different positions in the school's management.

Section 2 explored the perceptions of respondents with regard to the enquiries they had conducted within their networks. Nine sub-sections required enquirers (only respondents who identified themselves as enquirers were asked to complete section 2) to select the most appropriate answer(s) from a choice of up to fifteen responses per question. Respondents were asked to select answers that most closely matched their experiences or attitudes towards enquiry. In addition, for each of the nine questions respondents were asked to record their own views in open-ended questions.

Section 3 used opposing statements to record the attitudes of all respondents towards enquiry-based issues. Opposing statements provided a semantic differential for respondents, whose responses were separated into a scale of five positions relative to the two statements. These statements provided opposing views of one particular aspect of networked enquiry and, in conjunction with section 1, were designed to allow comparison of the attitudes of respondents from different networks and subgroups towards networked enquiry.

THE SCOPE AND RELIABILITY OF THE QUESTIONNAIRE

This section explored the scope and reliability of the questionnaire. The scope of the questionnaire was described in terms of the sample of respondent, and the reliability of the questionnaire was described through tests conducted on responses to sections 2 and 3.

Respondent characteristics

Each of the six case study networks were provided with sufficient copies of the questionnaire for all network personnel, with some spares. In total, 651 completed questionnaires were returned, which forms the sample for the analysis described here. The actual number of responses varied by network, in part in response to the nature of the network and in response to the willingness of personnel to complete and return the questionnaire. These response rates are compared in Table A.1.

Reliability tests

Sections 2 and 3 of the questionnaire were subjected to tests of reliability. These tests were administered to explore the statistical reliability of the answers given on the questionnaire.

Section 2 Reliability test: Kuder–Richardson coefficient

Section 2 of the questionnaire required respondents to select from multiple choice answers to questions concerning enquiry. As this section was only intended to be completed by enquirers, only respondents identifying themselves as enquirers were included in this reliability test and in any subsequent analysis quoted below. As respondents could choose from as many suitable answers as appropriate, each possible response was coded as a separate dichotomous item (i.e. boxes left unticked were coded one, those ticked were coded two). The Kuder-Richardson coefficient was used to test reliability, as it is intended for use with dichotomous items, rather than Chrombach's alpha, which is intended for use with multiple response items. The response of this test provided a coefficient of 0.9306 for 345 cases (NB enquirers

Table A.1 Response rate by network

Network	Frequency	Sample percentage
SUPER	238	36.6
Surrey LIFE	160	24.6
Bristol	38	5.8
Hartlepool	131	20.1
SW London	38	5.8
Blackburn	46	7.1
Total	651	100.0

only) and 104 items. This is considerably above the 0.7 threshold for reliable responses.

Section 3 Reliability test: Chronbach's alpha

As section 3 provided respondents with multiple responses, Chronbach's alpha was used as a test for reliability. This test produced an alpha value of 0.9047 for 539 cases and 20 items. Once again, this is considerably above the 0.7 threshold for reliable responses.

QUESTIONNAIRE ANALYSIS

This section explored comparisons of the responses of different groups, including members of different networks. This was achieved through analysis of tables and graphs of responses to section 3. As these showed a near-normal distribution, an analysis of variance (ANOVA) was used to compare the mean responses of different groups to questions in section 3. Although it is recognised that ANOVA utilises a comparison of means, some writers have suggested that this is useful for data from an ordinal level, and that, although the Kruskall–Wallis test provides a non-parametric alternative, comparisons of analysis using ANOVA and Kruksall–Wallis have shown very similar results. As a result, ANOVA was selected as it provided an increased complexity of analysis in comparison with Kruskall–Wallis.

Appendix 2

Evidence to support individual case studies

Evidence to support case study of Blackburn and Darwen NLC

Schools visited	• three out of nine in total
Interviews	• sixteen formal, comprising:
	• one co-leader (x3); one chair of steering group; one head teacher; two deputy head teachers; two heads of department; six teacher enquirers; one communications officer
Observations	• observed one half-day meeting of enquiry group
Archives/Documents	• enquiry group logs; CD of reports of enquiry; other general documents; NLC submission document
Questionnaires	• a sample of teachers in all schools were given questionnaires, forty-six returned

Evidence to support case study of Bristol NLC

Schools visited	• five in total, comprising:
	• one infants; one juniors; two JMIs; one secondary
Dates of visits	• November 2004–May 2005
Interviews	• ten formal, tape recorded and transcribed, comprising:
	• five teachers (all 'leading links', including two lead leading links); four head teachers; Director of EAZ/network co-leader)
	• various informal conversations recorded in note form, including:
	• Deputy Director of EAZ, teachers, children, support staff
Observations	• three in total, comprising:
	• one leading link network meeting, involving one teacher from each school
	• two teaching sessions, demonstrating research into practice
Archives/Documents	• network level, including: bid to become NLC; Spring Enquiry (February 2004); A Framework for Sustainability; BPRS and other research topics; research reports/leaflets; website information; newsletters: etc.
	• school level, including: prospectuses; policy documents etc.
	• classroom level, including: teaching and learning materials etc.
Questionnaires	• a sample of teachers in all schools, thirty-eight returned

Evidence to support case study of Hartlepool NLC

Schools visited	• five out of twelve in total
Interviews	• thirty-three formal, comprising: • three co-leaders (three interviewed x 2); two network facilitators; twenty-five teachers
Observations	• two, comprising: • two conference days
Archives/Documents	• enquiry group logs; enquiry reports; articles written about networks; other general documents
Questionnaires	• teachers in all schools were given questionnaire, 131 returned

Evidence to support case study of SUPER

Schools visited	• Schools have been visited by the critical friends at least half-termly, and these visits have been research occasions as well as development times
Dates of visits	• September 2000–July 2005
Interviews	• interviews with TRCs, SVCs, head teachers, critical friends, students, teachers and university lecturers
Archives/Documents	• partnership plans, writings by SUPER members, SUPER research reports
Questionnaires	• 600 teachers, 238 returned

Evidence to support case study of Surrey LIFE NLC

Schools visited	• two
Dates of visits	• November 2004–March 2005
Interviews	• five formal, tape recorded and transcribed, comprising: • two teachers; one TA; one head teacher; one NLC facilitator • various informal conversations recorded in note form, including: • head teacher; teachers; TAs and other support staff; children
Observations	• four in total, comprising: • one head teachers' steering group meeting; one network 'development day' conference (research co-ordinators and head teachers); one research co-ordinators' meeting; one pupil voice co-ordinators' meeting
Archives/Documents	• network level, including: bid to become NLC; agendas and minutes for meetings; research protocols; research support papers; network review/evaluation materials; materials from network conference; LEA website information etc. • school level, including: website information; teaching and learning/research materials; pupil voice 'sharing' materials/papers etc.
Questionnaires	• 650 teachers and TAs, 159 returned

Evidence to support case study of South West London NLC

Schools visited	• three, comprising:
	• one junior and two secondary
Dates of visits	• November 2004–May 2005
Interviews	• ten formal, tape recorded and transcribed, comprising:
	• one headteacher; two assistant head teachers; six teachers; two network co-leaders (one is also an assistant head teacher)
	• various informal conversations recorded in note form, including:
	• co-leaders, teacher researchers from all six schools, NLC facilitator
Observations	• two, comprising:
	• one network meeting, including ten teacher researchers;
	• one network research presentation at NLC conference
Archives/Documents	• network level, including: bid to become NLC; Spring Enquiry (February 2004); Year 2 review for NLC; Research Support Programme 2003–4 (Hounslow LEA and St Mary's College University); research summaries etc.
	• school level, including: prospectuses; policy documents etc.
	• classroom level, including: teaching and learning materials devised by teachers researchers from each school; CD-ROM and paper format
Questionnaires	• 600 teachers, twenty-eight returned

Questionnaire used across sample of Network Learning Communities (2004–5)

EXPLORING SCHOOL-BASED PRACTITIONER RESEARCH AND ENQUIRY

SCHOOL STAFF QUESTIONNAIRE

Introduction

Thank you for completing this questionnaire. It forms part of a current research project undertaken by members of the Faculty of Education at the University of Cambridge, on behalf of the Networked Learning Community Group. It has been given to staff in about 70 schools across England.

Instructions

- The questionnaire focuses on school-based practitioner research and enquiry. It may be that you may prefer other ways of describing these activities, such as 'action research' or 'evidence based practice'. However, to avoid unnecessary repetition in the questions we have used the general term 'enquiry' throughout.

- Because different schools have different ways of doing things, some of the questions may be more or less relevant to your work. However, please answer as many of them as you are able.

- We are interested in your views and what you do.

- We expect the questionnaire to take about 10 minutes to complete.

- Please return the completed questionnaire to the Faculty of Education, University of Cambridge, using the Freepost envelope attached. Please do so within two weeks of receiving the questionnaire.

- Members of the research team at the faculty will analyse the results. Each school will be given some general feedback but no individual school or member of staff will be identifiable. All responses are confidential.

THANK YOU FOR YOUR HELP

Section 1: This section asks for some information about you, your school and your work

1. **For how many years have you worked in your current school?**

   (a) Fewer than 5 ☐

   (b) 5 to 10 ☐

   (c) 11 to 15 ☐

   (d) 16 + ☐

2. **For how many years have you worked in schools altogether?**

   (a) Fewer than 5 ☐

   (b) 5 to 10 ☐

   (c) 11 to 15 ☐

   (d) 16 + ☐

3. **Are you ...?**

   (a) Male ☐   (b) Female ☐

4. **How old are the pupils with whom you are currently working?
   Tick all which apply**

   (a) Foundation stage ☐

   (b) KS1 ☐

   (c) KS2 ☐

   (d) KS3 ☐

   (e) KS4 ☐

   (f) 16+ ☐

5. **Which of following describe your job / responsibilities?
   Tick all which apply**

   (a) Class teacher ☐

   (b) Teaching assistant ☐

   (c) Deputy headteacher ☐

   (d) Head teacher ☐

   (e) Key stage co-ordinator ☐

   (f) Subject co-ordinator / head of department ☐

   (g) Pastoral responsibility ☐

   (h) Learning support teacher ☐

   (i) Other…Please explain: _____

6. **Do you mainly work in one curriculum or subject area?**

   (a) Yes ☐   (b) No ☐

   If 'yes' please write its name here: _____

Section 2: This section is about any enquiry activities in which you have been engaged during the last THREE years

1. **Have you been engaged in any form of school-based practitioner enquiry activities during the last three years?**

   (a) Yes ☐   (b) No ☐

   - If you have ticked 'Yes' please answer the rest of the questions in this section.
   - If you have ticked 'No' please go straight to Section 3.

(a) How would you describe your practitioner enquiry activities?

2:1 Tick any of the following which describe activities in which you have been involved.

   (a) Practitioner research ☐   (b) Action enquiry ☐

   (c) Educational research ☐   (d) School-based enquiry ☐

   (e) Action research ☐   (f) Classroom enquiry ☐

   (g) Evidence based practice ☐   (h) Investigation ☐

   (i) Reflective practice ☐   (j) None of these is appropriate ☐

2:2 Please write below how you would prefer to describe your enquiry activities: using either one from the above or your own words.

3. **What is the main focus of your enquiry activities?**

3:1 Tick any of the following which describe a main focus of any of your enquiry activities.

   (a) Whole school issues ☐   (b) School management ☐

   (c) Pupils' classroom learning ☐   (d) Subject / key stage focus ☐

   (e) Classroom management ☐   (f) Pupils' pastoral / behaviour ☐

   (g) Special education needs ☐   (h) Assessment of learning ☐

   (i) Parents / carers issues ☐   (j) None of these is appropriate ☐

   (k) Use of technology in classroom ☐

3:2 Please write below how you would chose to describe your main or most important enquiry focus: using either one from the above or your own words.

(a) Why do you get involved in enquiry activities?

4:1 Tick any of the following which describe reasons why you have been involved in enquiry activities.

(a) Improve own classroom practice ☐   (b) Own professional concerns ☐

(c) Support own school improvement ☐   (d) Raise school standards ☐

(e) Increase subject knowledge ☐   (f) Improve chances of promotion ☐

(g) Enhance job satisfaction ☐   (h) Promote social justice / inclusion ☐

(i) Support pupils' learning ☐   (j) Support enquiry of colleagues ☐

(k) Establish best practice ☐   (l) Directed to do enquiry by others ☐

(m) Support other schools'   (n) None of these reasons is
    improvement ☐   appropriate ☐

(o) Part of accredited course ☐

4:2 Please write below the main or most important reason why you have been involved in enquiry activities: using either one from the above or your own words.

---

5. Where do people work who support your enquiry?

5: 1 Tick any of the following which describe the workplace of people who have supported your enquiry.

(a) Own school ☐   (b) Networked Learning Communities ☐

(c) School other than my own   (d) Professional body / association
                                              ☐   ☐

(e) Higher education / University ☐   (f) Outside consultant ☐

(g) DfES / Other governmental   (h) I have not used support from any
    organisation ☐   of the places named here ☐

(i) Local education authority   (j) I have not used support for my
                                              ☐   enquiry ☐

5:2 Please write below the place where people work who have given you the most useful support for your enquiry: using either one from the above or your own words.

6. What kinds of support for enquiry have you been given?

6:1 Tick any of the following which describe ways in which you have been supported by others when undertaking your enquiry.

(a) Finding an enquiry focus ☐   (b) Ethics of enquiry ☐

(c) Writing an enquiry report ☐   (d) Given time to do the enquiry ☐

(e) Methods for collecting and analysing evidence ☐   (f) Given other resources to support the enquiry ☐

(g) Opportunity to discuss, learn and be challenged, within own school ☐   (h) Opportunity to discuss, learn and be challenged, outside own school ☐

(i) Sharing the findings with others ☐   (j) I have had none of these supports

6:2 Tick any of the following which have been PARTICULARLY helpful for you. ☐

(a) Finding an enquiry focus ☐   (b) Ethics of enquiry ☐

(c) Writing an enquiry report ☐   (d) Given time to do the enquiry ☐

(e) Methods for collecting and analysing evidence ☐   (f) Given other resources to support the enquiry ☐

(g) Opportunity to discuss, learn and be challenged, within own school ☐   (h) Opportunity to discuss, learn and be challenged, outside own school ☐

(i) Sharing the findings with others   (j) None of these has been particularly helpful

6:3 Please write below the most helpful kind of enquiry support you have had: using either one from the above or your own words.

---

7. What type of written information have you used to support your enquiry?

7:1 Tick any of the following types of written information you have used to support your enquiry.

(a) Internet / web ☐   (b) Text books ☐

(c) Journal articles ☐   (d) Times Educational Supplement ☐

(e) Materials provided by academic/ tutor in university ☐   (f) Radio /TV / non-specialist newspapers / magazines ☐

(g) Professional association publications ☐   (h) Government publications (e.g. DfES) ☐

(i) Networked Learning Community publications ☐   (j) I have used none of these forms of information ☐

(k) Union publications ☐

7:2 Please write below the most useful type of written information you have used to support your enquiry: using either one from the above or your own words.

8. With whom do you share the findings of your enquiry work?

8:1 Tick any of the following people with whom you have shared, or expect to share, the findings of your enquiry.

(a) Colleagues in own school ☐

(b) Children / students in other school ☐

(c) Senior management in own school ☐

(d) Professional body / association ☐

(e) Curriculum subject / key stage team own school ☐

(f) Staff in higher education / universities ☐

(g) Children / students in own school ☐

(h) LEA staff ☐

(i) Parents in own school ☐

(j) Networked Learning Communities ☐

(k) Governing body at own school ☐

(l) Do not share my findings ☐

(m) Colleagues in other school ☐

(n) None of these people is applicable

8:2 Please write below the main person/people with whom you have shared, or intend to share the findings of your enquiry work: using either one from the above or your own words.

9. How do you share the findings of your enquiry work?

9:1 Tick any of the following ways in which you have shared, or intend to share, the findings of your enquiry work.

(a) Informal discussion in own school ☐

(b) Informal discussion in other schools ☐

(c) Formal discussion / presentation in own school ☐

(d) Formal discussion/presentation in Other schools ☐

(e) Written report for own school ☐

(f) Written report for other schools ☐

(g) Own school intranet ☐

(h) Internet/web ☐

(i) Conference presentation ☐

(j) Local network's publication ☐

(k) Journal article ☐

(l) None of these ways is applicable ☐

(m) National Networked Learning Community publications ☐

9:2 Please write below your preferred way of sharing your enquiry work: using either one from the above or your own words.

Section 3: This section comprises pairs of statements about school-based practitioner enquiry.

- Please tick ONE box in the middle columns for each pair to show which of them you agree with most and how much.
- The very central column can be used if you neither agree nor disagree with either statement or if both statements are irrelevant to your experiences in school.

STATEMENT 1	TICK ✓ ONE BOX ONLY					STATEMENT 2
1. Being involved in practitioner enquiry is currently a high priority for me professionally						1. Being involved in practitioner enquiry is currently a low priority for me professionally
2. I frequently use published research to support my work in this school						2. I rarely use published research to support my work in this school
3. Teaching should be an enquiry-based profession						3. Teaching should not be an enquiry-based profession
4. Most of my school colleagues are currently engaged in enquiry activities						4. Very few of my school colleagues are currently engaged in enquiry activities
5. Enquiring collaboratively with school colleagues usually generates more useful results than individual enquiry						5. Individual enquiry usually generates more useful results than enquiring collaboratively with school colleagues
6. Educational research should be done mainly by practitioners in schools						6. Educational research should be done mainly by academics in universities
7. I can usually find the time to do school-based enquiry						7. I rarely find the time to do school-based enquiry
8. When my school colleagues undertake enquiry they usually share their findings with me						8. When my school colleagues undertake enquiry they rarely share their finding with me
9. Most school-based enquiry needs to include the views of pupils as part of its evidence						9. Most school-based enquiry does not need to include the views of pupils as part of its evidence
10. Engaging in enquiry is a particularly useful form of staff development						10. Engaging in enquiry is not a particularly useful form of staff development

STATEMENT 1	TICK ✓ ONE BOX ONLY					STATEMENT 2
11. Engaging in enquiry supports practitioners to be more reflective about their work generally						11. Engaging in enquiry does not really support practitioners to be more reflective about their work generally
12. The senior management give great support to enquiry work in this school						12. The senior management give very little support to enquiry work in this school
13. Enquiry work in this school has helped to improve pupils' performance in national tests						13. Enquiry work in this school has made little difference to pupils' performance in national tests
14. I have made changes to my classroom practices as a result of my engagement in enquiry work						14. I have not made any changes to my classroom practices as a result of my engagement in enquiry work
15. I am confident that I have the necessary skills to do practitioner enquiry work well						15. I am not really confident that I have the necessary skills to do practitioner enquiry work well
16. For enquiry work to be most useful it should involve practitioners from more than one school						16. For enquiry work to be most useful it should involve practitioners from one school only
17. The enquiry findings of colleagues have resulted in me making changes to my classroom practices						17. The enquiry findings of colleagues have not resulted in me making changes to my classroom practices
18. The senior management team in this school place a high priority on staff involvement in enquiry activities						18. The senior management team in this school place a low priority on staff involvement in enquiry activities
19. Engaging in enquiry is essential to develop practitioners' professional judgement						19. Engaging in enquiry is not essential to develop practitioners' professional judgement
20. Even though engaging in enquiry is demanding, I expect that it will always be a part of my work						20. Since engaging in enquiry is demanding, I do not expect it always to be a part of my work

References

Abercrombie, J. (1989) *The Anatomy of Judgement.* London: Free Association Books.

Achinstein, B. (2002) 'Conflict amid community: The micropolitics of teacher collaboration.' *Teachers College Record*, 104(3): 421–55.

Anderson, G. (1998) 'Toward authentic participation: Deconstructing the discourse of participatory reforms in education.' *American Educational Research Journal*, 35: 571–603.

Anderson, G. (1999) 'The politics of participatory reforms in education.' *Theory into Practice*, 138(4): 191–200.

Ball, S. J. (1987) *The Micro-Politics of the School: Towards a Theory of Social Organisation.* London: Routledge.

BASRC (2004) http://www.basrc.org/about_basrc

BASRC (2007) http://www.basrc.org

Baumfield, V. (2001) The north east school based research consortium: An overview of the changing nature of the roles and relationships between the universities, schools and LEAs. Paper presented at the British Educational Research Association Conference, University of Leeds, September 2001.

Baumfield, V. and McGrane, J. (2000) Teachers using evidence and engaging in and with research: One school's story. Paper presented at British Educational Research Association Annual Conference, University of Cardiff, September 2000.

Black-Hawkins, K. (2003) Are school-university friendships critical? Developing professional and institutional research relationships. Paper presented at the British Educational Research Association Conference, Heriot-Watt University, Edinburgh, September 2003.

Blasé, J. and Blasé, J. (1999) 'Principals' instructional leadership and teacher development: Teachers' perspectives.' *Educational Administration Quarterly*, 35(3): 349–78.

Bolam, R. and Weindling, D. (2006) *Synthesis of Research and Evaluation Projects Concerned with Capacity-Building through Teachers' Professional Development.* London: General Teaching Council.

Bradley, H., Conner, C. and Southworth, G. (eds) (1994) *Developing Teachers, Developing Schools.* London: David Fulton Publishers.

Brown, S. (2005) 'How can research inform ideas of good practice in teaching? The contributions of some official initiatives in the UK.' *Cambridge Journal of Education*, 35(3): 383–405.

Campbell, A., McNamara, O. and Gilroy, P. (2004) *Practitioner Research for Professional Development in Education.* London: Paul Chapman.

Carmichael, P., Fox, A., McCormick, R., Procter, R. and Honour, L. (2006) 'Teachers' networks in and out of school.' *Research Papers in Education*, 21(2): 217–34.

Carr, W. and Kemmis, S. (1986) *Becoming Critical: Education, Knowledge and Action Research*. London: Falmer Press.

Castells, M. (2000) *The Rise of the Network Society,* 2nd edn. Oxford: Blackwell.

Center for Research on the Context of Teaching (2002) *Bay Area School Reform Collaborative Summary Report, Phase 1 (1996–2001)*. Stanford, California: Stanford University.

Church, M., Bitel, M., Armstrong, K., Fernando, P., Gould, H., Joss, S., Marwaha-Diedrich, M., de la Torre, A. L. and Vouhé, C. (2002) *Participation, Relationships and Dynamic Change: New Thinking On Evaluating The Work Of International Networks*. Working Paper 121. London: Development Planning Unit, University College.

Claxton, G. (2002) *Building Learning Power*. Bristol: TLO.

Cochran-Smith, M. and Lytle, S. L. (2001) Beyond certainty: Taking an inquiry stance on practice. *In:* Lieberman, A. and Miller, L. (eds) *Teachers Caught in the Action: Professional Development that Matters*, pp. 45–60. New York: Teachers College Press.

Cohen, L., Manion, L. and Morrison, K. (2000) *Research Methods in Education*, 5th edn. London and New York: Routledge Falmer.

Copland, M. A. (2002) *Leadership of Inquiry: Building and Sustaining Capacity for School Improvement in the Bay Area School Reform Collaborative.* Stanford, California: Centre for Research on the Context of Teaching, Stanford University.

Cordingley, P. and Bell, M. (2002) School-Based Research Consortium Initiative: An overview report. Paper presented at the TTA Conference on Working and Learning in Partnership, London, March 2002.

Cordingley, P., Baumfield, V., Butterworth, M., McNamara, O. and Elkins, T. (2002) Lessons from the School-Based Research Consortia. Paper presented at the British Educational Research Association Conference, University of Exeter, September 2002.

Cordingley, P., Bell, M., Evans, D. and Firth, A. (2003*) What do Teacher Impact Data Tell us about Collaborative CPD?* London: DfES/EPPI/CUREE.

Dadds, M. (1993) 'The feeling of thinking in professional self-study.' *Educational Action Research*, 1(2): 287–303.

Dadds, M. (1995) *Passionate Enquiry and School Development.* London: Falmer Press.

Darling-Hammond, L. (ed.) (1994) *Professional Development Schools*. New York: Teachers College Press.

Darling-Hammond, L. and McLaughlin, M. W. (1996) Policies that support professional development in an era of reform. *In:* McLaughlin, M. W. and Oberman, I. (eds) *Teacher Learning: New Policies, New Practices*, pp. 202–18. New York: Teachers College Press.

Dewey, J. (1929) *The Sources of a Science of Education*. New York: Liverright.

DfES (1999) Excellence in Cities programme, www.standards.dfes.gov.uk/sie/eic (accessed September 2005).

DfES (2002a) Leading Edge Partnership programme, http://www.standards.dfes.gov.uk/leadingedge/ (accessed September 2005).

DfES (2002b) www.dfes.gov.uk

DfES (2004a) *Five Year Strategy for Children and Learners: Maintaining the Excellent Progress*. Nottingham: DfES.

DfES (2004b) *Primary Strategy Learning Networks: An Introduction*. Nottingham: DfES.

Earl, L. and Katz, S. (2005) *Learning from Networked Learning Communities – Phase 2 – Key Features and Inevitable Tensions.* Toronto: Aporia Consulting.

Ebbutt, D. (2000) The development of a research culture in secondary schools. Paper presented at the European Conference on Educational Research, Edinburgh, September 2003.

Ebbutt, D. (2002) 'The development of a research culture in secondary schools.' *The Journal of Educational Action Research*, 10(1): 123–40.

Elliott, J. (1981) *Action Research: A Framework for Self-Evaluation in Schools.* Cambridge: Cambridge Institute of Education.

Elliott, J. (1991) *Action Research for Educational Change.* Buckingham: Open University Press.

Elliott, J. (2002) 'Working 'against the grain': A conversation piece from the academy about the experience of sustaining collaborative research with teachers.' *Pedagogy, Culture and Society*, 10(2): 323–48.

Elliott, J. and Adelman, C. (eds) (1974) *Ford Teaching Project Reports and Documents.* Norwich: Centre for Applied Research in Education, University of East Anglia.

Elliott, J. and Sarland, C. (1995) 'A study of 'teachers as researchers' in the context of award-bearing courses and research degrees.' *British Educational Research Journal*, 21(3): 371–86.

Elliott, J., Chambers, P. and Powney, J. (1982) 'School-based curriculum research.' *British Educational Research Journal*, 8(2): 133–9

Elliott, J., Maclure, M. and Sarland, C. (1996) *Teachers as Researchers in the Context of Award Bearing Courses and Research Degrees: Summary Report.* REGARD. Available online at: http://www.regard.ac.uk (accessed 2 April 2005).

Elliott, J., Maclure, M. and Sarland, C. (1997) *Teachers as Researchers in the Context of Award Bearing Courses and Research Degrees: Summary of Research Results.* Norwich: Centre for Applied Research in Education, University of East Anglia. Available online at: http://www.uea.ac.uk/care/research/tar.html (accessed 31 May 2005).

Fielding, M. (1998) Students as researchers: From data source to significant voice. Paper presented at the Eleventh International Congress for School Effectiveness and Improvement, School of Education, University of Manchester, December 1998.

Fielding, M. (1999) 'Radical collegiality: Affirming teaching as an inclusive professional practice.' *Australian Educational Researcher*, 26(2): 1–34.

Fielding, M. and Bragg, S. (2003) *Students as Researchers: Making a Difference.* Cambridge: Pearson Publishing.

Fielding, M., Bragg, S., Craig, S., Eraut, M., Gillinson, S., Horne, M., Robinson, C. and Thorp, J. (2005) *Factors Influencing the Transfer of Good Practice.* London: DfES.

Freire, P. (1970) *A Pedagogy of the Oppressed.* New York: Seabury Press.

Frost, D. and Durrant, J. (2003) Bottom up? Top down? Inside-out? Joined-up? Building capacity for school improvement through teacher leadership. Paper presented at the International Congress for School Effectiveness and Imporovement, Sydney, Australia, January 2003.

Frost, D., Cullen, J. and Cunningham, H. (2003) 'Making a difference: Building a research community of practice.' *Professional Development Today*, Spring: 13–22.

Frost, D., Durrant, J., Head, M. and Holden, G. (2000) *Teacher-Led School Improvement.* London: Routledge-Falmer.

Fullan, M. G. (1992) *Successful School Improvement.* Buckingham: Open University Press.

Furlong, J., Salisbury, J. and Coombes, L. (2003) *Best Practice Research Scholarships: An Evaluation.* DfES, Cardiff: Cardiff University.

Gardner, J. W. (1991) *Building Community.* San Francisco: Independent Sector.

Gardner, H., Csikszentmihalyi, M. and Damon, W. (2001) *Good Work: When Excellence and Ethics Meet.* New York: Basic Books.

Gardner, H., Csikszentmihalyi, M. and Damon, W. (2006) The Good Work Project: An Overview, http://www.goodworkproject.org (accessed January 2006).

Gibbons, M., Limoges, C., Nowotny, H., Schwartzman, S., Scott, P. and Trow, M. (1994) *The New Production of Knowledge.* London: Sage Publications.

Gilchrist, A. (2004) Developing the well-connected community. *In:* McCarthy, H., Miller, P. and Skidmore, P. (eds) *Network Logic: Who Governs in an Interconnected World?*, pp. 143–54. London: Demos.

Gramsci, A. (1971) *Selections from the Prison Notebooks.* New York: International Publishers.

Granovetter, M. (1973) 'The strength of weak ties.' *American Journal of Sociology,* 78(6): 1360–80.

Gray, J., Hopkins, D., Reynolds, D. S., Wilcox, B., Farrell, S. and Jesson, D. (1999) *Improving Schools.* Buckingham: Open University Press.

Groundwater-Smith, S. (2002) Evidence based practice in school education: Some lessons for learning in museums. Paper presented at the Why Learning? Seminar, University of Technology, Sydney, Australia, November 2002.

Groundwater-Smith, S. (2004) School-based enquiry: A worthwhile and legitimate exercise. Paper presented at the Master of Education Conference, University of Western Sydney, Sydney, Australia, January 2004.

Groundwater-Smith, S. (2006) The Coalition of Knowledge Building Schools: A Market Place for Developing and Sharing Educational Practice. Paper presented at the British Educational Research Association Conference, Warwick, England, September 2006.

Groundwater-Smith, S. and Dadds, M. (2004) Critical practitioner inquiry: Towards responsible professional communities of practice. *In:* Day, C. and Sachs, J. *International Handbook on the Continuing Professional Development of Teachers*, pp. 238–64. Maidenhead: Open University Press.

Groundwater-Smith, S. and Kelly, L. (2003) As we see it: Improving learning at the museum. Paper presented to the Annual Conference of the British Educational Research Association, Edinburgh, September 2003.

Groundwater-Smith, S. and Mockler, N. (2002) Building knowledge, building professionalism: The Coalition of Knowledge Building Schools and teacher professionalism. Paper presented to the Australian Association for Educational Research Conference, University of Queensland, December 2002.

Groundwater-Smith, S. and Mockler, N. (2003) *Learning to Listen: Listening to Learn,* Sydney: MLC School and the Centre for Practitioner Research, University of Sydney.

Groundwater-Smith, S. and Sachs, J. (2002) 'The activist professional and the reinstatement of trust.' *Cambridge Journal of Education*, 32(3): 341–58.

Hannon, V. (2005) Network-based reform: Adaptive challenges facing the English education system. Paper presented at the Conference for the American Educational Research Association, Montreal, April 2005.

Hargreaves, A. (1991) Contrived collegiality: The micropolitics of teacher collaboration. *In:* Blasé, J. (ed.) *The Politics of Life in Schools*, pp. 46–72. Thousand Oaks, California: Corwin Press.

Hargreaves, A. (1993) Individualism and individuality: Reinterpreting the teacher culture. *In:* Little, J. W. and McLaughlin, M. W. (eds) *Teachers' Work: Individuals, Colleagues and Contexts*, pp. 51–76. New York: Teacher College Press.

Hargreaves, A. (1994) *Changing Teachers, Changing Times*. New York: Teachers College Press.

Hargreaves, A. (1998) 'The emotional practice of teaching.' *Teaching and Teacher Education*, 14(8): 835–54.

Hargreaves, A. (1999) 'Fielding error? Deepening the debate about teacher collaboration and collegiality: Response to Fielding.' *Australian Educational Researcher*, 26(2): 45–53.

Hargreaves, A. and Dawe, R. (1990) 'Paths of professional development: Contrived collegiality, collaborative culture, and the case of peer coaching.' *Teaching and Teacher Education*, 6(3): 227–41.

Hargreaves, D. (2004) Networks, knowledge and innovation: Reflections on teacher learning. *In:* McCarthy, H., Miller, P. and Skidmore, P. (eds) *Network Logic: Who Governs in an Interconnected World?*, pp. 77–88. London: Demos.

Hargreaves, D. H. (1994) 'The new professionalism: The synthesis of professional and institutional development.' *Teaching and Teacher Education*, 10(4): 423–38.

Hargreaves, D. H. (1996) *Teaching as a Research-based Profession: Possibilities and Prospects*. London: Teacher Training Agency.

Hargreaves, D. H. (1999) 'The knowledge creating school.' *British Journal of Educational Studies*, 47(2): 122–44.

Hargreaves, D. H. (2003a) *Working Laterally: How Innovation Networks Make an Education Epidemic*. Nottingham: DEMOS in partnership with NCSL DfES Publications.

Hargreaves, D. H. (2003b) *Education Epidemic: Transforming Secondary Schools Through Innovative Networks*. London: Demos.

Hart, S., Dixon, A., Drummond, M. J. and McIntyre, D. (2004) *Learning without Limits*. Maidenhead: Open University Press.

Hillage, J., Pearson, R., Anderson, A. and Tampkin, P. (1998) *Excellence in Research on Schools*. London: Institute for Employment Studies/DfEE/HMSO.

Holly, M.L. and McLaughlin, C.S. (eds) (1989) *Perspectives on Teacher Professional Development*. Lewes: Falmer.

Holmes, D. (2004) *Nuts, Bolts, Levers and Cranks: Designing Enquiry-Based Learning in Hartlepool*. Cranfield: National College for School Leadership Networked Learning Group.

Hopkins, D. (2000) Schooling for tomorrow: Innovation and networks. Paper presented at CERI/OECD Portuguese Seminar, September 2000.

Hopkins, D., Ainscow, M. and West, M. (1994) *School Improvement in an Era of Change*. London: Cassell.

Hord, S. H. (1997) SEDL (Southwest Educational Development Laboratory): Professional learning communities: Communities of continuous inquiry and improvement, http://www.sEd.l.org/pubs/change34; http://newportal.ncsl.org.uk/networked_learning/networked_learning_communities/nlg-nlc-developmentresearch (accessed April 2007).

Hoyle, E. (1974) 'Professionality, professionalism and control in teaching.' *London Educational Review*, 3(2): 13–9.

Huberman, M. (1993) The model of the independent artisan. *In:* Little, J. W. and McLaughlin, M. W. (eds) *Teachers' Work: Individuals, Colleagues, and Contexts*. New York: Teachers College Press.

ILEA (1977) *Keeping the School Under Review.* London: ILEA Learning Resources Centre.

Jackson, D. (2002a) 'De-mystifying enquiry for school improvement.' *BUSIP Newsletter.*

Jackson, D. (2002b) Networks and networked learning: Knowledge management and collaborative enquiry for school and system improvement. Paper presented at the Annual SCETT Conference on Professional Learning Communities, Grantham, October 2002.

Jackson, D. (2002c) The creation of knowledge networks: Collaborative enquiry for school and system improvement. Paper presented at the Conference on Knowledge Management in Education and Learning, Oxford 2002.

Jackson, D. (2004) Networked Learning Communities: Characteristics of 'networked learning' – what are we learning? Paper presented at the International Congress for School Effectiveness and Improvement, Rotterdam, The Netherlands, January 2004.

Jackson, D. (2006) Networked Learning Communities: Setting school-to-school collaboration within a system context. *In: Centre for Strategic Education Seminar Series,* Paper No 159, December 2006. Jolimont, Victoria, Australia: Centre for Strategic Education.

Jackson, D. and Leo, E. (2003) Knowledge Management in Networked Learning Communities. Paper presented at the American Educational Research Association, Chicago, Illinois, April 2003.

James, M. and Worrall, N. (2000) 'Building a reflective community: Development through collaboration between a higher education institution and one school over ten years.' *Educational Action Research,* 8(1): 93–114.

Johnson, B. (2003) 'Teacher collaboration: Good for some, not so good for others.' *Educational Studies,* 29(4): 337–50.

Johnson, D. W. and Johnson, F. P. (2006) *Joining Together,* 10th edn. London: Allyn and Bacon.

Johnson, K. (1998) Reflections on collaborative research from the realms of practice. Invited Keynote Address at the Second International Practitioner Research Conference, University of Sydney, Sydney, Australia.

Kaplan, G. R. and Usdan, M. D. (1992) 'The changing look of education policy networks.' *Phi Delta Kappan,* May: 664–72.

Kelly, K. (1995) *Out of Control: The Rise of Neo-Biological Civilization.* Menlo Park, CA: Addison-Wesley.

Kemmis, S. (1995) Some ambiguities in Stenhouse's notion of 'The Teacher as Researcher': Towards a new resolution. *In:* Rudduck, J. (ed.) *An Education that Empowers: A Collection of Lectures in Memory of Lawrence Stenhouse,* pp. 73–114. Clevedon: BERA Dialogues, 10 Multilingual Matters.

Kirschner, B. W., Dickinson, R. and Blosser, C. (1996) 'From co-operation to collaboration: The changing culture of a school/university partnership.' *Theory into Practice,* 35(3): 205–13.

Koshy, V. (2005) *Action Research for Improving Practice: A Practical Guide.* London: Paul Chapman.

Leeds Consortium (2001) *Final Report of the Leeds Consortium.* London: TTA.

Leitch, R. and Day, C. (2000) 'Action research and reflective practice: Towards a holistic view.' *Educational Action Research,* 8(1): 179–95.

Lieberman, A. (1996) Practices that support teacher development: Transforming conceptions of professional learning. *In:* McLaughlin, M. W. and Oberman, I. (eds) *Teacher Learning: New Policies, New Practices.* New York: Teachers College Press.

Lieberman, A. (1999) 'Networks.' *Journal of Staff Development*, 20(3): 1.

Lieberman, A. (2005) *Networks*. Nottingham: NCSL.

Lieberman, A. and Grolnick, M. (1996) 'Networks and reform in American Education.' *Teacher College Record*, 98(1): 7–45.

Lieberman, A. and McLaughlin, M. W. (1992) 'Networks for educational change: Powerful and problematic.' *Phi Delta Kappan,* May: 673–7.

Lieberman, A. and Miller, L. (1984) *Teachers: Their World and their Work.* Alexandria, Virginia: Association for Supervision and Curriculum Development.

Lieberman, A. and Miller, L. (1990) The Social Realities of Teaching. *In:* Lieberman, A. *Schools as Collaborative Cultures: Creating the Future Now*, pp. 153–65. London: Falmer Press.

Lieberman, A. and Wood, D. (2001) When teachers write: Of networks and learning. *In:* Lieberman, A. and Miller, L. (eds) *Teachers Caught in the Action: Professional Development that Matters*, pp. 174–88. New York: Teachers College Press.

Lieberman, A. and Wood, D. (2003) *Inside the National Writing Project: Connecting Network Learning and Classroom Teaching*. New York and London: Teachers College Press.

Lieberman, A. and Wood, L. (2004) Untangling the threads: Networks, community and teacher learning in the National Writing Project. *In:* McCarthy, H., Miller, P. and Skidmore, P. (eds) *Network Logic: Who Governs in an Interconnected World?*, pp. 63–76. London: Demos.

Lima, J. A. (2001) 'Forgetting about friendship: Using conflict in teacher communities as a catalyst for school change.' *Journal of Educational Change*, 2(2): 97–122

Little, J. W. (1982) 'Norms of collegiality and experimentation: Workplace conditions of school success.' *American Educational Research Journal*, 19(3): 325–40

Little, J. W. (1990a) Teachers as colleagues. *In:* Lieberman, A. (ed.) *Schools as Collaborative Cultures: Creating the Future Now*, pp. 165–95. Basingstoke: Falmer Press.

Little, J. W. (1990b) 'The persistence of privacy: Autonomy and initiative in teachers' professional relations.' *Teachers College Record*, 91(4): 509–36.

Little, J. W. (1999) 'Colleagues of choice, colleagues of circumstance: Response to M. Fielding.' *Australian Educational Researcher*, 26(2): 35–43.

Little, J. W. (2002a) 'Locating learning in teachers' communities of practice: Opening up the problems of analysis in records of everyday work.' *Teaching and Teacher Education*, 18(8): 917–46.

Little, J. W. (2002b) Professional community and the problem of high school reform. Paper presented at the SUPER (Schools–University Partnership for Educational Research) Conference, Faculty of Education, University of Cambridge, June 2003.

Little, J. W. (2005) *Nodes and Nets: Investigating Resources of Professional Learning in Schools and Networks*. Working Paper for National College of School Leadership, Nottingham, UK. Berkeley, California: University of California and National College for School Leadership – Networked Learning Communities.

Little, J. W. and McLaughlin, M. W. (1993a) Introduction: Perspectives on cultures and contexts of teaching. *In:* Little, J. W. and McLaughlin, M. W. (eds) *Teachers' Work: Individuals, Colleagues and Contexts*, pp. 1–8. New York: Teacher College Press.

Lortie, D. (1975) *Schoolteacher: A Sociological Study*. Chicago: University of Chicago Press.

MacBeath, J. (1999) *Schools Must Speak for Themselves: The Case for School Self-Evaluation.* London: Routledge.

MacBeath, J., Demetriou, H., Rudduck, J. and Myers, K. (2003*) Consulting Pupils: A Toolkit for Teachers.* Cambridge: Pearson Publishing.

McCarthy, H., Miller P. and Skidmore, P. (2004) Network logic. *In:* McCarthy, H., Miller, P. and Skidmore, P. (eds) *Network Logic: Who Governs in an Interconnected World?*, pp. 11–22. London: Demos.

McCormick, R. and Fox, A. (2006) 'How can networks support the professional learning of teachers.' Unpublished paper. Milton Keynes: The Open University.

McIntyre, D. (2005) 'Bridging the gap between research and practice.' *Cambridge Journal of Education*, 35(3): 357–83.

McIntyre, D. and Black-Hawkins, K. (2006) Reflections on Schools–University Research Partnerships. *In:* McLaughlin, C., Black-Hawkins, K., Brindley, S., McIntyre, D. and Taber, T. *Researching Schools: Stories from a Schools–University Partnership for Educational Research,* pp. 182–98. London: Routledge.

McLaughlin, C. (2003) 'The feeling of finding out: The role of emotions in research.' *Educational Action Research*, 11(1): 65–79.

McLaughlin, C. and Black-Hawkins, K. (2004) 'A School–University research partnership: Conditions, paradoxes and tensions.' *British Journal of In-Service Education*, 30(2): 265–85.

McLaughlin, C. and Black-Hawkins, K. (2007) 'School-University partnerships for educational research-distinctions, dilemmas and challenges.' *The Curriculum Journal*, 18(3): 327–41.

McLaughlin, C., Black-Hawkins, K., Brindley, S., McIntyre, D. and Taber, K. (2006) *Researching Schools: Stories from a Schools–University Partnership for Educational Research.* London: Routledge Falmer.

McLaughlin, M. W. and Talbert, J. (2001) *Professional Communities and the Work of High School Teaching.* London: University of Chicago Press.

McLaughlin, M. W. and Zarrow, J. (2001) Teachers engaged in evidence-based reform: Trajectories of teachers' inquiry, analysis, and action. *In:* Lieberman, A. and Miller, L. (eds) *Teachers Caught in the Action: Professional Development that Matters*, pp. 79–102. New York: Teachers College Press.

Maddock, M., Cunningham, M., Hargreaves, L., McIntyre, D. and Pell, T. (in press) 'Teachers' conceptions of teacher professionalism in England in 2003 and 2006.' *British Educational Research Journal.*

Mockler, N. (2002) Challenging practice through practitioner enquiry. Paper presented at the British Educational Research Association Annual Conference, University of Exeter, September 2002.

Mosley, J. (1998) *Quality Circle Time in the Primary Classroom.* Cambridge: LDA.

Nardi, B. A., Whittaker, S. and Schwarz, H. (2000) It's not what you know, it's who you know: Work in the information age, http://www.firstmonday.org/issues/issue5_5/nardi/index (accessed December 2006).

NCSL (National College for School Leadership) (2002a) *Networked Learning Communities: Learning from Each Other . . . Learning with Each Other.* Nottingham: NCSL.

NCSL (National College for School Leadership) (2002b) *Why Networked Learning Communities?* Cranfield: NCSL.

NCSL (National College for School Leadership) (2005) *Networked Learning Communities: Learning about Learning Networks.* Cranfield: NCSL.

Networked Learning Communities (2005) *Learning about Learning Networks.* Cranfield: National College of School Leadership – Networked Learning Communities.

Nias, J. (1993) Changing times, changing identities: Grieving for a lost self. *In:* Burgess, R. G. (ed.) *Educational Research and Evaluation: For Policy and Practice*, pp. 139–56. London and New York: Falmer Press.

Nias, J. and Biott, C. (eds) (1992) *Working and Learning Together for Change.* Buckingham: Open University Press.

Nias, J., Southworth, G. and Yeomans, A. (1989) *Staff Relationships in the Primary School.* London: Cassells.

Norwich Area Schools Consortium (2001*) Norwich Area Schools Consortium Final Report to the Teacher Training Agency.* London: TTA.

Ofsted (2001) *Inspection of Blackburn with Darwen Education Action Zone, January 2001.* London: Ofsted.

Ofsted (2005) *Interpreting Data: Training Material for Inspectors.* London: Ofsted.

Parker, A. (1977) 'Networking for innovation and problem-solving and their use for improving education: A comparative overview.' Unpublished manuscript. School Capacity for Problem Solving Group, National Institute of Education, Washington, DC.

Presage, S., Perks, P. and Soares, A. (2003) 'Developing Critical Intelligence: Tensions in the DfES model for Best Practice Research Scholarships.' *Educational Review*, 55(1): 55–63.

Ratcliffe, M., Bartholomew, H., Hames, V., Hind, A., Leach, J., Millar, R. and Osborne, J. (2005) 'Evidence-based practice in science education: The researcher-user interface.' *Research Papers in Education*, 20(2): 169–86.

Resnick, L. http://www.ifl.lrdc.pitt.edu/ifl/index.php?section=learningwalk (accessed May 2006).

Richards, J. (2003) A case study of a researching school: Sharnbrook Upper School. Paper presented at the British Educational Research Association Conference, Heriot-Watt University, Edinburgh, September 2003.

Richert, A. (1996) Teachers research on school change: What teachers learn and why that matters. *In:* Kent, K. (ed.) *Breaking New Ground: Teacher Action Research, a Wealth of Learning*, pp. 9–18. Redwood City, CA: Bay Region IV Professional Development Consortium.

Richmond, G. (1996) 'University/school partnerships: Bridging the culture gap.' *Theory into Practice*, 35(3): 214–8.

Rudduck, J. and Flutter, J. (2004) *How to Improve Your School: Giving Pupils a Voice.* London: Continuum Press.

Rudduck, J., Chaplain, R. and Wallace, G. (1996) *School Improvement: What Can Pupils Tell us?* London: David Fulton.

Rudduck, J., Berry, M., Brown, N. and Frost, D. (2000) 'Schools learning for other schools: Co-operation in a climate of competition.' *Research Papers in Education*, 15(3): 259–74.

Ruthven, K. (2005) 'Improving the development and warranting of good practice in teaching.' *Cambridge Journal of Education*, 35(3): 407–26.

Sampson, R. J. (2004) Networks and neighbourhoods: The implications of connectivity for thinking about crime in the modern city. *In:* McCarthy, H. Miller, P. and

Skidmore, P. (eds) *Network Logic: Who Governs in an Interconnected World?* pp. 155–67. London: Demos.

Salzberger-Wittenberg, I. Henry, G. and Osborne, E. (1983) *The Emotional Experience of Teaching and Learning.* London: Routledge and Kegan Paul.

Senge, P. (1990) *The Fifth Discipline.* London: Random House Business Books.

Sergiovanni, T. J. (1994) *Building Community in Schools.* San Francisco: Jossey-Bass.

Simons, H., Kushner, S., Jones, K. and James, D. (2003) 'From evidence-based practice to practice-based evidence: The idea of situated generalisation.' *Research Papers in Education*, 18(4): 347–64.

Somekh, B. (1994) 'Inhabiting each others' castles: Towards knowledge and mutual growth through collaboration.' *Educational Action Research*, 2(3): 357–81.

Springboard Schools http://springboardschools.org (accessed January 2007).

Stenhouse, L. (1975) *An Introduction to Curriculum Research and Development.* London: Heinemann.

Stenhouse, L. (1979) Research as a basis for teaching. Inaugral lecture, University of East Anglia.

Stenhouse, L. (1981) 'What counts as research?' *British Journal of Educational Studies*, 29(2): 103–14.

Street, H. and Temperley, J. (eds) (2005) *Improving Schools Through Collaborative Enquiry.* London: Continuum.

Symonds, K. (2003) After the test: How schools are using data to close the achievement gap, http://www.basrc.org

Szulanski, G. (2003) *Sticky Knowledge.* London: Sage.

TTA (1998a) *Evaluation of Research-Based Consortia Initiative.* Mimeo, London: Teacher Training Agency.

TTA (1998b) *Summaries of Annual Reports of the Four TTA School-Based Research Consortia for the First Year of the Initiative.* Mimeo, London: Teacher Training Agency.

TTA (2000a) *TTA/CfBT School-Based Research Consortia. Annual Review, 1998.* London: Teacher Training Agency.

TTA (2000b) *TTA/CfBT School-Based Research Consortia. Annual Review, 1999.* London: Teacher Training Agency.

Watkins, C. (2005) *Classrooms as Learning Communities.* London: Routledge.

Wellcome Trust (2006) *Believers, Seekers and Sceptics: What Teachers Think about Continuing Professional Development.* London: Wellcome Trust.

Wenger, E. (1998) *Communities of Practice: Learning, Meaning and Identity.* Cambridge: Cambridge University Press.

Winter, R. (1989) *Learning from Experience.* London: Falmer Press.

Yinger, R. (1988) The conversation of teaching: Patterns of explanation in mathematics lessons. Paper presented at Meeting of the American Educational Research Association, Washington, DC.

Zeichner, K. (2003) 'Teacher research as professional development for P-12 educators in the USA.' *Educational Action Research*, 11(2): 283–301.

Zeichner, K. and Noffke, S. (2001) Practitioner research. *In*: Richardson, V. *Handbook of Research on Teaching*, 4th edn. pp. 298–332. Washington, DC: American Educational Research Association.

Glossary and acronyms

BASRC	Bay Area School Reform Collaborative
BPRS	Best Practice Research Scholarship
Beacon school	Beacon schools are schools that have been identified as among the best performing in the country and represent examples of successful practice that are to be brought to the attention of the rest of the education service with a view to sharing and spreading that effective practice to others. (http://www.standards.dfee.gov.uk/beaconschools)
CARE	Centre for Action Research in Education
CERI	Centre for Educational Research and Innovation
CfBT	Centre for British Teachers
CORE	Consortium of Reading Excellence
DfES	Department for Education and Skills
EPIC	Educating Professionals for Informal Classrooms
GCSE	General Certificate of Secondary Education
HEI	Higher Education Institution
ICT	Information and communication technology
IQEA	Improving the Quality of Education For All
LA	Local Authority
NCSL	National College for School Leadership
NLC	Network Learning Community
NWP	National Writing Project
OECD	Organisation for Economic Cooperation and Development
Ofsted	Office for Standards in Education
PANDA	Performance and assessment data
PAT	Pupil achievement tracker
PGCE	Post Graduate Certificate in Education
RAE	Research Assessment Exercise
SAT	Standard Assessment Task
SMT	Senior Management Team
SUPER	School–University Partnership in Educational Research
SVC	Student Voice Co-ordinator

TDA	Teacher Development Agency
TIPS	Technology Integrated Pedagogic Strategies
TRC	Teacher Research Coordinator
TTA	Teacher Training Agency

Index

Note: page numbers in **bold type** refer to figures and tables.